CABARET PERFORMANCE

Volume II: Europe 1920–1940

CABARET PERFORMANCE

Volume II: Europe 1920–1940

Sketches, Songs, Monologues, Memoirs

Selected and translated, with commentary, by

Laurence Senelick

THE JOHNS HOPKINS UNIVERSITY PRESS

Baltimore and London

© 1993 The Johns Hopkins University Press
All rights reserved
Printed in the United States of America on acid-free paper

The Johns Hopkins University Press
2715 North Charles Street
Baltimore, Maryland 21218–4319
The Johns Hopkins Press Ltd., London

Library of Congress Cataloging-in-Publication Data

Cabaret performance / selected and translated, with commentary, by Laurence
    Senelick.
        p.   cm.
        Contents: —v.   2. Europe 1920–1940, sketches, songs, monologues,
    memoirs.
        ISBN 0-8018-4378-2 (v. 2 : alk. paper)
        1. Music-halls (Variety-theaters, cabarets, etc.)—Europe.   I. Senelick,
    Laurence.
        PN1969.C3C3   1993
        792.7'094—dc20   88-62672

*To the memory of John Brode, a citizen
of the world*

CONTENTS

PREFACE

IN 1908, THE RUSSIAN POET ALEKSANDR BLOK DIAGNOSED the malaise of his times: "The most vital, the most sensitive children of our century are afflicted by a disease unknown to physicians of body or mind. This disease, akin to psychological ailments, may be called 'irony.' Its manifestations are fits of exhausting laughter, which begin with a diabolically mocking provocateur's smile and end in rebellion and blasphemy" ("Iro-niya," *Rech,* 7 December 1908).

The ironical mode was characteristic of the European cabaret, whose history seems to reflect the Blokian evolution from provoking smile to blasphemous rebellion. Irony is essentially an oblique weapon, and the *fin de siècle* "artistic" cabaret had to exploit its many facets, predominately parody, in its sorties on social and aesthetic flanks, because censorship greatly hampered it from making frontal attacks on the Establishment, particularly in the political realm. Cabaret remained a peripheral means of expression, usually limited to its bohemian sphere of influence.

The Great War changed all that. The collapsed Hohenzollerns, Habsburgs, and Romanovs were supplanted by governments in central and eastern Europe which, at least at first, permitted broad latitude of expression in the performing arts. Long-dammed-up protest and dissent spilled over into a cataract of political satire.

During the war itself, this dissent had taken shape in the cabaret as Dadaistic anarchy; but with the new order in Europe, Dada seemed too cryptic and irrelevant. Cabaret audiences demanded and got direct reference to current events. The excitement of what was happening in the streets was mirrored on the cabaret stage not as abstract opposition but as specific and circumstantial criticism.

As if to draw a line between the prewar and postwar cabarets, Kurt Tucholsky, a leading exponent of satire in song and *feuilleton*, espoused the adoption of the word *Kabarett*. Unlike *cabaret*, whose prime function was to entertain, the Kabarett, in Tucholsky's view, had a duty to maintain an adversarial stance in order to change society: "Nothing is harder and takes more character than to stand in open opposition to one's time and loudly say: No!" ("Political Satire," *Weltbühne,* 9 October 1919). In his view, there were no bounds to satire, whose mandate stretched to everything under the sun.

Tucholsky's prescription as administered in his own work and that of such colleagues as Walter Mehring and Klabund leaves a residual impression that most cabaret of the 1920s and '30s was politically engaged in earnest. But the truth is otherwise. It is a mistake to consider that the average commentary from the cabaret stage was programmatic in its attacks. As the cabaret grew from an underground or avant-garde form to a genuinely popular entertainment, the heterogeneity of its audiences compelled it to dilute its message. The twenties was a period of considerable instability in Europe, and the larger public, wanting to forget its troubles in the theater, preferred satire to be glancing and sarcastic; the more the political situation became embroiled, the more the public sought light entertainment and diversion in the cabaret. Tucholsky's nay-saying came to be condemned by activists as futile negativism, and irony turned more and more to cynicism.

While left-wing cabaret moved increasingly towards agitprop to counteract the rise of fascism, the run-of-the-mill cabaret offered witty song-and-dance, tinged perhaps by liberal sympathies but by no means doctrinaire in its form or content. This enabled the mass audience to feel *au courant* but basically unchallenged. And gradually censorship resumed, in the form of libel suits instigated by indignant private individuals, obscenity prosecutions by state's attorneys, and harassment by the right-wing governments that came to power in the 1930s.

The cabaret was, moreover, omnivorous. It shoveled in great helpings of whatever was exciting and innovative—North American jazz and South American tango, "expressive" and undraped dancing, cinematic and radio techniques, the latest literary fashions—and regurgitated them, often in an only partially digested form. There was no consistency in the cabaret's attitude to these novelties: jazz, for instance, which was first introduced to Europe in a revue act by the Algerian Gaby Deslys and the American Harry Pilcer, might as easily shape a dance fantasia like the Blue Bird's *Advertising Agency Affair* as inspire a sardonic comment on the Americanization of European home life like Louis Davids's *Mother Is Dancing*. This ingestion of anything that proved attractive and alluring led many cabarets to adopt a revue format, a well-organized sequence of acts ostensibly grouped around a given theme. As a result, the *conférencier* of the prewar cabaret, who had given a distinct personality to the performance, often dwindled into a mere master of ceremonies, although certain outstanding talents like Fritz Grünbaum and László Békeffi managed to maintain their primacy. What was increasingly lost was the amateur or bohemian atmosphere of the cabaret, which grew ever more "professional" in its slickness and appeal to a more broadly based audience.

Despite the growing attendance of the cabaret by a general public, its personnel and creators continued to be drawn from peripheral groups whose viewpoint remained ironic. The proliferation of cabarets allowed minority concerns to infiltrate popular entertainment. Throughout central and eastern Europe, a large percentage of performers, composers, authors, and impresarios were Jews; and although there were only a few exclusively Jewish cabarets, comedy and political commentary were permeated with Yiddish rhythms, attitudes, and words. Liminal views on national concerns were provided by Hungarians working in Austria, Germans working in Czechoslovakia, and emigré Russians working in Germany and France. In Weimar Berlin, not only were many public favorites openly gay (Wilhelm Bendow, Claire Waldoff), but homosexual haunts also became must-sees on the itinerary of every urban tourist.

In general, the interwar cabaret was less venturesome and formally experimental than its precursors, but its slicker techniques enabled its messages to be more easily absorbed by the public.

Consequently, cabaret satire, even at its most anodyne, was viewed by totalitarian governments as a serious threat. The cabaret's basically antinomian stance could not be exploited to promote state policy. Rudolf Weys's inability to preserve satire in Nazi-occupied Vienna, despite his credentials as a fellow-traveller of the National Socialists, illustrates how inimical cabaret was to the fascist establishment. But as the pressures of Nazi incursion forced cabaret out of its usual venues, the cheeky, irrepressible urge to say No thrived among emigrés, fugitives, resistance workers, and even in concentration camps.

This book, like its preceding volume, attempts to provide a sampler of material performed in European cabarets from the end of World War I to the official ban on cabaret commentary pronounced by Reichspropagandaminister Goebbels. The selection is representative rather than exhaustive and opts for shorter pieces over extended ones. Much of the best cabaret writing was highly topical and loses a great deal of its meaning out of context, but I have tried to choose works which require a minimum of annotation. Similarly, cabaret songs work best when accompanied by their music, so that most of the items included here are prose pieces. However, when I have rendered a song or verse, I have retained the original meters and rhyme scheme.

When this anthology was first planned in West Berlin in 1985, the world was a very different place. The Wall still stood, giving the impression that it would do so in perpetuity. Many of the nations represented in this volume still dwelled in the shadow of Soviet hegemony. Friends I visited in the U.S.S.R. that year were suffering from injustice and repression imposed by the Brezhnev and Andropov regimes. This book therefore celebrates the hopeful beginnings of the 1990s, even as it may serve as a reminder that similar hopeful beginnings in 1920 came to a bad end. A strong dose of irony is therefore highly recommended.

This volume, like the earlier one, is greatly indebted to many persons who have offered advice, encouragement, and assistance. These include Berlin companions who accompanied me on cabaret jaunts on both sides of the Wall: Henry Akina, Christoff Bleidt, Alain Courtney, Dagmar Höher, Roy Kift, Joachim Klein, and Helen Palmer; and those friends whose linguistic expertise was immensely helpful: E. M. Beekman, Barry Jacobs, Peter Jelavich, Robert Konski, Joshua Rifkin, and Robi Sarlos. A preliminary translation of the Voskovec and Werich play was prepared by Karen von Kunes, preceptor in the Department of Slavic Languages and Literatures at Harvard University, and her students Iva Kalus and Stephen C. Sally. Gesine Bottomley, Librarian, and her staff at the Wissenschaftskolleg zu Berlin; Birgitta Walin, Librarian of the Drottingsholm Teatermuseum, Stockholm; and Dr. Jeanne Newlin, Curator, and the staff of the Harvard Theatre Collection helped locate obscure material. My editors, Gautam Dasgupta and Bonnie Marranca, have shown great fortitude and patience throughout a lengthy process; their pointed criticism and enthusiasm have made this collection broader and deeper than it might otherwise have been.

Recently an interest in Weimar cabaret has led to the performance of some of these translations. I should like to thank the Theatre Project of St. Louis and its artistic director, William Freimuth, for including certain of these pieces in its production *A Kurt Weill Cabaret*. A wider selection was adapted for *Cabaret Verboten* by Jeremy Lawrence, and my special thanks go to Mr. Lawrence, Mark Solomon, and Leon Katz of the Mark Taper Forum, Los Angeles, and Carey Perloff and Patricia Taylor of CSC Rep, New York City, for involving me in the project. Friedrich Hollaender's heirs, Blandine Ebinger and Melody Hollaender, have given their blessings to my versions of his songs.

I

CABARET DANCING

1920–1925

JEAN COCTEAU (1891–1963) HAD ALREADY WRITTEN THE scenario for the ballet *Parade* (1917) when he conceived the idea of a dance pantomime to be performed to the latest musical novelties. Darius Milhaud had concocted a fantasia of maxixes, sambas, and tangos which he called *Le Boeuf sur le Toit,* allegedly after a popular Brazilian dance "O Boi No Telhado." Milhaud thought it might make an accompaniment to a Chaplin comedy, but Cocteau coopted the music for a project of his own; even so, the silent film influence persists in what Cocteau called an "American farce." He himself admitted he had never been to America, but like Brecht, he fertilized his fancy with images from American popular culture. The jerky poses and slow-motion slapstick borrowed from the movies were to give his pantomime a dreamlike quality.

Typically, Cocteau announced it, sold out the house, and only then sat down to write what he called a farce with modern equivalents of commedia dell'arte characters. He cast it with clowns from the Cirque Médrano, although the critics were to complain that the oversized false heads the clowns had to wear neutralized their ability to be funny. The "jolly divertissement" shared a bill with other short musical pieces by Georges Auric, Francis Poulenc, and Eric Satie. The French audience was enthusiastic, as was the London public at the gigantic Coliseum music hall a few months later. Cocteau claims to have overheard a Cockney workingman commenting on the show: "You can't say it's funny, but it's fun because it's different."

The Ox on the Roof connects with the cabaret movement because of its adaptation of an older tradition of popular entertainment to new American trends. Its alliance of traditional ballet-pantomime with the knockabout of a Mack Sennett farce is characteristic of the cabaretic hybrid of sophistication and vulgarity. And in its own way it inspired a cabaret. In 1922, a nightclub called Le Boeuf sur le Toit opened in Paris with Cocteau's blessing, and in short order became the fashionable watering place, where Tristan Tzara read poetry and virtuoso pianists played everything from Mozart to Gershwin. It was closed by the Germans in 1943, but reopened after the war.

The Ox on the Roof
(Le Boeuf sur le toit)
or The Nothing Doing Bar
Farce conceived and arranged by Jean Cocteau

Costumes by G.-P. Fauconnet. Sets and cardboard properties by Raoul Dufy. Music by Darius Milhaud. Twenty-five-piece orchestra conducted by Wladimir Golschmann.

First performed in Paris on Saturday, 21 February 1920, at the Comédie des Champs-Elysées and in London, 12 July 1920, at the Coliseum.

PARIS CAST

The Bartender	*Paul Fratellini*
The Red-headed Lady	*François Fratellini*
The Lady in the Low-Cut Gown	*Albert Fratellini*
The Policeman	*Busby*
The Black Boxer	*Cyerillo*
The Bookmaker	*Roberts*
The Gentleman in Evening Dress	*Pinocchio*
The Billiard-Playing Black	*Boda the Dwarf*

The Ox on the Roof is a garishly lit bar. A yellow wooden screen is set up to conceal the offstage-right area. The corner of a billiard table extends beyond the wing-piece, left, on which a garnet-red drapery is painted. Down left a leather armchair. Down right a table. Table and armchair, visible in front of the curtain, act as a kind of prologue to forecast the immensity of the stage-set. They take their place in the ensemble as soon as the curtain rises. Ceiling fan. The fan turns slowly and casts shadows on the characters. They wear cardboard heads three times life-size. They act in the style of the scenery. They are *moving set pieces*. Each one, "in slow motion," against the current of the music, performs the gestures essential to his role with the ponderousness of deep-sea divers.

The props—bottles, glasses, straws, cigarettes, chalk, saucers—are the same scale as the fake heads.

Along the downstage sky-border, painted with multicolored drapes, hang five smoke rings made of tulle, emerging from the armchair and heading center-stage. As the curtain rises, the bartender is alone, stark white, stark pink. He is shaking his cocktail shakers behind his bar. A cigar, big as a torpedo, burns on a table behind the armchair. Enter left from the billiard room the black boxer in a sky-blue turtleneck sweater. He orders a cocktail, flexes his muscles, falls into an armchair, crosses his legs, and picks up his cigar. All at once the smoke rings become his. A black pygmy, in shirt-sleeves, backs out of the billiard room. He chalks a billiard cue. The boxer asks the bartender to clip his cigar, which is drawing badly. The bartender clips it with a revolver. The shot knocks the pygmy over backwards. Throughout this first part he can be glimpsed in the billiard wing, lifting one leg, aiming, just like in American lithographs.

Enter, one after another, the lady in the low-cut gown, in a red frock, very affected, very vulgar; the red-headed lady, with paper hair, pretty but masculine in manner, somewhat stoop-shouldered, her hands in her pockets; the gentleman in oilcloth evening dress, looking at his wristwatch (he will not leave his barstool until his exit); a scarlet bookmaker, with golden teeth, who wears a gray derby and an ascot fixed by a pearl the size of a crystal garden globe.

All these beautiful people settle in, shoot craps. (The dice game between the gentleman and the bookie must be a mechanical tableau composed of their heads, the head of the bartender behind a newspaper with poster-sized letters, the two dice, veritable cardboard boxes which are moved by spinning them on their axes.) The elegant lady powders herself, notices the pygmy. He leaps onto a stool. She hoists him onto her shoulder and carries him into the billiard room. The red-headed lady crosses the stage, puts the

smoke rings over her arm, slips them over the neck of the bartender, and vamps the boxer. The boxer leaves his chair to follow her.
The bookmaker observes them, gets annoyed, stamps his foot,
slinks over to them, pulls out his pearl, and strikes a blow at the
head of the black, who collapses. The pygmy drops his billiard
cue, helps the boxer, lays him in the armchair, fans him with a
napkin.

Little triumphal dance of the bookmaker. The women tango. A
whistle blows. It is the police. Everyone trembles. The bartender
hangs up a sign—*Only drink available here is milk*—hides bottles,
glasses, hands out bowls, and froths milk in a churn.

The giant policeman sticks his head in. He enters. He gives the
place the once-over. He approaches each one to smell his breath.
He tastes the milk.

Influenced by the bucolic mood, he dances a friendly ballet.

While he is twirling center-stage with the grace of a ballerina,
the bartender pulls a lever. The fan comes down and decapitates
the policeman. He staggers. He looks for his head, tries to put it
on backwards and falls dead.

Nothing surprises the night owls. After some brief rejoicing in
which the pygmy sings a song, hand on heart, the bartender presents the head on a platter to the red-headed lady, who is indifferent and stares offstage left.

She dances. Her dance is a general caricature of most Salome
dances. She stretches, she smokes, she shakes the policeman's head
like a cocktail. At last, she walks on her hands like the Salome on
Rouen Cathedral, circles the head, and still on her hands, leaves
the bar, followed by the bookmaker.

Before disappearing after them, the lady in the low-cut gown
turns around, takes the rose the gentleman in evening dress wears
in his buttonhole, and tosses it to the bartender. The gentleman
pays, and they leave.

The boxer wakes up, rises, staggers, and leaves in turn, followed by the pygmy, who refuses to pay the bartender.

Alone, the bartender straightens things up. He sees the policeman's body. He drags it as best he can to a chair behind the table.
The dead body tries to recover its balance. Once the body is
propped up, the bartender brings piles of saucers and puts them
on the table, then a bottle of gin, which he empties into the body.

He picks up the head, shoves it between the shoulders. He tickles and hypnotizes it. The policeman comes back to life. Then the bartender unrolls a bill four yards long.

P.S.—*The title "The Ox on the Roof" was a Brazilian sign-board. It was given me by Paul Claudel.*

Translator's Notes

French cast. The performers were all popular clowns in the Parisian circus. The Fratellini brothers were fixtures at the Cirque d'Hiver: François (1879–1951) was the elegant, smooth-talking white clown; Paul (1877–1940), the Auguste, or shabby-genteel fall guy; and Albert (1886–1961), the grotesque Bozo-like *contre-Auguste,* who specialized in "drag" comedy. The dwarf Boda worked with them. Busby and Cyerillo were a team; and Pinocchio (Arturo Biaggoni, 1880–1951) was another Auguste.

Salome dance. The Canadian dancer Maud Allan introduced "The Vision of Salome" in London in 1908, in which she danced barefoot in an abbreviated costume around a papier-mâché head of John the Baptist. She was widely imitated in European and American variety.

IN GERMANY, THE POSTWAR SENSE OF RELEASE FOUND ONE form of expression in a dance craze. Dance halls proliferated; tangos, foxtrots, one-steps, and Bostons were introduced weekly; and the frenzy of the inflation period worked itself out in complicated steps imported from America. One private citizen, driven frantic by the fluctuations between civil war and everlasting carnival, plastered the advertising kiosks with a poster reading "Berlin, your dance is death."

Berlin's dance was also nude. The factors that contributed to this phenomenon of *Nakttanz* included reaction against the prudery of the Wilhelmine era and release of tension in the wake of wartime depression. Certain progressive groups sponsored nudism as a healthy way of life; others vaunted voyeurism as a legitimate activity of the modern city-dweller. And finally, at a time when maimed war veterans were to be seen begging on every street and prostitution of all kinds throve as an economic necessity, the body objectified was regarded as a fitting medium of entertainment.

The naked dance was introduced after the German revolution by Celly de Rheydt (Cäcilie Schmidt), mistress of an army officer who pimped for her performances. The artistic pretensions of her recitals at the Berlin Chat Noir were pure kitsch, but taking the cue from her, almost every cabaret and nightclub featured unclad dance, often with Salome as a pretext. (One such Salome appeared at the White Mouse, where the guests were masked.) The censors' annoyance became outrage when nudity was enhanced by a sadomasochistic theme, as in the whip dance called "A Night of Love in the Harem."

The most sensational nude dancer of the time was Anita Berber (1899–1929), whose life and creations—*Horror, Depravity, Ecstasy,* and *Cocaine*—incarnated the new generation's thirst for untrammeled experience. Berber was a beauty who appeared in silent films and modeled for painters and porcelain makers, a lesbian who set the fashion by appearing in public in a tuxedo and mon-

ocle, a media celebrity who hung out with bicycle racers and box-
ers. As one song complained,

> What does the audience want to see?
> Starving millions and misery,
> Thousands in prison going rotten?
> Is that what the audience wants to see?
> Alas, Anita Berber's naked bottom
> That's what the audience wants to see.

Her dance partner and second husband, Sebastian Droste
(Willy Knoblauch), who had worked with Celly de Rheydt, introduced her to cocaine. He succumbed to it; she declined under its
influence and died impoverished at the age of thirty.

A Naked Dance Club

(Nakttanz)

1920

by

Felix Langer

The master of ceremonies made heavy weather of extolling his artistic aims; but then that's his business. He warbled: "We want pure art (he pronounced it 'ort'), beauty, beauty, and more beauty. We want pure morality, ideal pleasure, the immanent aesthetics of the feminine body." The fellow aestheticized away for quite a while. But then came the punch line. He said something like, "Our highest aim is to procure for our downtrodden ('dahntrawn') people the pure ideal of beauty and to 'upraise it in its need.'" But the exploited German people were not to be seen in great numbers. The high admission fees were within the means only of those who are not wholly exploited. So there they all were, those gentlemen who can be found wherever "a man can afford to indulge himself." Obese old duffers, tacticians of market fluctuations, and heroes of foreign exchange, whose need to see pure art is to be regarded in the same light as the master of ceremonies' need to present pure art. But here we go. The hall was dimmed, a magic beam of light hit the platform, the curtains parted. Something vague, monk or Pierrot, was fiddling on a pedestal. The dance was supposed—how poetic—to evolve out of his playing. And now the priestess of pure joy was drifting in, followed by two acolytes, all enveloped in makeshift silk crepe; you could see everything.

It is cold in the hall. Influenza is raging. They dance a kind of drilled ballet. But don't hold your breath waiting for art. She knows what the exploited people need: a good mood, bucking up.

So she comes right in in three-quarter time and to the infernal cancan from "Orpheus in the Underworld." Contact is made; the public is excited; the ladies are unrestrained in their movements; no one still regrets the high admission fee. And outside, people are starving to death.

COCAINE
(Kokain)
1922
A Dance by Anita Berber

CONCEPTION BY SEBASTIAN DROSTE

Walls
Table
Shadows and cats
Green eyes
Many eyes
Millions of eyes
The woman
Movements nervously craving
Life flaring up
Lamps smouldering
Shadows dancing
Little shadows
Big shadows
The shadows
Oh—the leap over the shadows
It torments, does this shadow
It tortures, does this shadow
It devours me, does this shadow
What does this shadow want
Cocaine
Scream

Beasts
Blood
Alcohol
Pain
Much pain
And the eyes
The beasts
The mice
The light
This shadow
This horrible big black shadow

DESCRIPTION BY JOE JENČIK

(From Schrifttanz, 1:10, 1931)

Curtain. On stage an undraped body in an empty space suffused with the dim blue-gray light of dawning. The majesty of death throughout. Above, below, before, behind, perhaps in the motionless shape as well. In every detail just as when, hand in hand with an ex-girlfriend she had chanced to meet, she entered the room where she was to scream on finding Droste's body in its death agony, lying delirious after an overdose of cocaine . . . With this remembrance of an obscene episode whose sorry hero was her second husband, Anita Berber begins one of her finest creations—COCAINE.

Still as death and in a deep swoon! Evidently the first impact of the dreadful crippling poison. Somewhere the soul is striving tensely to regain its former mastery of the body. The convulsive creature reveals barely visible spasms in different parts of the body, the porcelain-tinted limbs recover their self-control, and the wretched drugged woman unwittingly comes to, for the love of life is indestructible. At least insofar as the muscles must obey, with tremors resembling the swings of a long pendulum the body rights itself; or more correctly, a remarkable coil of flesh, with two indescribable slits for eyes and a blood-red orifice for mouth, takes shape. The coil unwinds extremely slowly, taking orders from something for the moment halfway between mind and sodden cerebral cortex. The dancer impersonally gets to her feet. She looks like a marionette in a cruel state of serenity suspended between narcotic and heartbeat. The blood, coursing through the veins by the will of nature, pulses from one part of the body to another. The narcotic, administered by human will, hinders and obstructs hopelessly; it forces itself by brute strength into a place which is the domain of life's great mystery. The body looks frightfully, absurdly, and embarrassingly bloated. Something is boiling inside it, although it is coated with hoarfrost. Imaginary attempts to scream dissolve around the mouth, wondering at the sudden vague grimaces: these dissolve again before the scream, and so the dancer torments both herself and the creations of her sick fantasy. The healthy body struggles with the poisoned one, and the poisoned body rages again in the healthy one. The heartbeat will finally be paralyzed, as the monster of cocaine addiction overwhelms its voluntary victim. The dancer's body pitches about in a monstrous tumble. Further agonies—this time reminiscent of the sweet sleep of one freed from the torments of hell . . .

All this is carried out with a simple technique of natural steps and uncontrived poses. The attitudes in this dance are initiated tragically, and the arabesques demoniacally protracted. The incredibly slow movements of the body on its axis, like a leap recorded by a slow-motion camera—a lash of the tawse—always end with a supple *port de bras,* as conceived by a sculptor. Abrupt backward movements of the head seem to act as an unbearable counterweight. Position of the feet: chiefly a broad fourth position, which is the distinguishing feature of the idiosyncratic art of this original dancer. The whole technique is directed by the dynamic of dreams, which, freed from the weight of the mundane, atomizes the dancer's whole corporal being into the finest nuances of agility. Cocaine and Morphium are Anita Berber's most important and most personal artistic emanations, now and then resembling pathological studies by a famous mime—a mime, however, who understands how to subordinate herself to the dance form at the proper moment, without abandoning herself to it.

THE *AUSDRUCKSTANZ*, OR EXPRESSIVE DANCE, DEVELOPED by Rudolf Laban and Mary Wigman, is one of the major movements in modern dance history. Its cousin-german, the grotesque dance-pantomime as practiced by Lotte Goslar and Pina Bausch, was created by a cabaret performer, Valeska Gert (Gertrud Samosch, 1892–1978). She made her debut in Berlin in 1916 and, as she tells it, astonished audiences by her choice of material and presentation. Whores, mummies, corpses, and debauched little girls peopled her repertory, and her toughness and wit made a frightening impact. Calling it a pinnacle of art, one critic wrote of her *Death:* "She does nothing. She stands and dies." And Kurt Tucholsky said of her slut's dance *Canaille,* "the most audacious thing ever done on a stage."

After many engagements at cabarets in Munich and Berlin, including the second Schall und Rauch and Brecht's Rote Zibebe (Red Raisin), Gert toured Europe and the Soviet Union, appeared in Friedrich Hollaender's revue *Laterna Magica* (1926) and in films (as Louise Brooks's sadistic dorm matron in *Secrets of a Soul,* as Mrs. Peachum in *Threepenny Opera*), and made regular appearances at the Tingeltangel-Theater, the Katakombe, and her own cabaret, the Kohlkopp (Cabbage Haid). An egoist of monstrous proportions, Gert jealously regarded every other dancer, including Kurt Jooss, as her epigone, and declared that when she asked Brecht what he meant by epic acting, he replied, "What you do."

My Dance Pantomimes
(*from* Ich bin eine Hexe, *1950*)
by
Valeska Gert

I performed theater, I longed for the dance; I danced, I longed for the theater. I was in conflict until the idea occurred to me to combine them: I wanted to dance human characters. I invented an intricate fabric, one of whose strands was modern dance-pantomime; another strand was abstract dance; other strands were satiric dances, dances to sounds, expressionistic dances. I exploded a bundle of stimuli on the world; other dancers would make a whole program out of a single strand, but for me they were loud, whizzing little rockets, shooting around the world.

My dances were short and clear. I did no variations as other dancers do. For me the only important things were attack, tragic or comic climax, subsidence, nothing more. Because I didn't like solid citizens, I danced those whom they despised—whores, procuresses, down-and-outers, and degenerates.

. . . So far, streetwalkers had not been portrayed on the dance stage. People were too noble, though later it became an epidemic. But other dancers only endorsed the society I condemned. I called the character *Canaille;* without my being aware of it, it was the first socially critical dance-pantomime.

I wiggle my hips provocatively, hoist the black, very short skirt, and for an instant show white flesh above long, black stockings, pink garters, and high-heeled shoes (a scandal at a time when dancers, if they weren't dancing ballet, hopped across the stage barefoot). I am an ultra-refined whore. My movements are sleek and voluptuous. My white face is almost entirely covered by strands of black hair falling over my forehead. I bow my head deeply; my chin disappears up to the garish red mouth in a red collar which hangs loosely round my neck. Then I bend my knees slowly, spread my legs wide and sink down. In a sudden spasm, as if bit by a tarantula, I twitch upwards. I sway back and forth. Then my body relaxes, the spasm dissipates, the jerking becomes ever gentler, ever feebler, the intervals longer, the excitement ebbs away, one last twitch, and I'm down to earth again. What's been happening to me? I've been exploited. My body's been abused because I need money. Wretched world! I spit one disdainful step to the right and one to the left; then I shuffle off.

I was dancing coitus, but I "alienated" it, as people say nowadays. Art is always an alienation of reality. My *Procuress* was the whore grown old, capable of doing business only with the bodies of the young. Still, she spurted keen venomous lust, clutched her fat belly, staggered in drunkenness, and mumbling, begged for money, all together.

Brecht invited me to Munich. He presented an evening at the Kammerspiele: Ringelnatz recited, glass in hand; Brecht played the lute and recited his ballads. I danced *Canaille* to organ music. . . . At the Romanesque Café there was a lot of talk about modern dance. One scrawny girl with a pockmarked face and sharply jutting cheekbones said, "We want the 'outlandish' in dance." That's what I wanted too. What's outlandish? Birth, love, death. Nobody had previously dared to portray them barefaced and truthfully. I wanted to do it. This is how I did *death:* Motionless I stand in a long, black dress on a glaringly lit platform. My body slowly stretches, the struggle begins, the hands ball into fists, ever tighter, the shoulders hunch, the face is twisted with pain and agony. The pain becomes unbearable; the mouth opens wide to a soundless scream. I bend the head back; shoulders, arms, hands, the whole body stiffens. I try to protect myself. No use. For seconds I stand there motionless, a pillar of pain. Then, slowly, life withdraws from my body, which relaxes very slowly. The pain goes into remission, the mouth slackens, the shoulders droop, the arms hang loose, so do the hands. I feel the people staring in the audience; they want consolation. A glint of life glimmers in my face, a smile is already forming from very far away. Then it suddenly subsides; the cheeks grow flabby; the head falls quickly, the head of a puppet. Over. Gone. I have died. The stillness of death. No one in the audience dares to breathe. I am dead.

VALESKA GERT MADE HERSELF ENEMIES THROUGH HER AS-
sertions that she had been the firstest with the mostest in the fields
of modern dance, epic acting, or any theatrical innóvation one
cared to mention. Her fondness for self-advertisement was parodied by suave Paul Nikolaus (Steiner, 1894–1933), among the
sharpest and politically most uncompromising conférenciers in
the Weimar Republic. His nightly comments on current events
delivered at the KadeKo (Comics' Cabaret) were fueled by his
morning's perusal of Berlin's many newspapers.

Valeska Gert Her Own Publicity Agent!
(Jeder sein eigener Nachrufer!—Valeska Gert)
1924
by
Paul Nikolaus

She was not only the greatest dancer of her time, she was also the greatest actress. She was not only the greatest actress of her time, she was also the greatest singer, the greatest film star, the greatest director. If life had been long enough, she could have proven to our day and age that she would have put every practitioner of every field of sport in the shade. But beyond all this talent, we must not forget that she was also a wonderful person. She was the best spouse and housewife, the most passionate lover, and the most faithful daughter, sister, and friend. Since it is a pity to cremate or commit to earth all these splendid qualities, during her lifetime in shrewd acknowledgment of the rare value of her personality she left behind a wish in writing that her earthly remains be preserved by embalming in their approximate form for at least a couple of centuries for the sake of admiring posterity. May the embalming fluid lie lightly on her!

A sketch by Jean Cocteau of the entrance of the visitors in Le Boeuf sur le toit.

A sketch by Raoul Dufy for the setting of Le Boeuf sur le toit.

Celly de Rheydt, who introduced naked dancing. Photograph by Badekow.

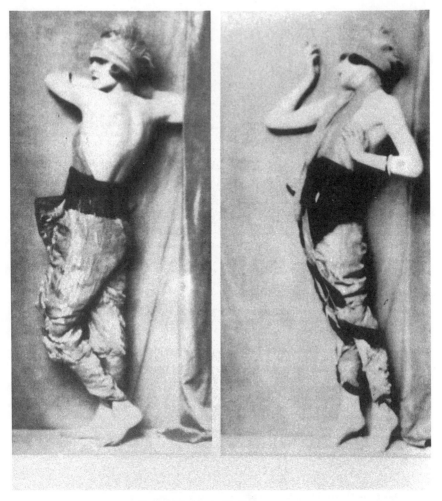

Anita Berber in Cocaine.

Valeska Gert.

II

Cabaret in Weimar Germany

1921–1928

THE FIRST GERMAN CABARETS, *ÜBERBRETTLS,* AND POETS' cafés never reached a large public; they remained, for their short lifetimes, limited in appeal, hamstrung by Wilhelmine censorship and their own aesthetic programs. But, as Max Halbe noted, "the examples in Berlin and Munich were so influential that within a few years the revolutionary transformation of the mental and artistic habits of the Germans was already complete . . . they longed for color, disorder, and the unleashing of the arts of the theater."

This thirst was slaked after the war. The overthrow of the kaiser, the revolutionary tumult that resulted in the establishment of a Social-Democratic republic, and the hardships of the inflation period were the troubled waters in which cabaretists could fish with spectacular success. Berlin became a maelstrom, sucking in the energies and talents of the rest of Germany. The Austrian writer Stefan Zweig provides a lurid description of the cultural capital of the Weimar Republic: "Berlin transformed itself into the Babel of the world. Bars, amusement parks, pubs shot up like mushrooms. [It was a veritable] witches' sabbath, for the Germans brought to perversion all their vehemence and love of system. . . . Amid the general collapse of values, a kind of insanity took hold of precisely those middle-class circles which had hitherto been unwavering in their orderliness." Amid this breakdown, the cabaret, once regarded as the haunt of a certain type of liberated individual, now lured a bourgeois as well as a bohemian audience. What New York in the 1920s was to jazz and speakeasies, Berlin was to cabaret.

There was a close collaboration between the cabaretists and the journalists of the Weimar Republic. Many of the leading columnists of the liberal paper *Die Weltbühne* wrote for the cabaret stage, and the conférenciers interpreted to the public the events that had just been reported in the newspapers. But under the froth of democracy and innovation, much of the old German witch's brew of narrow-mindedness, authoritarianism, and prejudice still seethed. Theo Hanns's sketch about the government bureaucracy portrays the persistence of old ways of thinking in the new republic.

Democratizing the Bureaucracy
(Demokratisierung der Verwaltung)
A Comedy from the Revolutionary Period in One Act
1922
by
Theo Hanns

Government building. Council chamber of a ministry. Civil service committee meeting.

CHARACTERS

The minister, Schewening

Civil service councilors

Speaker for the senior civil servants, Privy State Councilor Baron von Rawfoot-Doonix

Speaker for the intermediate civil servants, Senior Privy Councilor Krinkly

Speaker for the junior civil servants, Senior Privy Administrative Assistant Threatlog

Bysitter, an administrative servant

SCENE ONE

THE MINISTER: Gentlemen! I-uh have come to your meeting to confer with you on how best to implement the democratization of my department. I-uh must declare that the removals of the key to the toilet and the Kaiser's portrait have provoked a certain opposition on the part of my administrative staff which I-uh—let us say—*deliberately* as a democrat cannot understand and—let us say—*again deliberately* as a Social Democrat could not understand. I-uh hope that today we shall succeed in clearing up these matters so that we can proceed with democratization. I-uh must tell you that as a democrat or—let us say—as a Social Democrat I cannot impose the will of the masses on everyone, but, because it is still unfortunately the parliamentary custom to do so, I wish to give the floor first to the representative of the junior civil servants.

THREATLOG: Eggzelenzee! De abolition of de key is a sign dat de Refolution has sugzeeded. Ve can do very vell vitout it. From 8 to 9 our colleaks go, from 9 to 11 de zekretaries go, and from 11 to 12 de hets of de adminiztratif debartments go. If Nature vill haf it odervise, den no key can stay in blace. Dere must be no talk of a privy counzilor's toilet being prostiduded by a chunior zivil zervant. Also, ve don't care vedder de paper chafes. Vit regard to de Kaiser's bortrait ve don't gare vich vun you hang: His Machesty or Ebert.

THE MINISTER: I-uh see that the gentlemen you have the honor to represent have already grasped the new era to some extent. I-uh must, however, learn the views of the other administrative representatives.

SCENE TWO

KRINKLY: Herr Minister, Excellency! The question of the key has never concerned us. The colleagues in our groups have scant interest in using the toilet. The majority are proprietors of suburban garden-lots, which explains their restraining themselves for the enhancement of the local countryside. I emphasize that in this case we are unconcerned with the measures the authorities have taken. Whether this function is democratized or socialized leaves us quite indifferent.

The removal of the Kaiser's portrait we cannot agree to without further discussion. There is, for example, Senior Privy Castrator Mumble, who as his parents' seventh child has the honor to register His Majesty as his godfather, therefore has the right to consider himself a relation. Furthermore, there is Senior Privy Government Auditor Piffpaff, the Kaiser's former rifle loader, who can point to a picture of the Supreme Master of the Hunt inscribed in his own hand with the dedication, Vive l'empereur et ses chasseurs!—Your Excellency will understand that the feelings of these two colleagues, which depend on a kindred and long-standing patriarchal relationship to their former sovereign, must be considered. They are both at present good republicans and hope to remain so, depending on how things go. For these reasons we request that the removal of the portrait in question be restricted as far as possible.

THE MINISTER: I-uh understand that these gentlemen cannot be so easily converted. But as a democrat I-uh do not understand and—*deliberately*—as a Social Democrat I could not understand, how private affairs can so impinge on official matters. I-uh shall come back to this. I-uh am, however, delighted by your attitude regarding the key.

SCENE THREE

THE MINISTER: I-uh now request the representative of the Senior Administrative Officials . . .

VON RAWFOOT: Herr Mini . . . ! I first protest—eh—, that the question of the key—eh—and the removal of the portrait of His Majesty and the members of the Royal Family—eh—so to speak—are dealt with in the same breath.

THE MINISTER: I-uh—

VON RAWFOOT: Herr Mini . . . ! Eh—we wish to deal with the question of the key as it affects discipline and raising staff morale—eh—as we see it. Every gentleman should have his own . . .

THE MINISTER: I-uh—

VON RAWFOOT: Herr Mi . . . ! Eh—it will not do that a senior official has to wait until—eh—a messenger boy is pleased to vacate the place and—eh—then be offered a prewarmed opportunity to sit. Eh—the maintenance of operations in the service demands the greatest possible opportunity for comfort in that respect for the senior official staff, which sees its authority—eh—threatened by the question of the key, and all the more so since the spread of socialist propaganda in work places will be facilitated in this way.

THE MINISTER (*raising his voice*): I-uh please . . .

VON RAWFOOT (*very loudly*): Herr M——! Eh—the removal of the portraits of the Supreme Personage we do not agree to. As monarchists—eh—former monarchists we are not bothered by their hanging, and as good republicans we are reminded by them at all times of what we owe to Germany.

(*A Servant enters. He goes to the Minister.*)

SERVANT   (*in an undertone*): Your Excellency, your egg-drop bouillon. (*Exits.*)

THE MINISTER: I-uh have just been summoned to an important meeting. I-uh believe, gentlemen, a coalition commission—the democratization, I-uh—I-uh—have to go to an important meeting. (*Exits!*)

THE CURTAIN FALLS

Translator's Note

Threatlog. The dialect suggests that junior civil servants were drawn from the provinces or outer territories of the empire.

Friedrich Ebert (1871–1925), mildly socialist politician and leader of the Social Democratic party, was the first president of the Weimar Republic.

KARL VALENTIN (VALENTIN LUDWIG FEY, 1882–1948) WAS probably the greatest clown Germany ever produced. The difficulty in categorizing him is made clear by the subtitle of a collection of essays: *Karl Valentin: Folksinger? DADAist?* Valentin was firmly rooted in Bavaria's folk-song tradition, and yet his appeal is universal. Although his career began in turn-of-the-century Munich beer gardens, his material went over equally well in the elegant cabarets of the 1920s and '30s. Valentin shared Chaplin's ability to raise laughs from the groundlings and the intelligentsia alike; but his comedy, colored by his own brand of dour pessimism, also toyed with the vagaries of language.

The distinguishing feature of Valentin's monologues, songs, and sketches is misanthropy. His is a world infused with malice, in which human behavior, inanimate objects, and even words behave recalcitrantly. The grotesque nonsense of his routines mirrored all of life's perversities. Valentin's satire, though often set in proletarian or petit bourgeois milieux, was not political or social so much as phenomenological; he protested everything. With his constant partner from 1911, Liesl Karlstadt (Elisabeth Wellano, 1892–1961), he could portray a multitude of types. She, short, plump, dark, played both men and women of all ages; he, lanky, scrawny, albino-hued, was always out of sync with his surroundings.

Brecht was a great admirer of what he called Valentin's "lapidary art." After the Munich production of his prize play *Drums in the Night,* he established a midnight cabaret, the Rote Zibebe (Red Raisin), and chose for its second play Valentin's *The Christmas Tree Stand,* of which Brecht wrote: "It caught the era and the people of the era in a mirror of comedy. . . . One can learn from Valentin how to construct a play. The 'Christmas Tree Stand,' viewed from a literary standpoint, is, like Valentin's other plays, a dramatic creation of first rank." A later sketch, *At the Radio Station,* is a prime example of Valentin's farce of physical mayhem, deconstructing high culture by wreaking havoc on a Schiller classic.

The Christmas Tree Stand

(Das Christbaumbrettl)

1922

by

Karl Valentin

Poor working-class folk try to celebrate the holiday six months after Christmas. The set represents their wretched digs; through the big window, center, there is a splendid view of a spring landscape with trees in bloom. The household furnishings are strewn about in a muddle: a child's tricycle, broken crockery, a Victrola and an old iron stove, a kitchen clock, cheap chromos and a slide trombone on the walls, a table telephone, blotters, and sewing utensils with coarse yarn complete the chaos. That it is a holiday can be seen from the tasty-looking whipped-cream cake that stands on a chair beside the wardrobe. Twilight falls gradually. As the curtain goes up, a Christmas carol played on the Victrola can be heard.

THE MOTHER (*[Liesl Karlstadt] is sitting in a shabby housedress and a blue apron with patchwork shoes at a small round table, center stage, under an old-fashioned hanging kerosene-lamp; holding her head in her hands, she weeps and then says*): The Christmas chimes are ringing; oh, if only I had never lived to see this day. I can never be happy again. Oh, Alfred, how could you do this to me! He went to Oberammergau to be a tour guide; but when he got to Oberammergau, the Passion Play had been over for a long time. Oh, Alfred, could anything dumber have happened to you? My old eyes are weary with weeping, and your picture is so covered with dust that I can't see it any more! Ptooy! (*She spits on the picture and wipes it off with her handkerchief.*)—There, that's better, now he looks out at the world so calmly a person can enjoy it. (*She tosses the picture into the air a couple of times.*) Oopsy-daisy! (*She lights a cigar.*) What's keeping my husband so long? My dear husband—I sent that tiresome screech owl to the market today to bring home a little Christmas tree for the children, and it's taking him forever to get back. I think he's missed the house, the old nitwit. I hope nothing's happened to him. It's already so late, the sun will soon go down. One—two—three—ah, there it went. I'd better check up on his present whereabouts, the lazy dog. (*She picks up the telephone.*) Sebastian, where are you right now? So, you just got to the market?—Did you get a Christmas tree?—That's all right then—now come straight home! Watch out crossing streets that you don't run over some lady with the baby carriage. (*There is a knock.*) Come in!

Bye-bye then, Sebastian, come straight home!—I'm waiting for you—Bless you, Sebastian! (*There is a knock.*) Come in! (*She hangs up the receiver. At that very moment the Father [Karl Valentin] comes in with the Christmas tree. He is wearing a snow-laden raglan, eyeglasses, a snow-covered hat, mittens, and carries a Christmas tree.*) Oh, there he is! I was just talking to you on the phone and here you are already!

THE FATHER: Yep, I just hanged up and ran right over.

THE MOTHER: That's right—you've got the little tree too. Oh, isn't that nice—lovely.

THE FATHER: Yeah, well, it's child-size.

THE MOTHER: But it's for the children.

THE FATHER: Yeah, I went to two Christmas tree factories before I came up with this one.

THE MOTHER: But there's no Christmas tree stand with it; did you forget it? I told you specifically to get a tree with a stand.

THE FATHER: This one don't have none.

THE MOTHER: I can see it doesn't.

THE FATHER: How can you see it if it ain't there?

THE MOTHER: I even wrote it down: a tree *with* a stand!

THE FATHER: Yeah, they had nothin' but trees with stands. This was the only one *without*.

THE MOTHER: And you picked it out on purpose?

THE FATHER: But it looks so much more natural. It would grow in the woods without a stand.

THE MOTHER: It doesn't need one there. Now how am I going

to stand it on the table?

THE FATHER: This year we'll lay it down—for fifteen years running we stood it *up;* this year we'll lay it *down.*

THE MOTHER: I've still got to decorate the tree. I said to the children, I said, when you get home, there'll be a Christmas tree too. And now he brings a tree without a stand! I'd much rather you brought a stand without a tree.

THE FATHER: The children wouldn't get a kick out of a stand all by itself.

THE MOTHER: But there's no way I can set it up!

THE FATHER: Sure, just hold it up.

THE MOTHER: Don't be silly—you can't stand here till Twelfth Night holding up a tree.

THE FATHER: Why not? I don't have much to do right now; I'm out of work.

THE MOTHER: But there's two weeks to go; you can't hold up the Christmas tree night and day—you have to go out once in a while.

THE FATHER: Then I'll take it with me.

THE MOTHER: That's what you think—now you go right back to where you bought that tree and exchange it, say they should give you a different one.

THE FATHER: Naa, naa, he's glad he got rid of this one.

THE MOTHER: Then you gotta make a stand yourself.

THE FATHER: Sure, I'll go to the janitor and get a couple of boards from the yard, and we'll stick something underneath.

THE MOTHER: Get just a little board; that'll do.

THE FATHER: Just a little piece o' board.

THE MOTHER: But take your clothes off first.

THE FATHER: All of 'em?

THE MOTHER: Your hat and coat—but don't put your hat on the bed, or all the snow will melt on it.

THE FATHER: It won't melt; it's fake Christmas-tree snow.

THE MOTHER: Now go along with you.

THE FATHER: I'll put my housecoat on now and get the boards. (*He exits.*)

THE MOTHER: He brought home a lovely little tree; he is a good husband, but an awful dope—bringing home a tree without a stand.—(*Children scream.*) Ssh!—who turned the baby upside-down? All the blood'll flow to his head. (*More children scream-*

ing.) Be quiet now—you sons of bitches, listen to that, he's surely wet again. (*Puts the baby on the table.*) Yes, yes, I'll dry you off right away. (*She takes the ink-blotter and dries the baby with it. The baby keeps on screaming.*) Now be quiet—wait, I'll blow you a lullaby. (*She takes the trombone off the wall.*) Now, baby, pay close attention. (*She blows Brahms's Lullaby; by the last note the child is asleep. The Father comes in with two two-by-four planks, gets them stuck in the hanging-lamp, bangs into everything, the table falls apart, the flypaper sticks to his face, a ghastly mess results, the Mother tries to help him.*) Here, take the baby. (*She forces the baby on him and hangs the trombone back on the wall.*)

THE FATHER: Take the boards!

THE MOTHER: My God, the way he's holding the baby! My God, what a mess! (*She laboriously extricates him from the flypaper, the lamp-chain, etc.*)

THE FATHER: Are these boards all right? We can make enough Christmas tree stands out of these now to last us for at least twenty years.

THE MOTHER: Why did you get boards this long? Didn't they have anything longer?

THE FATHER: Naa, these were the longest.

THE MOTHER: All right, then take a saw and cut out a stand!

THE FATHER: Right, I'll just get a bit of a saw.

THE MOTHER: And meanwhile I'll heat things up.

THE FATHER (*comes back with a saw and lays the Christmas tree on its side on the board*): This'll make three Christmas tree stands.

THE MOTHER: Oh dear, oh dear, the stove's smoking again!

THE FATHER: Did you at least make a fire?

THE MOTHER: Don't talk stupid! For two years now I've told you to have in the chimney sweep.

THE FATHER: I'll phone him right now; do you know the chimney number? (*He phones.*) What's that? Neither of us know the number, Fräulein.

THE MOTHER: Who are you talking to?

THE FATHER: I got a wrong number. I think I just talked to King Herod.

THE MOTHER (*pulls the receiver out of his hand*): Who is this? What?—Oh, hello!

THE FATHER: Who is it?

THE MOTHER: It's the chimney sweep's wife! Hello, Frau Chim-

ney Sweep's good lady! Is your husband home? Please tell him
to come over here right away. (*The Father talks in between.*) Tell
him our stove is smoking.

THE FATHER: He should clean out the stove.

THE MOTHER: I already told him.

THE FATHER: I can tell him too.

THE MOTHER: Then tell *her* if you're so smart.

THE FATHER: Excuse me, wouldn't you like to take your ladder
and clean out our stove?

THE MOTHER: Rubbish, she knows that already; why mention
it?

THE FATHER: She says he'll definitely come maybe. (*He hangs up
the receiver in the cupboard.*)

THE MOTHER: Will you build that stand! (*She is still kneeling on
the floor by the stove. The Father takes the saw and sits down on the
Mother.*) What are you doing, can't you look, you blind jackass!

THE FATHER: How big should the stand be, as a matter of fact?

THE MOTHER: Haven't you ever seen a Christmas tree stand?

THE FATHER: Lots of times, but I never memorized it.

THE MOTHER: Then use last year's stand as a model. (*The Father
saws the board; the Mother helps him.*) Watch out you don't cut
yourself!

THE FATHER (*keeps talking*): The children will really get a kick
out of this. Now there's a knothole. —(*The Mother goes out and
gets a coffee service.*) Bring me some chitlings to grease it. (*The
Mother goes to the table. With the saw he pushes the board up in the
air and knocks the crockery out of the Mother's hand.*) I told you you
should hold the board.

THE MOTHER: What did you do with the little piece you already
sawed off?

THE FATHER: Here it is. (*He is still holding the long board in his
hand. The Mother steps on the other end. The board hits the Father in
the foot.*) Ow, ow, it fell on my foot.

THE MOTHER: Which foot?

THE FATHER: Our foot. (*He lifts the board. It slides up under the
Mother's dress.*) .

THE MOTHER: What are you doing? Today is Christmas Eve and
he gets up to such cunning stunts.

THE FATHER: It's only Christmas Eve Afternoon.

THE MOTHER: You've cut out such a little stand we can't use

it. Bring the old one over here, but you still have to bore a hole in it.

THE FATHER: Then I'll get the drill. (*He does so, and bores a hole in the stand; the stand keeps revolving on the drill.*)

THE MOTHER: Come on, let me give you a hand. Put the board here on the table. I'll hold it and you bore a hole. (*The Father drills and talks at the same time.*) Stop talking—keep your eye on your hole!

THE FATHER: I can talk and be boring at the same time!

THE MOTHER: Who needs it!

THE FATHER: There! (*He has drilled through the board and the table, so that the drill sticks out underneath.*)

THE MOTHER: Just look at that now! He drills a hole in that lovely table. You would come up with something like that; the nicest piece of furniture in the house is ruined now.

THE FATHER: Naturally.

THE MOTHER: And besides, the hole is too big: the Christmas tree will go right through it.

THE FATHER: We don't need the stand now. We can stick the Christmas tree right in the table.

THE MOTHER: You should have done that first; then we wouldn't have needed a stand.

THE FATHER: That's what I was saying; that's why I bought a Christmas tree without a stand.

THE MOTHER: Now decorate the tree, a couple of balls dangling from it, the children will enjoy that.

THE CHILDREN (*offstage*): Mama, can we come in?

THE MOTHER AND THE FATHER: No, not just yet.

THE MOTHER: Hurry up, the children want to come in.

(*The Father hangs a pair of glass Christmas-tree balls but in the process overturns the tree and table.*)

THE MOTHER: Jesus Christ, what are you up to now? (*The children scream again.*) Right away, children, don't scream so loud! (*To the Father.*) Hurry up, stick on the candles. (*The children scream again.*) Do be quiet—you sons-of-bitches, you little bastards!

THE FATHER: Sons-of-bitches is no sort of thing to call those friggin' retards! (*The children scream yet again.*)

THE MOTHER: Calm down, or else go to hell!

THE FATHER: Don't forget, if they go to hell, this whole job was for nothin'—

THE MOTHER: Never you mind. Hurry up!

THE FATHER: Tut tut! (*He howls horribly.*)

THE MOTHER: Be still, children; your father's gone crazy. (*To the Father.*) What's the matter with you? (*The Father has tacked a candle to his finger.*) For heaven's sake, another accident! (*The children scream again.*) Santa Claus'll be here any minute—(*To the Father.*) Now, light up the tree and I'll bring in children while you do it.

THE FATHER: She's brought enough children into the world already.

THE MOTHER: I mean, I'll bring them in here. (*She goes out. The Father takes a match and lights the tree. The Mother returns and screams.*) What are you doing, you're setting fire to the tree!

THE FATHER: You told me to light the tree!

THE MOTHER: I meant the candles.

THE FATHER: You said tree.

THE MOTHER: Well, it's just a figure of speech. (*She goes out. The Father lights the candles, rings the hand-bell, and turns on the Victrola. The Mother and the children come in.*) All right, children, now Santa Claus is going to come. (*They all stand around the tree.*)

CHILDREN: Oh, oh, it's so pretty!

THE FATHER: It's not as pretty as all that.

ALL (*sing*): "Hail, hail, the gang's all here, What the heck do we care!"

THE FATHER: Well, well, they're turning the place into a beer joint.

THE MOTHER (*to a child*): Now recite your poem. Can you do it? Now recite it so your father can enjoy it.

THE CHILD:
> "Saint Nicholas through the forest strode,
> And many fir trees were his load;
> Where'er he wandered, he left in the snow
> Many crumbs of food for hare and roe.
> He opens the door with never a sound,
> And gaily the little ones gather around:

What have you brought, Saint Nicholas?
What have the angels made for us?"

(During this, the Father and the Mother weep.)

THE FATHER: She recited that real pretty, real pretty!

THE CHILD: Now, mother dear, this is for you! *(She gives the Mother a bonnet.)*

THE MOTHER *(delighted)*: Oh, you dear child, thank you! Look, Father, isn't it lovely?

THE FATHER: Ah, a can of sardines!

THE MOTHER: Go on, open your old peepers. She gave me a bonnet. It's lovely, just what I wanted . . . Did you make the bonnet yourself?

THE CHILD: No, I didn't, Mother, I stole it.

THE FATHER: What'd you say?

THE MOTHER: What? Where did you steal the bonnet?

THE CHILD: Oberpollinger's.

THE FATHER: Not bad!

THE MOTHER: Oberpollinger's, hmmm? So they've got such lovely bonnets? You dear child, everything's so expensive nowadays, nobody can buy anything any more.

THE FATHER: Of course not; that's the way to go into debt.

THE MOTHER: I hope nobody saw you?

THE CHILD: No, Mother, nobody saw me.

THE MOTHER: Then go back next week and get me another one.

THE FATHER: And on your way past Henne's, pick me up a Mercedes.

THE MOTHER: You are a dear child—soon you'll be ready for the penitentiary.—Now out of my way. See what Santa Claus brought, a mouth organ.

THE CHILD: Oh, thanks, Mother!

THE MOTHER *(to the second child)*: And a jump rope for you.

THE CHIMNEY SWEEP *(incredibly tall, with a high black top hat, axes, ladder, and brooms, suddenly enters)*: Greetings to all! *(The children scream in terror of him.)*

THE MOTHER: Calm down, children, he won't hurt you. *(To the Chimney Sweep.)* For goodness' sake, Herr Chimney Sweep, you might have knocked; we have no time for you now, we're just handing out the presents.

THE FATHER: He would come right this minute. I phoned specially to say you should come tomorrow on the holiday. Specially for a chimney sweep you're s'posed to have such good manners you won't scrape the stove now.

THE CHIMNEY SWEEP: We can do it right away. I'm good and ready. (*He begins very noisily to pound and scrape the stove.*)

THE MOTHER: Hold on a minute! Can't you see we're just handing out the presents? Nobody can hear a single word with all this noise. (*The children are also clamoring.*) Shut up, you brats!

THE FATHER: Hang on a minute, Herr Chimney Sweep. (*To the Mother.*) Looky here, you get a photo of yourself; I had it enlarged. (*He hands her a paper kite.*)

THE MOTHER: What, a kite? I think you're trying to get my goat. Am I s'posed to go fly it? All right, here, Father, your Christmas present from me is a Cockerel-brand motorbike—but this year you gotta walk it yourself. You don't get the accessory motor till next year. (*She gives him the child's tricycle which has stood covered up on stage. To the Chimney Sweep.*) Herr Chimney Sweep, please sit down for a minute.

THE CHIMNEY SWEEP: If I may! (*He sits down backwards on the chair where the cream cake is, right on top of it.*)

THE CHILDREN (*scream*): Mother, the chimney sweep sat on the whipped-cream cake!

THE CHIMNEY SWEEP: Jaysus Keerist! That would have to happen to me on Midsummer's Night. (*He turns around and wipes the cream off his pants with his hand.*)

THE FATHER (*has meanwhile sat on his bike and ridden around the stage, knocking over everything—lamps fall over—a dreadful tumult ensues. The Mother and the children scream. He stops suddenly center stage, agape, in stupefied astonishment.*) Whadya mean, Midsummer's Night?

THE CHIMNEY SWEEP: What else; today is June the 24th!

THE FATHER: Hellsbellsandbotheration! My tear-off calendar must be running slow!

THE MOTHER: Go look at it right away!

THE FATHER: Guess what, old girl—that must be why I got the Christmas tree so cheap!

CURTAIN

At the Radio Station

(Im Senderraum)

1926–1934

by

Karl Valentin

A light gray curtain forms the backdrop, brightly lit from above by several large spotlights above the stage screened off from the audience. A large sign in a black frame reads in big letters:

Warning! When the red light is on, dead silence!

Stage center stands a large table with lots of machines and circuit break-ers. We can also make out a calibrated beaker, a plate with bits of tin and, in the middle of the table, a mushroom-shaped siren. On the right edge a big bell hangs from a wooden frame, a long black thong attached to its clapper, just like at the fire station. Next to the table and at the back is a stand with the big drum-shaped cylinder of the wind machine, and further right a stand for the thunder sheet and its mallet. On the left side of the table, three dented tin buckets, a chair, a hatrack, and a standing microphone with its electric cords.

At the rise of the curtain the stage is fully lit but empty; the red light is on, however.

Liesl Karlstadt enters. She is wearing a white smock with an unbut-toned turn-down collar over her dark day-dress. She goes to the microphone and speaks.

LIESL: Dear ladies and gentlemen of the listening audience! After that scientific lecture on the sex life of the mayfly, we shall now take a brief intermission. We will be back in three minutes. (*She turns off the red light.*) Ah, here comes our actor from the national theater. But I'd like to know why the sound man is taking so long. He should have been here long ago. (*She shouts into the wings.*) Fräulein Anna, would you call into the booth and tell the sound man to get to the broadcasting studio right away! (*To the audience.*) I can't do the sound effects all by myself. (*She looks over the props and puts them in order.*) Is everything set? We can cut in with the next lecture afterwards. (*She calls into the wings as before.*) What's the matter? Isn't the sound man there? Oh, I'd better take a look for myself. (*She exits.*)

(*Karl Valentin comes in, crosses center, and stands at the table. He is wearing an old-fashioned straw hat, the type known as a "boater." He has a bristly red wig and on his incredible duck's bill of a nose a pair of black horn-rimmed glasses with circular lenses. His shiny black suit is out at the elbows and knees; the jacket, old-fashioned and countrified, has bunched-up coattails in back and at his waist. From under his trousers, altogether too narrow and short, stick out thick woollen socks and enormous elastic-sided boots.*
Liesl Karlstadt enters left and sees him.)

KARL VALENTIN: Hello!

LIESL: Hello! What do you want?

KARL: I'd like twenty-five yards of longish antenna wire.

LIESL: Say what?

KARL: Twenty-five yards of antenna wire is what I need.

LIESL: Yes, excuse me, how did you get into the broadcasting studio?

KARL: Through that door over there.

LIESL: Yes, I can believe that. But we don't sell anything here.

KARL: A friend of mine of my acquaintance wants to build hisself a radio, so he sent me here for antenna wire.

LIESL: He must certainly have sent you somewhere else. You're in the wrong place. This is the broadcasting studio at the radio station. We don't have twenty-five yards of antenna wire.

KARL: How about twenty yards?

LIESL: No, we don't sell anything; we only transmit.

KARL: Then transmit my friend the wire.

LIESL: We don't have anything for sale.

KARL: But I got the money on me. (*He picks up a roll of wire lying on the table.*) This would do.

LIESL (*takes the wire away from him*): No, I'm telling you, this wire is for another purpose!

KARL: Oh yeah? What'd you need the wire for?

LIESL: Look, would you please go away!

KARL: Then maybe you got some nice tender screws . . .

LIESL: No, all we do is put on programs.

KARL: You got hearers?

LIESL: What?!

KARL: Have you got hearers, maybe?

LIESL: You have a funny way of putting things. Naturally, we've got hearers, several thousand listeners.

KARL (*shows on his head what he means*): No, I just need one.

LIESL: Oh, you mean earphones.

KARL: No, a black head.

LIESL: You've got blackheads?

KARL: No, a black headset with two boxes like so.

LIESL: That's what I said, earphones. That's radio supplies.

KARL: Yeah, we're building us a radio up on the roof.

LIESL: You can't get that here; you have to go to a radio supply store.

KARL: Can you maybe supply me with a radio supply store?

LIESL: There are plenty of radio supply stores. There's one right around the corner, and there you can get everything you need.

KARL: Why?

LIESL: Because it's a store that specializes in radio supplies. But for all I care, you can go somewhere else.

KARL: Yeah, I'd rather do that.

LIESL: Look, just make sure you go. We have work to do here. You can get out right over there.

KARL: Yeah, that's right. But sell it to me anyways. (*He picks up the roll of antenna wire again.*)

LIESL: No, no way.

KARL: Éclair de la loony—Mademozell from Armentières—par-ley-voo—toot sweet—lundi mardi.

LIESL: What do you mean?

KARL: Lundi mardi.

LIESL: You're talking French? What's that supposed to mean?

KARL: Lundi mardi—lend it to me.

LIESL: No, no, now hurry up and get out of here! This very minute! Right out that door! (*She exits hurriedly.*)

KARL (*takes a couple of steps, stops, goes back to the table, and stares at the antenna wire*): Dog in the manger! She got the wire and she won't hand it over. And that's just the kind my friend needs. But you can keep your junk! (*He looks over the machinery on the table.*) Now what's all this stuff? The things they come up with nowadays! On'y thing they ain't come up with is a cure for the common cold! Ah, that must be the motor for the broadcasting studio! (*He pushes a button. Suddenly the storm machine starts up and winds begin to howl.*)

LIESL (*rushes back in, in a temper*): What's going on in here?

KARL (*points to the button*): That thing.

LIESL: But it can't go on all by itself! (*She pushes the button and turns off the wind machine.*)

KARL: It did.

LIESL: But that's impossible!

KARL: Of course it went off by itself. I was just standing here and it started up all of a sudden.

LIESL: You must have touched something.

KARL: No, I didn't touch nothing, I would certainly have noticed if I touched anything.

LIESL: Then you didn't touch anything?

KARL: No.

LIESL: You think I'm dumb enough to believe that?

KARL: Sure—no—

LIESL: Of course you touched it, I can see it.

KARL: Never.

LIESL: So you didn't touch anything here.

KARL: No, just a little bit.

LIESL: You're lying in your teeth.

KARL: Yes.

LIESL: This is our storm machine; this is how we make wind.

KARL: You need a special machine for making wind?

LIESL: Naturally! What do you think! If the microphone had been switched on, the whole world would have heard you making wind.

KARL: As loud as that?

LIESL: Absolutely. And this is our microphone. (*She shows it to him.*)

KARL: Pleased to meet you. (*He bows.*)

LIESL: It's a lucky thing for you that nothing happened! Can you imagine! The entire apparatus generates a current of five hundred thousand volts.

KARL: That expensive!

LIESL: You could have been killed!

KARL: Heavens to Betsy! To die so young and beautiful!

LIESL: What's taking that sound man so long? My nerves are beginning to fray! (*She shouts into the wings.*) Fräulein Annerl, what's happening with the sound man? (*She hearkens.*) What? He can't come today? That's wonderful. What am I supposed to do in that case? (*Karl Valentin slowly heads out the other side. Liesl suddenly has an idea and calls him back just as he is about to disappear into the wings.*) Stop! Are you doing anything at the moment?

KARL: I gotta get some wire.

LIESL: But you don't have anything important to do right now? I'll get you your antenna wire later on if you help me out now. You can also earn five marks real fast.

KARL (*stares at her goggle-eyed*): What do you mean?

LIESL: Now pay close attention. This is how things stand: we urgently need the sound man this very minute, but he isn't here, he just didn't show up, and that's why I'm asking you if you would like to stand in for him and do a few things with the stuff on the table. Could you do that?

KARL: No! Nothing doing! At this moment absolutely not. (*He prepares to leave.*)

LIESL: Now just stay here. You could too. (*Karl comes closer, intrigued.*) Now pay close attention: here's the situation: our speaker will be coming in at any moment to recite a poem into the microphone, and we have to make all the sound effects that go with it. That's what the sound man usually does. Because he didn't show up today, you have to help me out. First, put your hat away! (*She picks up her script.*)

(*Karl doesn't know what to do with his hat, puts it on the edge of the table, it falls off, then he sticks it under his arm, but realizes that he can't move his hand, so he puts it under his chin.*)

LIESL (*grabs the hat and flings it on the floor*): Will you stop fussing with that beat-up old hat! Now pay close attention . . .

(*Karl stares sorrowfully at his hat.*)

LIESL (*carrying on*): Now, our speaker . . .

(Karl keeps staring at his hat.)

LIESL: You aren't paying attention. What's the matter with you?
KARL: My hat!
LIESL: It's not going to go anywhere.
KARL: But what if somebody steps on it?
LIESL: Who's going to step on it?
KARL: Me.
LIESL: But you know it's lying there.
KARL: But what if I forget?
LIESL: Then simply pick up your hat! You are so aggravating!

(Karl immediately and hastily picks up his hat.)

LIESL: Now will you put that hat away once and for all!

(Karl searches feverishly for somewhere to hang his hat. He slips it over the bell; the hat slides off. He holds it in his hand in every possible physical contortion and adjustment; finally, he supports himself, holding the hat in his left hand with his right elbow on it, and balances on one leg while the other is twisted around it.

Liesl fumes with rage and snatches the hat away from him. Karl wavers, then recovers his balance.)

LIESL *(angrily tosses the hat on the table. The hat is crushed. She screams.)*: Will you get rid of that hat?

(Karl takes his hat off the table with a look of patience and mutely and reproachfully shows Liesl his smashed hat.)

LIESL: I'm sorry, but it's your own fault; you'll have to get a new one. Now will you pay close attention! Our speaker will come in and stand in front of the microphone . . .

(Karl absentmindedly stares at the floor around him.)

LIESL: Now what's the matter?
KARL: My hat!
LIESL: But it isn't here any more; it's over there. *(She points at the hat lying on the table.)* Now listen: the actor stands in front of the microphone and recites his poem into it, and we have to make all the sound effects that go with it. You don't have to say anything, but you have to do everything that's underlined in my script in red.
KARL: When?

LIESL: When I tell you. For instance, when the speaker says "thunder," we have this machine over here. (*She shows him the thunder sheet.*) Then you have to make the thunder. Or when he says, "The storm wind howls"—

KARL: I gotta howl?

LIESL: No, we have two storm machines here, the big one (*she indicates the manual wind machine*) for big winds (*Karl turns it a few times, and a terrible typhoon can be heard*). And this is the little one for little winds. (*She points out the appropriate button.*)

KARL: I already tried that one. (*He steps closer to the apparatus and touches it.*) And what's all this? (*He rings the bell.*) That's for chow time?

LIESL: No. Leave those machines alone! I'll explain them all to you! I'll stay here in the room with you.

KARL (*looks in the script*): Oh, that's how it works. When he says, "Benignant is the might of Flame"—I gotta light a fire!

LIESL: Of course not. I just told you: all you have to worry about is what's underlined in red! You don't have to do anything else. It's all very simple! Just like in the theater.

KARL: I gotcha. I did that once at a lodge show; there was s'posed to be a waterfall, so I did it with emery paper.

LIESL: What was the name of the play?

KARL: "Snow White and the Seven Little Pigs."

LIESL: Not that it matters, but the title is "Snow White and the Seven Dwarfs."

KARL: Maybe that's what it used to be called, but one of them's dead now.

LIESL: It's almost time! We have to start! Oh, something else! I almost forgot the most important thing.

KARL: My five marks!

LIESL: No, listen: when the red light is on . . .

KARL: I know what that means. It means there's a whorehouse around here.

LIESL: No! No! It means the microphone is running.

KARL: Where to?

LIESL: It means the microphone is plugged in, and from that moment the whole world can hear what's going on in this room.

KARL: You don't say!

LIESL: Therefore, when the red light is on, you mustn't cough, you mustn't sniffle, you mustn't make a sound but be dead silent, like the sign says. (*She points it out to him.*) Now let's begin. I'll get the speaker. He's been waiting outside long enough. (*She exits.*)

KARL (*stays on stage and opines dolefully*): I think I'm gonna crumble into nice little bits.

LIESL (*comes back in with the Speaker*): Won't you please . . . ?

(*The Speaker wears a dark jacket with striped gray trousers and a brightly colored floppy bow tie. He makes a very elegant impression. A handkerchief flutters coquettishly from his breast pocket.*)

SPEAKER: Say, how long am I supposed to wait! I'm in a hurry; I have to get back to the theater! I'm playing Hamlet today.

LIESL: Just a moment! Take it easy in the meanwhile. (*To Karl.*) That man over there is the speaker. So pay close attention, we're about to begin!

(*Karl pulls an empty hand out of his pocket and holds it out to Liesl, claiming his five marks; makes a gesture of counting money, paints a big five in the air and keeps his hand out. Liesl turns on the red light, puts her finger to her lips, and points at the shining red light.*)

KARL: Ah! It's on already! (*He stumbles over the microphone, knocks over a bucket, and makes a terrific racket. Liesl angrily pushes him away and places her index finger imperiously to her lips. She places herself in front of the microphone.*

(*Karl stands in front of the speaker and in mute gestures asks him how much money he's getting, while at the same time trying to make it clear with gestures that he—Karl—gets only five marks.*)

LIESL (*yet again looks around with pleading finger to her lips*): Attention! Attention! This is the Bavarian Broadcasting System. Ladies and gentlemen of the listening audience! You will now hear a performance of one of our great German classics, recited by the State actor Herr Heperdepernepi.

THE SPEAKER (*strides to the microphone and bows*): Dear ladies and gentlemen of the listening audience! Today I offer you a few excerpts from our great German classics and I shall begin with the speech of the old companion from Schiller's "Song of the Bell."

(*Karl vigorously strikes the bell, which rings out a shrill ding-a-ling. Liesl, outraged, pulls back his arm.*)

THE SPEAKER:

"Benignant is the power of Flame,
When Man keeps watch and makes it tame,
In what he fashions, what he makes,
Help from this Heaven's force he takes.
But fearful is this heaven's force,
When all unfettered in its course
It bursts forth, its own law to be,
Thy daughter, Nature, wild and free.
Woe! when once accelerated,

(Karl blows an auto horn. The Speaker and Liesl stare at him in fury and wave at him.)

THE SPEAKER:

With nought her power to withstand,
Through the streets thick populated,—

(Karl makes the sounds of a crowd murmur; we hear "Rhubarbrhubarb-rhubarb," etc. The Speaker and Liesl wave again, in shock.)

THE SPEAKER:

High she waves her monstrous brand!
By the elements is hated
What is formed by mortal hand.
From the heavens
Blessing gushes,
The shower rushes:

(Karl pours water out of the calibrated beaker into a bucket. It sounds hollow and tinny.)

THE SPEAKER:

From the heavens, all alike,
Lightnings strike.

(Karl takes the drumstick for the bass drum and beats a violent thunder-clap on the thunder sheet. Liesl waves at him. Karl, however, is not distracted and keeps beating all the harder, till Liesl leaps on him and tears the drumstick out of his hand. She violently pulls Karl away from the thunder sheet, so that he bumps his head on the bell, which starts swaying and bonging.)

THE SPEAKER:
> Hark! the droning from the spire!

(Karl uses a bird whistle to make the twitching of larks.)

THE SPEAKER:
> That is fire!

(Karl turns on the little wind machine.)

THE SPEAKER:
> Blood-red now Heaven is flushing:
> That is not the daylight's glow!
> What a rushing,
> Streets along!
> Smoke rolls on!
> The fire column, flick'ring, flowing,
> Through the long streets swiftly growing:
> With the wind is onward going—

(Karl turns on the big wind machine.)

THE SPEAKER:
> As from out a furnace flashing,
> Glows the air, and beams are crashing,

(Karl breaks slats of wood over his knee.)

THE SPEAKER:
> Pillars tumble,

(Karl tosses a board on the floor.)

THE SPEAKER:
> Windows creaking,

(Karl throws the plate of tin bits on the floor.)

THE SPEAKER:
> Mothers fleeing,

(Karl twirls the whirligig on the end of a string.)

THE SPEAKER:
> Children shrieking,

(Karl screams in falsetto: "Mammaaa, Mammaaa!")

THE SPEAKER:

> Cattle moaning,
> Wounded, groaning,

(Karl howls like a dog.)

THE SPEAKER:

> All is fleeing, saving, running,
> Bright as day the night's becoming;
> Through the chain of hands, all vying,
> Swiftly flying,
> Goes the bucket:—

(Karl tosses three tin buckets at the backdrop. In shock, Liesl tries to prevent it, rushes at him again, but catches his arm only by the third bucket and stops him.)

THE SPEAKER:

> Bowlike bending,
> Spouts the water, high ascending.

(Karl takes a glass of water, fills his mouth with water, and spritzes the Speaker.)

THE SPEAKER:

> Howling comes the blast, befriending.

(Karl turns on the siren. The Speaker is seen to scream but cannot be heard. He tries to turn off the siren but can't find the button. Karl also tries to find it, feverishly, while the Speaker tears his hair out in despair. Liesl, stupefied, wrings her hands; the Speaker tosses his script at Karl's head and dashes out yammering. Liesl feverishly pushes all the buttons but in vain. Finally, Karl leaps onto the table and sits on the mushroom head of the siren, which instantly stops. He bows to the audience, whereupon the siren immediately starts up again; he quickly sits on it a second time; it stops. Liesl has finally found the button and leans on it so that it goes off audibly. The curtain falls quickly but is rung up again immediately. Karl bows, triumphantly takes the roll of antenna wire from the table, and exits. Slowly the curtain falls for the second time.)

BERLIN IN THE 1920S WAS FILLED WITH REFUGEES FROM the Russian Revolution, and not surprisingly, one of these emigrés, I. E. Duvan-Tortsov, a former Moscow Art Theater actor, brought with him a cabaret, Der Blaue Vogel (Blue Bird). It had originally developed in Russia in imitation of the Bat, and like its model, the Blue Bird dealt in picture-book scenes from Russian folklore, heavily stylized and picturesquely costumed. Toy soldiers, idealized peasant girls, and the famous *Volga Boatmen* vignette, copied from the Bat, were stocks-in-trade. A certain amount of contemporary criticism was available, as in the satire on American advertising given here. (This was a standard butt: Evreinov had already presented at the St. Petersburg Crooked Mirror an "American" farce couched entirely in commercials.) Its author, Nikolay Agnivtsev, had emigrated from the Kievan cabaret Crooked Jimmy (see Part III, below) and would later found the Tilting-Doll (Vanka-Vstanka) Russian Theater in Paris. Between the more than seventy numbers in the Blue Bird's repertory, the conférencier Yu. D. Yushny undercut the colorful exoticism and nostalgia with his broken German and down-to-earth prattle. "An enchanting cabaret, but rather too harmless," was the verdict of critic and revue writer Alfred Polgar.

Advertising Agency Affair
(Reklama-dvigatel torgovli)
An American Romance
1923
by
Nikolay Agnivtsev

MASTER OF CEREMONIES:
>To Miss Alice Bolivar

AD-MAN:
>Of the theater "Chat-Noir,"
>Silk-lined cape, very nice,
>Fifty dollars, bargain price,
>Dress in style of "Belle Hélène"—
>Hat of color "Crème de Chine"
>Exclusive by "Madame Nadine,"
>Pale pink corset, underclothes
>From the shop "La Petite Chose,"
>Pumps are sold by "Johns and Co."
>Sunshade style is"Rococo,"
>Hairdo and decolleté—
>Signed "Institut de Beauté,"
>Teeth supplied by "Cook and Son,"
>Telephone 7-0-1.

MASTER OF CEREMONIES:
>Strode, doffing his bowler hat,

AD-MAN:
>Hatters "Whiting, Black and Pratt,"
>Five gold medals, two first prizes,

Phone 6-9-3, fits all sizes.

MASTER OF CEREMONIES:

Mister William Forrestal.

AD-MAN:

In gas and oil he made his haul,
Tidy income—free and clear,
3-0-5 million a year,
Broadway Hotel, Penthouse Suite,
Telephone is 5-2-8.

FORRESTAL:

I am rich and forty, so
"Time is money." Yes? or No?

MASTER OF CEREMONIES:

Declared Mister Forrestal.

AD-MAN:

In gas and oil he made his haul,
Trademark "Gray Owl" on the sign,
Telephone 2-7-9.

MASTER OF CEREMONIES:

But, in reply, she said

MISS ALICE:

No.

MASTER OF CEREMONIES:

Did Miss Alice Bolivar.

AD-MAN:

From the theater "Chat-Noir"
Silk-lined cape, very nice.
Fifty dollars, bargain price,
Dress in style of "Belle-Hélène"
Hat of color "Crème de Chine"
Exclusive by "Madame Nadine,"
Pale-pink corset, underclothes
From the shop "La Petite Chose,"
Pumps are sold by "Johns and Co."
Sunshade style is "Rococo,"
Hairdo and decolleté
Signed "Institut de Beauté,"
Teeth supplied by "Cook and Son,"
Telephone 7-0-1.

MASTER OF CEREMONIES:

And, having donned his bowler hat

AD-MAN:

From hatters "Whiting, Black and Pratt";
Five gold-medals, two first prizes
Phone 6-9-3, fits all sizes.

MASTER OF CEREMONIES:

The chagrined multimillionaire
Brandished a pistol in the air.

AD-MAN:

From the new firm "Smith Premier,"
Chairman of the Board John Nevin,
Phone number is 3-8-7.

MASTER OF CEREMONIES:

Stared at it, then, bang, he shot
Miss Alice in her beauty spot.
And she fell upon the street

AD-MAN:

Paved by "Jenkinson Concrete"

MASTER OF CEREMONIES:

Said Miss Alice Bolivar

AD-MAN:

From the theater "Chat-Noir,"
Dress in style of "Belle-Hélène,"
Hat of color "Crème de Chine,"
Exclusive by "Madame Nadine,"
Pale-pink corset, underclothes
From the shop "La Petite Chose,"
Pumps the wares of "Johns and Co."
Sunshade style is "Rococo"
Hairdo and decolleté
Signed "Institut de Beauté,"
Teeth supplied by "Cook and Son"
Telephone 7-0-1.

MASTER OF CEREMONIES:

In a whisper ere expiring.

MISS ALICE:

I forgive you everything . . .
But, besides my head, you know,
You shot a hole in my chapeau,

AD-MAN:
>
> Hat of color "Crème de Chine"
>
> Exclusive by Madame Nadine,

MASTER OF CEREMONIES:
>
> The open-handed billionaire
>
> Quickly hid his gun somewhere,

AD-MAN:
>
> From the new firm "Smith Premier,"
>
> Chairman of the Board John Nevin,
>
> Phone number is 3-8-7

MASTER OF CEREMONIES:
>
> And once more doffing bowler hat

AD-MAN:
>
> From hatters "Whiting, Black and Pratt,"
>
> Five gold medals, two first prizes,
>
> Phone 6-9-3, fits all sizes.

MASTER OF CEREMONIES:
>
> He remarked with visage drear,

COMMISSIONER:
>
> 3-0-5 million a year,
>
> Broadway Hotel, Penthouse Suite,
>
> Telephone is 5-2-8.

FORRESTAL:
>
> I'm very sorry about that.
>
> For the lead-ventilated hat

AD-MAN:
>
> Of the color "Crème de Chine,"
>
> Exclusive by "Madame Nadine,"

FORRESTAL:
>
> Please accept, I must insist,
>
> My check for two million, miss.

MASTER OF CEREMONIES:
>
> And, donning then his bowler hat,

AD-MAN:
>
> From hatters "Whiting, Black and Pratt,"
>
> Five gold medals, two first prizes,
>
> Phone 6-9-3, fits all sizes.

MASTER OF CEREMONIES:
>
> So exits Mister Forrestal

AD-MAN:

> In gas and oil he made his haul,
> Tidy income—free and clear—
> 3-0-5 million a year,
> Broadway Hotel, Penthouse Suite,
> Telephone is 5-2-8.

MASTER OF CEREMONIES:

> And flying to a distant star
> She murmured one last "Au revoir,"
> Did Miss Alice Bolivar.

AD-MAN:

> From the theater "Chat-Noir,"
> Silk-lined cape, very nice,
> Fifty dollars, bargain price,
> Dress in style of "Belle-Hélène"
> Hat of color "Crème de Chine"
> Exclusive by "Madame Nadine,"
> Pale pink corset, underclothes
> From the shop "La Petite Chose,"
> Pumps are sold by "Johns and Co.—,"
> Sunshade style is "Rococo,"
> Hairdo and decolleté
> Signed "Institut de Beauté,"
> Teeth supplied by "Cook and Son,"
> Telephone 7-0-1.

END

OF THE MAJOR TALENTS WRITING FOR THE BERLIN CABARET, Kurt Tucholsky (1890–1933) is probably the best-known outside of Germany, for his humorous essays and songs have been translated into English, and a revue based on his work was staged in New York. Like many of his colleagues, Tucholsky was primarily a journalist, contributor to the militant review *Die Weltbühne* for many years. He was a leading proponent for a political cabaret whose every song would be a *Gebrauchslyrik* (an "applied lyric," Erich Mühsam's term) satirizing modern urban life. Under such pseudonyms as Peter Panther, Theobald Tiger, Ignaz Wrobel, and Kaspar Hauser, he attacked nationalism, militarism, philistinism, organized religion, the bureaucracy, the blindness of justice, the wishiwashiness of the liberal press, and the opportunism of the Social Democratic party. Briefly associated with a socialist splinter group, Tucholsky tried to remain unaffiliated and seldom attacked even the Nazis directly because he considered them too low to be satirized. His motto was, "Yea, though a man preach with the tongues of angels and have no hatred—he's no satirist."

Tucholsky collaborated in a number of cabaret shows, including *Bite Please* and *Madame Revue,* in which his songs and sketches were introduced by Gussy Holl, Rosa Valetti, Paul Graetz, and other brilliant performers. Since his skits are less well known than his songs, I have included two sketches from a revue written with Alfred Polgar. The first, featuring his normative bourgeois couple the Wendriners, parodies the entertainment cabaret the Blue Bird and its audiences. The second more pointedly assails the pervasive bullying and toadying of the German character, while the "blond lady" in the satiric song that follows is Germania herself.

The Wendriners Have a Box Seat

(Wendriners setzen sich in die Loge)

1927

by

Kurt Tucholsky

HE: We should have taken a cab.

SHE: That's what I told *you*. You didn't want to.

HE: *You* didn't want to.

SHE: That's marvelous! Who didn't want to? When we were standing on the corner of Geisberg Street, and one came along—it's a real pleasure going to the theater with you.

HE: Anyway, it hasn't started yet.

SHE: Of course it started long ago! Look at all the people—didn't they all make it on time! We've missed at least three scenes. Have you got the program?

HE: No. They were out of programs—

SHE: You never buy a program. Give me the opera glasses. What's on now?

HE: Something Russian.

SHE: Russian? I can't take any more of that stuff. Wait and see—they'll stick their heads through a piece of scenery and sing "The Volga Boatman" . . . don't I know it.

HE: Don't be silly!

SHE: Say, did you turn off the light in the bedroom?

HE: No. You were the last one out of there.

SHE: So! Now you forgot to turn the light off! And then you wonder why the electric bills are so high! Sssss . . . ha!

HE: Well, maybe you turned it off—?

SHE: No, that's your job, turning off lights. The Regierers are over there.

HE: Where?

SHE: There, on the left.

HE: That's not the Regierers.

SHE: Of course it's the Regierers. Don't always contradict! Why're you humming along with the music? You don't know that tune at all.

HE: Well, that's why I sing along!

SHE: When I think of that light, I could just burst.

MASTER OF CEREMONIES (*before the curtain*): We shall begin with a moving vignette taken from the life of the Russian peasant: "The Volga Boatman."

SHE: There, what did I tell you. But you always have to argue!

CURTAIN RISES

A cabaret scene. A quartet sticks its head through a scene curtain of a Russian landscape with painted-on little bodies and sings slowly and very, very solemnly a verse of "The Volga Boatman."

CURTAIN

(Wendriners in their box)

SHE: Just like at the Blue Bird with Yunitz.

HE: Yushny.

SHE: What do you mean Yushny? I mean the M.C. at the Blue Bird.

HE: His name is Yushny.

SHE: Yunitz.

HE: For chrissake, I know what it is!

SHE: Don't keep arguing. I wonder if it's hard to stand so long holding your head like that.

HE: Go backstage and look.

SHE: You always act as if I couldn't. All I have to do is say the word to Levy, the one who knows the house doctor's cousin, and he'll take me backstage!

HE: Yeah, and you know what you'd see there?

CURTAIN RISES

The same scenery as before, but seen from behind. The four singers stand on a little step and expressively sing "The Volga Boatman" again. Nearby stands the manager talking to another actor; they are drinking cognac and telling each other jokes. The performers scratch; one of them drops a notebook he's pulled out of his pocket; the one standing next to him draws it over with his foot; a foot-fight breaks out. The manager goes by and paternally pats a female singer on the tush.

CURTAIN

WENDRINERS (*in their box*): That's what!

Life Is a Dream
(Der Traum—Ein Leben)
1927
by
Kurt Tucholsky

SCENE ONE

Before the Counter

The public room of a post office. Cross-section: the audience can see both in front of and in back of the counter. Behind the counter a post office clerk in a partially unbuttoned uniform jacket. The clerk is impolite, gruff, and cold, and doesn't put himself out. Instead, he is punctiliously unpleasant and disobliging. Before the counter a little girl, who has to stand on tiptoe to reach him, behind her a man, behind him Pallenberg, who shifts impatiently from foot to foot, behind him a lady.

THE LITTLE GIRL (*in a whining monotone*): Two five ten-cent stamps—

THE CLERK: What was that again?

THE LITTLE GIRL: Two five ten-cent stamps—

THE CLERK: There's no such thing!

THE LITTLE GIRL: But Mama said—

THE MAN: Maybe you got it wrong?

THE LITTLE GIRL: No, Two five ten-cent stamps.

PALLENBERG: Let's get this line moving! How about chairs for the ladies and gentlemen! . . . I still have to send a telegram after I'm done here, an urgent telegram!

THE WOMAN: My God!

THE CLERK: Next.

THE MAN: Oh, just a minute! This little girl—

THE CLERK: That's none of your business! What do you want—
quick now!

THE LITTLE GIRL: Two five ten-cent stamps!

PALLENBERG: I'm in a hurry, because I'm a businessman in a
hurry! We Berlin businessmen are always in a hurry. First we
wait three months, and on the last day we send a telegram! Is
this line moving?—

THE MAN: You might at least show some courtesy to little children! This little girl—

LITTLE GIRL: Two five ten-cent—

PALLENBERG: Naturally! Bravo! At least little children! Little
children have no business at the post office! The man is absolutely right. What's this all about? (*To the Woman behind him.*)
Will you stop treading on my heels?

THE WOMAN: I'm not.

(*Now all together:*)

THE CLERK: I didn't ask you—quick now!

THE LITTLE GIRL: Two five ten-cent—

THE MAN: With little children you should at least—!

PALLENBERG: Bravo! I'm in a hurry! Is this moving? Stop treading on my heels!

THE WOMAN: My God!

(*The Little Girl exits in tears. A distinguished gentleman joins the end
of the line.*)

THE MAN (*at the counter, finishing his business*): Quiet!

PALLENBERG: Is he still molesting little children? I'll get this
moving! (*Goes up to the counter.*) Two ten five-cent stamps!

THE CLERK: What . . . ah . . . get . . .

PALLENBERG: And a money order, three telegram forms, and the
complaint book!

CLERK: But first the stamps. Now, how many stamps?

PALLENBERG: Two fives and five twos and thirty-three thirty-
threes!

CLERK: Thirty . . . 65 . . . 75 . . . quick now: what else?

PALLENBERG: Next the money order.

CLERK: Do you care to pay the carrying charges?

PALLENBERG: Not if I don't have to.

CLERK: You don't have to. You may.

PALLENBERG: I may. Then I'd care to. Yes, I'll pay them.

CLERK: There's a blank on the form: "Carrying charges prepaid."

PALLENBERG: Yes, it is a blank: write it in.

CLERK: That's not my job.

PALLENBERG: Of course it's your job!

CLERK: It is not my job. You're the one who has to consign the consigned shipment ready for consignment.

PALLENBERG: You have got to write in it!

CLERK: No.

PALLENBERG (*fuming*): No? No? You think the public is something to sneeze at? I'll show you sneezing! I stand here as the public and if I stand here as the public—then you have to—

CLERK: Nothing—quick now.

PALLENBERG: But, my dear sir, you can write it in just as easily as I can! I'm in a hurry—but this is a matter of principle. My principles are at stake!

THE DISTINGUISHED PERSON: Unheard-of! Go away, you in front there!

PALLENBERG: What have you got to say about it! You'll stink up the business if you get involved! No thanks!

THE DISTINGUISHED PERSON: Shut your trap!

PALLENBERG: Shut yours! Sir! Shut yours!

THE DISTINGUISHED PERSON: Boor!

PALLENBERG: Oaf!

DISTINGUISHED PERSON: Probably some kind of Bolshevik!

PALLENBERG: Don't sell those comrades short—(*To the counter.*) Now write it down, I'm in a hurry! (*To the Distinguished Person.*) And what did you do in the war, sir?

DISTINGUISHED PERSON: I was probably deeper into enemy territory than you, sir! The impudence!

PALLENBERG: The audacity!

THE WOMAN (*crushed fore and aft*): My God!

PALLENBERG: So now write it in for me—carrying charges— with a capital *C*—Dear friend, do be reasonable—there's no pen back here. And the one over there doesn't write. And I've got arthritis in my feet—I definitely can't write!

THE CLERK: I am not obliged to perform secretarial duties of that kind. Quick now.

PALLENBERG: In other words, you want to get on somebody else's tits now? (*Turns to the Woman.*) I don't mean you!

THE WOMAN: My God!

PALLENBERG: My God! My God! (*To the counter.*) Aren't you writing it in? (*Behind him.*) My God! Who here are you calling God! This is the post office! (*To the counter.*) Aren't you writing it in?

CLERK: No. Quick now.

PALLENBERG: And suppose I took this all the way to the Kaiser! I mean, suppose I took this all the way to the Kaiser's surrogate—will you stop treading on my heels!—look how the general public is treated here! Then we'll see if you write it in—after all, it's a favor—As a businessman, I—

THE DISTINGUISHED PERSON: As a member of the National German League of (*he is overcome with a fit of coughing*), I must protest against this!

THE WOMAN: As a mother, I—my children are waiting at home alone!

PALLENBERG: As a businessman, I—as a businessman in a hurry (*To the counter.*) So far as I know, there was an ordinance passed about civil servants being civil—Goddamanblastit!

CLERK: That's none of your business!—quick now.

PALLENBERG: That's none of my business? That's none of my business? Look at how you're sitting there! Your jacket is open in front! You come to work half-naked like that? Well, I'm telling you—(*The wicket shuts down.*) Ahaa! Now he's having breakfast! Can you hear him having breakfast? He is unbelievable! He's smacking his lips. The doctor's forbidden me any overexcitement on medical grounds! I have health insurance! I'll sue the postal authorities, they can . . . (*The wicket goes up.*)

CLERK: Next?

PALLENBERG: Don't be so sure that things are going to go on like this. (*Wicket down.*) They won't. (*Wicket up.*) Are you writing it in? writing it up? writing it down?

CLERK: It is not part of my duties. And if it is not part of my duties, then it is not part of my duties. I am a civil servant.

PALLENBERG: So you aren't writing it in! Then I'll write it myself! But we'll see about this! I'll put an ad in the papers! Right in the middle! I know the publisher personally! There you'll be, large as life and on the front page! I'm telling you—hanit over—that money order—you!

THE DISTINGUISHED PERSON: Shocking!

THE CLERK: Here—quick now.

(The Woman goes to the counter to do her business.)

PALLENBERG *(collapses in total exhaustion on a bench and wipes the sweat from his brow)*: Oof! This is not to be believed! The nervous energy it drains from you! You could found two families on it! *(To the Distinguished Person, venomously.)* Well, are you satisfied now?

(The Distinguished Person doesn't answer.)

PALLENBERG: That's obvious. The general public at the post office—does the post office exist for the post office's sake or the public for the public's sake? I wonder. I'm so tired—standing all this time—and the highway in the heat—the public should be treated decently and with kindness—politely, urbanely as in other countries, for instance, in Posta Rica—if I were a civil servant—if I were a postal clerk—*(he falls asleep)*.

(Blackout. Soft music. Then:)

SCENE TWO

Behind the Counter

(Behind the counter Pallenberg as postal clerk: the jacket's just slung over his shoulders, his shirt is out in front, his cap tilted far back on his head, the wicket is down, and a step stool is leaned against it. Pallenberg has plates and coffeepots and cups and fruit peels in front of him. Before the counter the same persons as before, but now the postal clerk in civilian clothes is in Pallenberg's position. Wicket up.)

PALLENBERG: Hm?

LITTLE GIRL: Two five ten-cent stamps—*(Pallenberg hrrumphs, wicket down, wicket up again.)* Two five ten-cent stamps.

PALLENBERG: Aren't you ashamed? Yes, aren't you ashamed? How old are you?

LITTLE GIRL: Nine.

PALLENBERG: And you spout poppycock like that here? In a public office? March back home and stop bothering the civil service! Incredible! *(Wicket down. The little girl exits.)*

THE MAN: Tsk! Tsk! You might at least treat little children decently here—*(Wicket up.)*

PALLENBERG: What business is it of yours? It's none of your business! This is my job! Quick now! And since it's my job, I can be a pig and still keep my job! What do you want?

THE MAN: First of all, that you speak to me decently!

PALLENBERG: I am speaking decently to you, sir! I'm even speaking far too decently! Far too decently for such a big post office! What if my colleagues were to hear it—quick now.

THE MAN: All right—two insuredrubberstampremovalout-ofservicepostagedueexcisesstamps!

(Once served, he stands at the writing desk and writes.)

POSTAL CLERK *(now in civilian clothes)*: Here—this money order!

(Pallenberg hands it back without a sound.)

POSTAL CLERK: What's that supposed to mean?

PALLENBERG: Missing.

POSTAL CLERK: Missing? Who?

PALLENBERG: Missing something.

POSTAL CLERK: Yes, well then, what's missing, blast it!

PALLENBERG: Sir! No cursing here!

POSTAL CLERK: All right, what's missing?

PALLENBERG: This is missing: "Carrying charges prepaid"!

POSTAL CLERK: Yes, well, if it's missing, write it in please!

PALLENBERG: What? Me? I'm supposed to write it in! What do you take me for? Am I a letter writer? Am I a book writer? I'm a civil servant, sir! This is my job! A postal clerk in the civil service! Take note of that! *(Wicket down.)*

POSTAL CLERK *(to the others)*: Have you ever seen the like of this before?

THE WOMAN: Unbelievable!

THE DISTINGUISHED PERSON: The civil servant is quite within his rights! Order must prevail.

THE MAN: No! The gentleman is entirely correct—nowadays civil servants are so discourteous . . .

THE DISTINGUISHED PERSON: The lack of discipline brought on by the November days is now over and done with.

PALLENBERG *(feeding his face, behind the wicket)*: Bravo!

THE MAN: No wonder—nowadays when the reactionaries are back at the helm—a person's got to—

THE DISTINGUISHED PERSON: What has a person got to do! What is it a person has to do! I presume you support the position of the Communists on the last budget? Naturally—but when it comes to one's duties to the state—you're probably one yourself—

THE MAN: One of these days there'll be some changes made! Then you'll see (*Pallenberg, eating breakfast the while, reads the paper, tugs on his moustache*), then you'll see—your sort'll get it but good . . .

THE DISTINGUISHED PERSON: The bulwark of order must be erected once more—

THE POSTAL CLERK (*who is, despite it all, still in the middle, help-lessly*): But, gentlemen . . .

THE OTHER TWO (*fortissimo*): Shut your mouth! (*Simultaneously.*) The good old Prussian spirit—the courage of the masses—our noble German empire—the ruin of the exploited proletar-iat—

THE DISTINGUISHED PERSON: Nowadays everyone has to make a sacrifice! (*Wicket up.*)

THE POSTAL CLERK: Please, I have no pen—couldn't you do it; it's just these two words—

(*Pallenberg pulls wicket down, keeps eating.*)

THE POSTAL CLERK: People shouldn't be surprised if Russia comes here and imposes order. I'm certainly loyal to the em-peror—

THE DISTINGUISHED PERSON: Unheard-of!—(*Wicket up.*)

THE MAN: Bravo!

THE DISTINGUISHED PERSON: Scandalous!

THE MAN: Don't act so high and mighty! Quit it!

THE DISTINGUISHED PERSON: High and mighty!

THE MAN: Down! (*Wicket down.*)

PALLENBERG (*wicket up*): Hmm?

POSTAL CLERK: Oh, don't give me a hard time or make trouble . . .

PALLENBERG: A hard time? Trouble? As a somebody, let me tell you something, as a somebody I'm telling you something. Does the post office exist for your sake or our sake maybe, or do we exist for the post office's sake or do you exist for the general public's sake? Aha! This is a government office—do you under-stand me? If you want favors, go to the German Democratic party, which does all the world favors—maybe—

POSTAL CLERK: I'll register a complaint!

PALLENBERG: Ha! Haa! He'll register a complaint. I sit here on my pension rights—and where you sit, sir, is in no way clear! Have you ever registered a complaint against a Prussian civil servant? Just you try it! Two things will be set in motion: first the civil service and then the floor from underneath you!

THE POSTAL CLERK: I'll enlist the aid of the press!

PALLENBERG: Dear sir, what you read in the papers makes no difference at all! What they print is a joke! (*Wicket down.*) The public is not mature enough to deal with civil servants . . .

THE POSTAL CLERK: Most of all, these counters have to be abolished! They are the source of all the abuses!

THE DISTINGUISHED PERSON: Absurd!

THE MAN: Bravo!

THE WOMAN: My children are setting the house on fire!

PALLENBERG: What do my civil-serviceable ears hear? Abolish counters? Why, doesn't the civilian know what a counter is? (*Strokes the counter.*) The counter is the border line between civil servant and public. We counteract as we please.—The public just wishes it could peep back here into all the mysteries of the civil service (*a cup falls over*). Anyone with the tough luck to come into the world as general public—is beyond help.

THE WOMAN: I can't wait here any longer! (*Exits.*)

PALLENBERG: An honorable German is a civil servant and not a human being—anyone can be a human being. To stand in front of a counter is the German fate. To sit behind the counter is the German ideal. That's why there are counters! This nuisance— this spirit-sapping job—the responsibility—(*he falls asleep*).

(*Blackout. Soft music. The same scene as before.*)

SCENE THREE

Before the Counter

Pallenberg snoozing on the bench in the public room. People before the counter; the little girl is there too.

PALLENBERG (*jumping up in alarm*): Wha . . . what . . . where am I? Ah!—I stretched out for a nap on the bench—(*his handkerchief drops off*).

THE LITTLE GIRL (*helps him up*): Please. What's wrong with

you, uncle? There's such a funny look on your face. What was
it—?
PALLENBERG: It was a German dream.

Translator's Notes

Der Traum—Ein Leben. The title of a fairy tale play of 1834 by Franz Grill-
parzer, whose moral is "Greatness is dangerous and glory an empty jest."

Max Pallenberg (1877–1934). Pallenberg was Max Reinhardt's favorite comedian, equally at home in Molière and Gilbert and Sullivan. He was the original Schweik in Piscator's *Adventures of the Good Soldier Schweik.*

November days. The 1918 revolution of workers and soldiers which saw the
ousting of the Kaiser and the founding of the Weimar Republic.

The Blond Lady Sings
(Die blonde Dame singt)
1921
by
Kurt Tucholsky

For Gussy Holl

This Germany of mine much heed I've given,
When times were great and when they weren't so hot.
I've seen the Kaiser to the opera driven;
Now could that man wear ermine? He could not.
Those flunkeys! and those brass-hats in profusion!
With baggy minds, but uniforms well-cut . . .
My soul inquired with modest disillusion:
    "Now what . . . ?"

The cities teem and seethe with agitation.
The working class keeps toiling like a slave.
The bourgeois German lives in moderation,
Sips beer, drives bargains and attempts to save.
But artists and the younger generation
Need poverty and sorrow in their gut.
Will they succeed? They fade in enervation.
I wonder, once their noisy mouths are shut:
    "Now what . . . ?"

Then came the war; the price of food ascended.
The land went crazy. Revolution's come!
Scared stiff, the German middle class nigh ended,
The rug pulled out, it tumbled on its bum.

And everywhere idealists were calling,
Groups, councils, unions, started in to strut . . .
Bolshies and Sparticists, all parties brawling—
    "Now what . . . ?"

And now I stand before the Judge Almighty,
(At bottom God is only human too),
He lifts his flaming sword to make me fright; He
Speaks: "This wicked girl Mine eyes refuse to view!
Begone, thou shalt in hottest hellfire moulder!
Toss her in the deep pit where she must rot!"
I murmur wearily and shrug my shoulder:
    "Now what . . . ?"

Translator's Note

Gussy Holl (1888–1966). Blond, svelte actress and singer, co-founder of the Munich Bonbonnière before becoming a Berlin cabaret star. The high point of her fame was as Public Opinion in Reinhardt's production of *Orpheus in the Underworld* in 1921; then she married Emil Jannings and retired.

WALTER MEHRING (1896–1981) WAS CLOSELY ASSOCIATED
with the Berlin Dada group—Huelsenbeck, Grosz, and the
brothers John Heartfield and Wieland Herzfelde, makers of anti-
establishment photomontages—and as an art student, he wrote
the *Oresteia* parody for the second Schall und Rauch (see *Cabaret
Performance,* vol. 1). Despite (or because of?) the first-night scandal, Max Reinhardt hired Mehring to write songs for the next program, and between 1919 and 1921 he composed a series of mas-
terpieces, introduced by such outstanding performers as Blandine
Ebinger, Trude Hesterberg, Gussy Holl, and Paul Graetz. Although, like Tucholsky, he remained nonaligned politically, in his
sympathies Mehring was an anarchist with leftist tendencies, and
these sentiments show up in his numbers. His *Chorale for Seamen*
(1919), set to the tune of "It's a Long Way to Tipperary," became
a virtual folksong; and he composed the songs for Piscator's production of Toller's *Hoppla wir leben! (Hurray, We're Alive!).* Mehring is considered one of few real poets to emerge from the German
political cabaret.

The two songs given here come from his revue *Europäische
Nächte (European Nights,* 1924). "The Condemned Man Has the
Last Word" derives in part from Mehring's own trial in 1919 for
"circulating an obscenity," an antimilitarist song in the Dada jour-
nal *Everyman His Own Football* (he was acquitted on appeal). "The
Machines" was created by the great and phenomenally ugly Rosa
Valetti: she introduced Aristide Bruant's songs to Germany, was
the first Mrs. Peachum in *The Threepenny Opera,* and in 1928
opened her own cabaret Larifari (Poppycock). So powerful was
"The Machines" that even the Nazis sang it at their first mass
meeting, but without the optimistic final verse.

The Condemned Man Has the Last Word
(Der Angeklagte hat das letzte Wort)
1924
by
Walter Mehring

Before a black curtain, the accused is in the dock: he is a soigné, elderly gentleman, bald-spot, gold-rimmed eyeglasses, well-groomed beard dyed blue-black; dainty, slender, manicured hands in fetters. Two helmeted policemen on either side of him. From above a brash voice calls out:
The condemned man has the last word!

You call me guilty! Yes, I heard you say so!
Yet of this mischance I don't know the grounds—
I only know you've been and tried my case, so
It's 'cause of me the court wears wigs and gowns!
In all the papers my name is emblazoned:
But what's a murder to a journalist!
No murderer am I! Though it sounds brazen,
My last word is that I'm a moralist!

I wanted to devote myself to wisdom,
And wear bright medals on my chest some day,
I flunked out on account of logarithms,
But in theology I got an A!
I was compelled to roam the wide world over,
Because a bank ten thousand marks had missed!
But I'm still a good German, you'll discover;
In just one word: I am a moralist!

I shot the postman Schultz and heard him whimper!
I raped the virgin Anna Schmidt one night!

But I have never made God lose his temper,
I only straightened out his oversights!
The postman's legs were bowed like any wishbone,
The virgin's lips had never once been kissed!
For those rash deeds I see no need to atone!
In just one word: I am a moralist!

Where'd lawbooks be without me as a sample?
Without me what would judges referee?
I'm shown to faithful sheep as bad example
And that is how I serve the powers-that-be.
My misdeeds make a brightly lit arena
For showing off each legal casuist!
Of ten attorneys I am sole maintainer!
In just one word: I am a moralist!

A poet dies or else a great commander,
In marble will his effigy be hewn!
More dates to learn, more useless memoranda!
And facts and figures always made me swoon!
When dead, I'll educate like a lyceum!
My bones bequeathed to an anatomist!
My skull will ornament a wax museum!
In just one word: I am a moralist!

My beneficial corpse would make me prouder,
Did not my deeds appear to be half-hearted!
I'm sorry I did not invent gunpowder!
I'm sorry a world war I never started!
Great minds make art of murders and disasters,
Their deaths are honored by the State for sure!
Hats off to you! You are the perfect masters!
My last word: I was just an amateur!

(Muffled drumroll. The defendant with a jerk pulls his skull from his torso! When the two policemen try to grab him, they clutch empty clothes which drop to the ground.)

The Machines
(Die Maschinen)
1924
by
Walter Mehring

(To be sung by a chorus of men and women.)

(As dawn breaks, a perspective of dingy, eroded firewalls and smokestacks emerges. The sky is striped pink and mouse-gray. The factories suck in the work force while the hooters shriek.)

Without sleep, repose, or dreams,
Round the world and through the dark
Where no daylight ever gleams,
Man is hurried, harried, stark!
Where the falling hammers pound,
Iron shrills its hate-filled song—
Ever ringed by deaf'ning sound
The machines keep moving on!

When the final door is sealed,
When the final cheer grows still,
Fearful must the work force yield
To hooters shrieking from the mill.
Pained to earn his daily crust
Man crawls forth diseased and wan:
Through the poverty and dust
The machines keep moving on.

Of a sudden in the night
That gives neither sleep nor balm,

As awakened unto life,
Iron stretches out its arm,
From the cannons murders flash,
See! death's scythe is clashing yon.
While the human race goes smash,
The machines keep moving on.

From the deepest slavery,
Panic-stricken, near to drop,
The last mortal shouts a plea,
An order: Everything must stop!
Things stop! Yet even at the last,
When blood fills earth's greedy yawn,
Still across your graves they pass,
The machines keep moving on!

Round the earth no sleep, no dreams,
Through night's everlasting reign,
Where no daylight ever gleams,
Brightly blazes human pain!
When the last bombardment booms
And dead iron's strength is gone:
New-awakened from the tombs
Human life keeps moving on!

(While the last ones march by outside, the song rings out and the factory-hooters answer.)

THE MOST VERSATILE, PROLIFIC, AND ENDURING OF BERLIN songwriters was Friedrich Hollaender (1896–1976). Classically trained, a student of Engelbert Humperdinck, in 1919 he became the house composer and conductor for the second Schall und Rauch. There he wrote some of cabaret's greatest hits; there too he discovered Blandine Ebinger, for whom he wrote "Jonny, wenn du Geburtstag hast" (well known in English from Marlene Dietrich's rendition, "Johnny") and whom he married in 1921. Hollaender ran the Munich Bonbonnière in 1925, but the next year began to concentrate on "revuettes," turning the ordinary glamor revue into a far more politicized entertainment. He could compose scores for Reinhardt and Wedekind one week and turn out the German equivalent of Tin Pan Alley the next. Outside of Germany he is most famous for the saucy songs Dietrich launched in *The Blue Angel* in 1931. "Shag Tobacco," originally sung by Trude Hesterberg, is a spoof of the pose of decadence much affected in 1920s Berlin, when every smart young thing boasted of being "perverse."

Shag Tobacco
(Starker Tobak)
by
Friedrich Hollaender

I am so completely vice-ridden,
So crazily avid for fun!
I've tried all the thrills that are hidden,
There's nothing new under the sun.

On opium I teethed as a baby,
And hot molten tin I have drunk,
I'll madly slurp yoghurt, if maybe
Sulphur matches in it I can dunk.
In nursery school I'd spend the recess
Injecting my forearm with ink,
I buttered my bread with nose-candy, so—
Even with the best will in the world you can't come to me and
    say:
Who's this novice, this greenhorn, this wet-behind-the-ears
    kid?

Oh no!

My nerves crave as satiation
New sensations . . .
When night falls and electric lights glare crudely,
Why do my nostrils flare so rudely,
Even lewdly . . .

I read the Picture Post newssheet—haa!
I break my fast on uncooked meat—haa!

I may shack up with an all-in wrestler
Or a girl who looks like Marie Dressler!

Shag tobacco, shag tobacco,
Wild sensations, heady wine!
Ah, I'm what you'd call a per-,
A perverted filthy swine!

I am so completely vice-ridden,
So crazily avid for fun!
I've tried all the thrills that are hidden,
There's nothing new under the sun!

I've munched cigars mixed with molasses
And used honey for a shampoo.
I've wallowed in broken wineglasses,
A thrill for a minute or two.
I've gurgled mouthwash made of thumbtacks,
A sensation you never forget!
My pursuit of fresh vice reached a climax,
When cactus I kissed on a bet.
Down Main Street at noon I went jaunting,
Wearing granddaddy's specs, nothing more!
So what else can a person be wanting?
This sort of diversion is all very nice, it may be amusing at
    most twice or thrice,
But the thrill soon turns into a bore!

My nerves crave as satiation
New sensations . . .
When night falls and electric lights glare crudely,
Why do my nostrils flare so rudely,
Even lewdly . . .

I watch old films that predate sound,
I ride the trolley out of town,
I drop into the opera house,
And sleep like Alice's dormouse!

Shag tobacco, shag tobacco,
Wild sensations, heady wine!
Ah, I'm what you'd call a per-,
A perverted filthy swine!

I am so completely vice-ridden,
So avidly crazy for fun!
I've tried all the thrills that are hidden,
There's nothing new under the sun!

I dance at the reporters' ball.
That's the most perverse of all!
When I'm fed up with dance and jazz,
I haunt the Comédie Française!
Aroused, I come home with élan,
Put a Bach cantata on,
Dim the sultry lamp o'erhead,
Doze off before my hubby's said:
"L'amour, baby, l'amour!"
"Mon petit, cut the romance, mon petit, cut the romance!
Go to sleep!"

Shag tobacco, shag tobacco,
Wild sensations, heady wine!
Ah, I'm what you'd call a per-
A perverted filthy swine!

Translator's Note

According to Blandine Ebinger, the song's original ending was censored and never published. She has provided me with a manuscript of the original lines, which end the last verse; in translation, they go:

Dim the sultry lamp o'erhead,
And hear in dreams what Goebbels said:
"Some heads are going to roll!"

TRUDE HESTERBERG (1892–1967), THE DAUGHTER OF A
Berlin druggist, trained as an opera singer and gained plenty of
experience in operetta before she went into cabaret in 1914. After
the war, Hesterberg replaced an indisposed Gussy Holl at the second Schall und Rauch and won acclaim for her interpretations.
From 1921 to 1923 she ran her own cabaret, the Wilde Bühne
(Untamed Stage) in the cellar of the Theater des Westens; the first
program included Leo Heller's songs of Berlin lowlife, modeled
on the *chansons réalistes* of Aristide Bruant. The best writers, composers, and performers were showcased at the Untamed Stage,
winning it a reputation as the classiest cabaret after the Schall und
Rauch. Among the numbers Hesterberg introduced there were
Mehring's "The Aria of That Great Whore the Press" and Tucholsky's antimilitaristic "The Prince's Own Regiment." She also
presented young Bert Brecht to the Berlin public in January 1922,
when he sang "The Ballad of the Murderer Apfelböck" and "The
Legend of the Dead Soldier," provoking a riot in the process. A
few years later, Hesterberg created the Widow Begbick in Brecht
and Weill's opera *The Rise and Fall of the City of Mahagonny.*

Hesterberg's expert technique in delivering a cabaret song was
colorfully described by Hollaender: "She sang, she warbled, she
murmured the most devastating songs of the time. And they are
at their most devastating when they are murmured. But who, besides her, knew that? The blessed Yvette Guilbert had been rein-
carnated, and she was it! But with her own little kisser, her own
little schnoz, the very own gestures of her eloquent, teasing
hands."

Brecht and the Impact of Cabaret Songs

(*from* Was Ich Noch Sagen Wollte, *1971*)

by

Trude Hesterberg

The impact of cabaret songs comes especially from the personality who "puts it across." This can make even a trite verse turn into an experience. Naturally, just as an excellent role "carries" the actor in an outstanding dramatic play, so an extraordinary song carries the performer. But unfortunately, the selection of "wonderful" cabaret songs is even smaller than that of "good" roles. Cabaret artistry is the most subtle kind of miniature work. Its impact is either all or nothing. And so it is the most inexplicable and most difficult of all the arts. The precise effect a cabaret song may have is never to be predicted under any circumstances; it depends entirely upon the audience. . . .

At the Untamed Stage we had one day every week when young talent could present itself for comment. One day Walter Mehring brought me a young man whose name was Bert Brecht. Except for some pimples on his face and long, slender hands that stuck out of his jacket, which was much too short, there was nothing about him to make any special impression. In harsh Augsburg dialect he informed me that he wanted to sing cabaret songs to lute accompaniment. Since I was on my way out, I asked him to visit me at home any Sunday morning. I had long forgotten about him when one gray November morning Herr Brecht and Herr Mehring came knocking at my door. I showed them in and offered them seats, but it turned out that Herr Brecht had no instrument. So first, after much entreaty, one of my colleagues (Maximiliane Ackers) had to agree to lend a seventeenth-century lute which belonged to her. And then, in the melancholy November atmosphere of my rented middle-class flat, the first bars of "The Dead Soldier" and "Josef Apfelböck" rang out, and Bert Brecht's coarse voice cast a spell over it all. . . .

Soon afterwards he appeared on my stage [and sang the "Legend of the Dead Soldier"], and a bona fide theater riot resulted, during which the curtain had to be rung down. Quietly, amiably, young Brecht asked me why I had rung down the curtain. I said, "Didn't you hear what was going on out there?" And Brecht simply replied, "So what?"—The riot had broken out because these songs had blazed a totally new trail, and their content, moreover, was aggressive and forthright, and more than once he went up in his lines, which was received with whistling and hoots of derisive laughter. Then I came before the curtain and said rather sharply, "Calm down, people, and remember that once Wedekind was hissed too."

WILHELM BENDOW (1884–1950) WORKED IN A NUMBER OF Berlin cabarets, including his own, Tü-Tü (1924) and Bendows Bunte Bühne (Motley Stage, 1932), transferring in 1933 to the Kabarett der Komiker (KadeKo). Affectionately nicknamed "Lieschen," Bendow employed the stage persona of an outrageous and scatterbrained "fairy," whose naive questions punctured officialese or lent obscene connotations to flowery euphemisms. He often performed in drag, as in Tucholsky's monologue *The Tattooed Lady:* "Here on my breast is the political portion of my artworks. Here I have all the Impotentates of Europe . . . (*Points to her belly.*) Here I have the Reich's automatic justice machine. You put in the defendant up at the top, and five minutes later a ready-made judicial murder comes out through the bottom . . . On my left rear upper thigh I have the German war heroes . . . on my right rear upper thigh I have the decline of the West."

Like this monologue, the telephone conversation with the imprisoned bookie Max Klante was performed at Hesterberg's Untamed Stage. (Klante was a con man who used a Ponzi scheme to convince the Berlin public that he was infallible at picking winners.) When Bendow named names, as he does in this monologue with the discredited war hero Ludendorff, he was often interrupted by angry outbursts from the audience and was occasionally prohibited by the police from alluding to specific individuals. But like many comedians who have affected effeminate mannerisms, Bendow was beloved by both straight and gay audiences, and the Nazis allowed him to perform until 1944. He survived to play "Uncle Wilhelm" on German television.

Phoning the Bookie
(Telefongespräch mit Klante)
1925
by
Wilhelm Bendow

"Ah—Herr Klante! Where are you now?—Ah—You're still here!? I though you'd be far away by now! Well, yeah, I thought in Holland or some peaceful little country! And taken it all with you!—Where are you?—Where?—But Herr Klante!! In prison?! . . . Really? Is it all right there? A telephone on the night table! The new government thinks of everything!—Oh! Oh! the cell is furnished Biedermeier style!—How cosy! . . . Well, now you can sit it out nice and comfy!—Listen, how long do you have to stay there?—What! Six years!? Yipes!—And how long have you been there already?—Two weeks?—Would you look at that—how time flies!—No, just keep your shirt on! You're missing absolutely nothing!—Politics! Oh, we never talk about it!—You know I don't know anything about politics, and therefore I never talk about it!—Yes—yes! There used to be all sorts of people who didn't understand anything about it either—and they talked about it anyway!—No—I haven't a clue when it comes to politics! I just say whatever pops out of my mouth—and that way all the parties regard you as an incredibly intelligent person! . . . And then I always say, "Yes, you're absolutely right!" Recently, when I was passing through Munich, I went into a shop to buy a little souvenir.—So the man offered me a really enchanting little carved swastika—with a peephole—with really gorgeous views of Palestine!—Then, bold as brass, Herr von Ludendorff walks into the shop, because he wants to buy a fountain pen with a reversible nib for writing his memoirs. "Oh, good morning, Commander-in-Chief," I said to him. "Oh, please, come round to my right side, if you have something to say to me! I don't hear anything on the left any more!"—Then he started in shouting horribly and saying, "By the way! It's the Jews' fault that we lost the war!"—So I said polite as you please, "Oh, Herr von Ludendorff, I didn't know you were Jewish!"

WEIMAR BERLIN BOASTED (THAT IS THE CORRECT WORD) the most conspicuous and lively gay subculture in Europe. Despite a notorious law against homosexual activity between males, prostitution for all sexes and tastes was blatantly practiced. By the late 1920s, a saunter through the gay clubs was a standard item on the sightseer's agenda, offered even by Cook's tours. Many of these clubs housed their own cabarets. The Kabarett die Spinne (the Spider), for instance, offered on weekends such attractions as Luziana the Enigmatic Wonder of the Globe—man or woman?—and a male twin song-and-dance act. The Kurfürsten-Kasino featured the female impersonator Mieke parodying Ruth St. Denis and other famous dancers. The cynosure of the subculture was the Alexander-Palais (later Alexander-Palast), with its huge ballrooms, orchestra, and first-class cabaret.

Lesbian clubs were slightly more exclusive. The singer Claire Waldoff described the Pyramide in Berlin's West End in her memoirs: "One had to go through three house-doors before arriving at the clandestine Eldorado of Women, admission 30 pfennigs. Four brass musicians were playing the proscribed Club anthem. A room decorated with garlands, peopled with female painters and models. Famous male painters from the Seine were to be seen; beautiful, elegant women, who wanted to learn just a little about Berlin's seamy side, infamous Berlin; and amorous little secretaries; and there were petty jealousies and tears nonstop, and the loving couples always had to disappear to settle their conjugal differences outside. Every so often in the course of the evening, they would strike up the famous 'Cognac Polonaise,' which was celebrated by kneeling on the dance floor with a full glass of cognac in front of one. My pen quails before the unparliamentary verses of this polonaise."

The "proscribed anthem" to which Waldoff refers was the so-called "Lila-Lied," or "Lilac Song." *Lila* equates to the English *lavender* for the gay color, because of its muted, in-between nature; "Lilac Nights" alluded to the round of pleasure to be had in Berlin. In fact, Marcellus Schiffer (1892–1932), one of the most popular writers of cabaret hits, had composed it for Wilhelm Bendow to sing at the Untamed Stage, and Hesterberg promised the performer that his tuxedo, the band around his straw hat, and even the bar would be lilac to go with it. Bendow's success put his "Tattooed Lady" in the shade, and the song itself became known to all, especially from its lines, "We are different from the others" (*anders als die andern*), a reference to Bill Forster's 1904 novel of that name and to the gay-rights silent film of the same name which the authorities suppressed. The psychiatrist Charlotte Wolff recalls hearing it sung by Gussy Holl before a mixed audience at the KadeKo, when it brought the house down.

Despite Hesterberg's account and the attribution to Schiffer, the song had first been published in 1920, with words by Kurt Schwabach and a foxtrot tune by Arno Billing. At that time, it was dedicated to Dr. Magnus Hirschfeld, the proponent of homosexual rights.

The Lavender Lay
(Das Lila-Lied)
1928
by
Marcellus Schiffer

How civilized
That we're despised
And treated as something taboo,
Though wise and good, 'cause our selfhood
Is special through and through.
We're classified
Fit to be tried,
For the law forbids us too.
Since we're of different stripe,
They malign and fine our type.

REFRAIN:
After all, we're different from the others
Who only love in lockstep with morality,
Who wander blinkered through a world of wonders,
And find their fun in nothing but banality.
We don't know what it is to feel that way,
In our own world we're sisters and we're brothers:
We love the night, so lavender, so gay,
For, after all, we're different from the others!

Why the quarrels
Others' morals
Foist on us, torment bringing?
We, near and far,

Are what we are.
They'd love to see us swinging.
But still we think
Were we to swing,
You'd soon hear them complain,
For, sad their plight,
In just one night,
Our sun would shine again.
For equal rights we fought our bitter war!
We *will* be tolerated, and never suffer more!!

REFRAIN (*repeat*)

FRITZ GRÜNBAUM (1880–1941) WAS ONE OF THE MOST POP-
ular conférenciers of the German-speaking cabaret. Born in Vienna, he studied law there and performed at Hölle (Hell), where
he was seen by the German impresario Rudolf Nelson, who engaged him for the Berlin Chat Noir in 1907. Grünbaum served in
the Austrian army during the war and then performed sketches
at the Vienna Simplicissimus. In 1922 he and Karl Farkas developed the two-man *conférence,* a cross-talk act performed "in one"
before the curtain (for an example, performed with László Békeffi,
see Part III, below).

With his horn-rimmed glasses and bald head, Grünbaum came
on looking like a startled schoolteacher but erupted into witti-
cisms and sarcastic *bon mots.* Playing in a Berlin cabaret during the
inflation period, he improvised: "Ladies and gentlemen down
front. It's hard enough in these times to have to watch you eat,
but to *hear* you eat as well . . ." What made his sallies work so
effectively was his eminent plausibility. He traveled back and
forth between Germany and Austria, writing revues and acting
the M.C. in them, until the advent of the Nazis. For Grünbaum's
end, see Part V.

The Bill Collector
(Der Kassenbote)
by
Fritz Grünbaum

BOSS: What's with these bills, Fräulein? Here's another one! United Papermills wants 500 marks from me. They must be crazy.

SECRETARY: They've been dunning you now for four years, boss.

BOSS: So what? Does that bother you? Then you should have said something! After all, we're not married! Send them an answer: I won't pay; I never pay anybody. Anything else?

SECRETARY: There's a gentleman outside, in answer to the ad about hiring a new bill collector. He's been waiting.

STIFFNECK: Waiting is right! Talking about me? My name is Stiffneck. I've come about the bill collector job.

BOSS: Are you aware that nowadays bill collection is one of the toughest jobs there is? Because nobody pays anybody . . .

STIFFNECK: Everybody pays me.

BOSS: Nobody pays nowadays. I don't pay either.

STIFFNECK: You'd pay me.

BOSS: Then you'd be the first one to pry any money out of me. All right, once you're my bill collector, I'll pay you . . .

STIFFNECK: Not enough.

BOSS: I haven't said how much yet!

STIFFNECK: How much is always not enough. I'm a famous bill collector. You could even send me to the IRS, and I'd bring you money back.

BOSS: Stiffneck, now you're bragging!

STIFFNECK: All right, I'll prove it to you. Do you know someone who never pays anybody any more?

BOSS: Do I know someone? Me! Here, look: today, for instance, I got a bill from United Papermills, and they've been dunning me for 500 marks for four years. I don't pay.

STIFFNECK: You'll pay me. I'm a scientific bill collector. I deal with every debtor on an individual basis. I have a special method for each one. For some the sentimental dodge, for others the rough-and-tough one. Let me demonstrate. Let's assume you owe somebody money.

BOSS: Assume nothing—I do!

STIFFNECK: Then let's assume I've come to collect the debt.

BOSS: Ah, you want to do a trial run. An audition for the part.

STIFFNECK: That's right, I've already started.—Good morning!

BOSS: Good morning. What do you want?

STIFFNECK: Excuse me, can I speak to the boss?

BOSS: What about?

STIFFNECK: Excuse me, I have some money to give him.

BOSS: Give him?

STIFFNECK: Yes, but I have to hand it over to the boss personally.

BOSS: Well then, hand it over: I'm the boss in person!

STIFFNECK: Great! If you're the boss in person—you've fallen into my trap.

BOSS: Ah!

STIFFNECK: You see, that's how I find out whether I'm dealing with the debtor personally. You can't keep telling me the boss is out.

BOSS: Wonderful!

STIFFNECK: Let's go on! Now, if you're the boss in person, I have 500 marks from the Black and White Company to give you.

BOSS: Hand it over!

STIFFNECK: Oh dear, I just realized, I have only a 1,000-mark note on me.

BOSS: Oh, that's all right; I can change it.

STIFFNECK: Great! If you can change it, then you've fallen into my trap again. You can't keep telling me you haven't any money on you.

BOSS: I must admit that's clever. You're a first-class bloodhound! But I'm no idiot either.

STIFFNECK: Who says so?

BOSS: I say so.

STIFFNECK: Fine, let's go on!

BOSS: So, you have 500 marks for me. Hand it over. You can't imagine what a treat that is in times like these.

STIFFNECK: Which makes me all the more sorry to inform you that I've made a mistake. I don't have any money for you. I've come about something else.

BOSS: No!

STIFFNECK: I'm not here from the Black and White Company, but from Green and Blue, about your wife's fur. The little sum of 500 marks.

BOSS: Sorry, I have no money.

STIFFNECK: But you were just ready to make change for me!

BOSS: No, this money here is owing to the IRS for back income taxes. You see, you can't get any money out of me.

STIFFNECK: Unfortunately I do see. All right, goodbye!

BOSS: Goodbye!

STIFFNECK: And to have this happen in a firm where I knew the late lamented grandfather.

BOSS: Hang on a minute—you knew my grandfather?

STIFFNECK: Did I know him, that worthy patrician! Many's the time he said to me, "Stiffneck, look at my pants; that stain came from my little grandson." And now this little grandson is kicking me out. And all for a trifle . . . (*Weeps.*)

BOSS (*weeps too*): Stiffneck, come over here. Here, take it . . .

STIFFNECK: What, you'll really give me the money? Good old grandfather!

BOSS: No, you shouldn't have brought him up because now you'll get nothing. Grandfather put in his appearance in the nick of time. He would have turned over in his grave if I gave you any money. The sentimental dodge doesn't work!

STIFFNECK: You bastard, hand over that money right now!

BOSS: Ah, plan B, the rough-and-tough dodge. That won't help you either.

STIFFNECK: In that case—I give up! So long!

BOSS: Where are you going now?

STIFFNECK: To Doctor Fürst.

BOSS: Doctor Fürst? You mean the lawyer Doctor Fürst in this building? I know him!

STIFFNECK: Of course you know him; he's been having an affair with your wife.

BOSS: How dare you!

STIFFNECK: That's what *I* said. How dare he: he's paid all the blackmail installments so far when they fell due; this time he sent me here for you to pay. But now I'll go back to him . . .

BOSS: You will not go!

STIFFNECK: I will so go!

BOSS: You will not leave!

STIFFNECK: I will so leave!

(They argue loudly and incomprehensibly.)

STIFFNECK: So far as I'm concerned, the whole office can hear that your wife is having an affair with Doctor Fürst!

(Stiffneck shouts incomprehensibly again; the Boss is even louder.)

BOSS: Come here, come here—here, take the 500 marks.

STIFFNECK: Thank you kindly. You see, I did collect it!

BOSS: Ah—ah, I see; excellent! Now I get you—but of course I was on to it from the start!

STIFFNECK: Yes, you were on to it!

BOSS: Well, very good! I'll take you on as our bill collector. Come back tomorrow morning, and we'll draw up a contract.

STIFFNECK: Goodbye!

BOSS: Just a minute—I'd like my money back!

STIFFNECK: What money?

BOSS: Why, the money you extorted during that farce.

STIFFNECK: Ah, unfortunately, I can't give it back to you. I happen to be the bill collector for United Papermills, whom you've owed 500 marks for four years. Until they sent me. What do you say now?

BOSS: God, am I an idiot!

STIFFNECK: See, you wouldn't believe me when *I* told you!

ADOLF GONDRELL (GRELL, 1902–54) BEGAN AS A CHARAC-
ter comedian, but in 1923 did a stint as conférencier at Munich's
Simplizissimus and soon became the most important German
M.C. outside Berlin. When Kathi Kobus died in 1929, he
bought Simpl, where his party piece was a recitation of Ludwig
Thoma's "The Munich Native in Heaven." He also directed some
films of Karl Valentin's routines. In the article excerpted below he
attempted to elevate cabaret to the status of legitimate theater.

Directing Cabaret
(Kabarett-Regie)
by
Adolf Gondrell

If a cabaret aspires to be *more* than just a place of amusement with a traditional "variety" program, if the miniature stage therefore undertakes to achieve the status of "Miniature Art Theater," such an institution first requires an individual who will be its artistic director in a more influential, indeed decisive position. For cabaret in its present form should not be "improvised."

It is a widespread but on that account no less great mistake to think that a cabaret performance can be done off the top of one's head. If this misconception had not got into circulation, every Tom, Dick, and Harry wouldn't have had the brilliant idea of "opening a cabaret." The result, the natural and inevitable result, can now be experienced at plenty of sorry examples! The Work-Makes-Joy mass production of "art" in recent years has given many copycats the idea that they can be artists too, and the current cabaret inflation feeds not only this opinion but also those who hold it. The true cabaret expert will put the greatest possible value on the neat and conscientious staging of his sequence of acts. Running a modern cabaret properly requires, above all, experience of the laws of the theater. Anyone who wishes to present a mirror image of life and ordinary existence on the stage—whether in theater or cabaret—and in bright and lively colors, must put characters on stage in whom spectators (the ones with a sense of humor) can recognize and laugh at themselves. To achieve this, you need real actors. In cabaret too. Even in short scenes, the so-called sketches, it is simply not enough to recite the memorized text, relying on each performer's individual talents until the punch line in the protracted joke is more or less justified more or less artistically. The sketch too must be a dramatic play, though a miniature one, a small chamber scene. Conscientious detail-work is required to effect this. In short, it takes a director!

A good sketch requires the most concentrated performance art. . . . The subtle art of fashioning a cabaret song is very seldom practiced because there are so very few individuals capable of "rehearsing" cabaret songs. This is a gratifying field of activity for a good dialogue coach! A sharply pointed cabaret song, rich in subject matter, resembles polished diamonds. Only a master knows how to polish them. The leading performers of cabaret songs (we, unfortunately, have all too few!)—like Trude Hesterberg, Loni Heuser, and Tatjana Sais—have, as is only natural, not made a great fuss about the laborious detail-work which every good cabaret song requires. But they have declared to me that a cabaret song can never be improvised. The interpretation of a sophisticated song is so special, so difficult, dare I say, so elevated an art that even here no serious artist can dispense with the harmonizing and shaping collaboration of a director.

Translator's Note

Tatjana Sais (1910–81), a diseuse of the Yvette Guilbert school, played with Werner Finck at the Katakombe from 1931 until it was closed by the Nazis in 1937. Her husband-to-be, Günther Neumann, opened a nonpolitical revue at the KadeKo, which starred her and *Loni Heuser.* Both women remained active in cabaret after the war.

Curtain call for The Christmas Tree Stand, *with Valentin second from the right, and Liesl Karlstadt to his right.*

A performance of At the Radio Station, *with Liesl Karlstadt at the microphone and Karl Valentin behind the sound-effects table.*

The Volga Boatman *at the Blue Bird, parodied in the revue* Dialogues of the Courtesans.

Kurt Tucholsky als Theobald Tiger
Karikatur: Walter Trier

Caricature of Kurt Tucholsky as Theobald Tiger, by Walter Trier.

Caricature of Walter Mehring from his book The Political Cabaret, 1920.

Marlene Dietrich singing to Friedrich Hollaender's accompaniment.

Trude Hesterberg, around 1922.

A photo-portrait of Bertolt Brecht in 1917.

Wilhelm Bendow as the Tattooed Lady at the Wilde Bühne.

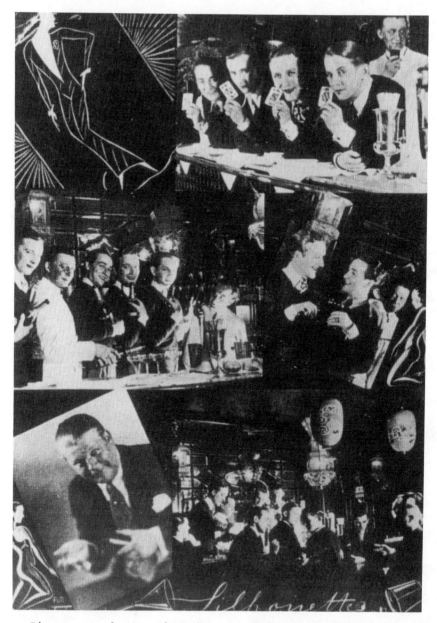

Photomontage advertising the Berlin gay bar Silhouette, much frequented by Marlene Dietrich.

Caricature of Fritz Grünbaum.

III

Cabaret in Central and Eastern Europe

1913–1934

AUSTRIAN CABARET BEFORE THE FIRST WORLD WAR HAD A hard time coming out from under the German shadow. In the spring of 1901 Felix Salten's Jung-Wiener Theater zum lieben Augustin (Young Vienna Theater at the Sign of Dear Augustin) was the first indigenous if half-hearted attempt. Marya Delvard and Marc Henry, veterans of Munich's 11 Executioners, tried to carry on that tradition at the Nachtlicht (Nightlight) and Der Fledermaus (the Bat) from 1905 to 1910. Their programs consisted largely of preexisting German material, although some Viennese talents like the raconteurs Roda Roda and Peter Altenberg were featured, and the Vienna Werkstatt artists Gustav Klimt and Oskar Kokoschka collaborated on the décor.

One of the local discoveries of the Bat was Egon Friedell (Friedmann, 1878–1938), a Ph.D. and literary historian, whose cabaret sketches were among the most successful ever played in Vienna. Coauthored with Alfred Polgar the most renowned of these sketches (which loses a great deal in cultural transmission), was *Goethe at the Exam,* an attack on German pedantry, in which Goethe, with a thick Weimar accent, comes back to life and finds, when tested by a schoolmaster, that he has all the facts about his own life wrong. Friedell was also acclaimed for his recitations of Altenberg's work and acted for Reinhardt both in Berlin and Vienna. *At the Linden Cabaret* relates Friedell's experiences when he tried to transfer his somewhat erudite style to a well-known light-entertainment cabaret in Berlin. Most Austrian provincial cabarets remained the kind of glorified music-hall that the poet Richard Hutter, who had been first conférencier at the Vienna Simpl, describes here in one of his prewar routines.

Friedell also worked at the Vienna Simplicissimus and Hölle (Hell). The basically apolitical Simpl opened in 1912, specializing in duets of composers and sopranos. There, Fritz Grünbaum (see Part II, above) and Karl Farkas developed the double-conférencier act; an example written by László Békeffi, another of Grünbaum's Hungarian partners, is given below. Hölle, despite its diabolical name, chiefly offered mini-operettas, among them a parody of *The Merry Widow,* framed by cabaret numbers.

The two leading satirical cabarets of the 1920s were geared for specific audiences: The Political Cabaret, a Social Democratic propaganda stage staffed mainly by amateurs; and the militant Zionist Jewish Political Cabaret, whose first program bore the startlingly ambiguous title "Jews Get Out!"

Not until 1931, with the rise of Austrian fascism, did a truly topical cabaret take root, reviving the name Der liebe Augustin. Again the inspiration came from Berlin, for the founders—the scurrilous poet Peter Hammerschlag (1902–43?) and the actress Stella Kadmon—sought to reproduce the Katakombe, where they had both worked. Opening on 7 November 1931 in the cellar of a café whose owner let them rent it for the price of 50 cups of coffee, Der liebe Augustin became an overnight hit, for Hammerschlag's lyrics were original and Kadmon's diseuse performance was picturesque. Hammerschlag billed himself as a "Lightning Poet" who made up verses on any subject on the spot, while the Hungarian cartoonist Sándor Szekely would cut out instant caricatures. The pianist Eugen Klein could parody any composer, pitting Richard Wagner on his right hand against Richard Strauss on his left.

Gradually, the short numbers evolved into one-act plays. One of the purveyors of these sketches was Berlin-bred Hugo F. Koenigsgarten (1904–75), who had been writting opera libretti for a living. He specialized in the Reinhardtian literary parody, including *Julius Caesar* as written by Hauptmann, *Three Times Faust* (as a stage adaptation, a movie and a radio play), and *Romeo and Juliet* as if written by Strindberg (Stella Kadmon played Juliet). As Der liebe Augustin became more politically acute, Hammerschlag failed to fit in as house author and, in 1934, moved successfully to the less engaged Literatur am Naschmarkt, founded by Rudolf Weys (see Part V).

At the Linden Cabaret
(Im Linden-Cabaret)
by
Egon Friedell

Before my first appearance:

"Now, Herr Doctor, we have naturally reserved the finale of the program for you, since it's the star slot. You are the linchpin of the whole program, which should be obvious from your place on the bill!"

Before my second appearance:

"With your kind consent we have made a little change in the line-up. Your routines are so elegantly and profoundly conceived that they ought to come a little earlier. Later on the audience is worn out and incapable of being receptive to your witty ideas. So middle of the first act!"

Before my third appearance:

"Well, you see, Herr Doctor, your brilliant personality stands out so much from the structure of an ordinary cabaret program that other conventional acts, if they precede you, spoil the whole atmosphere. The audience, coarsened by insipid jokes, can no longer get in tune with your style. Don't you think the best thing would be for you to introduce the evening?"

Before my fourth appearance:

TELEGRAM:"Most respected sir! With reference to clause 4, paragraph B, of our contract we venture to inform you that we forego your further involvement in our enterprise. The salary allotted for three nights follows by money order."

Cabaret in Graz
(Das Kabarett in Graz)
1913
by
Richard Hutter

(Author's note: I expressly declare that the following "true-life adventure" did not, of course, take place in Graz. I just say Graz, so that nobody will be able to figure out where it really did happen. I could say Linz just as easily, but then people would think right away it happened in Graz, so I'd rather go ahead and say Graz.)

I was once engaged by a cabaret in Graz. Oh, yes, Graz does have a cabaret. It is a very elegant saloon; one time even a sergeant-major came there in uniform. But he didn't want to go inside at first. You see, he asked at the door what it cost. And when he was told, "Cost? 20 heller program," he cried out in alarm, "What? 20 hellers per gram?! I ain't gonna go in; I weigh a good ninety-five kilos!"

Anyway, something very unpleasant happened to me in Graz. There I was, standing in front of the audience, and I said, "I am the well-known writer Richard Hutter." And as soon as I had said "I'm the well-known writer," a gentleman in the audience shouted at the stage, "Well, I ain't never heerd o' you!" Now instead of answering politely, "Oh, yes, you have!" or some similar courteous rejoinder, I thought as master of ceremonies it was my duty to be quick-witted, so I said, "Yes, but I'm only known to the intelligent members of the audience."

There's no special skill to being quick-witted. You've always got a supply of repartee; lots of put-downs come pouring out the minute a customer in the cabaret opens his mouth. As a rule I like it when a customer opens his mouth because I'm delighted to find there's an intelligent person in the house besides me. But if he talks too much, he starts to annoy the rest of the audience, and you have to say something to make him stop. So I usually ask him, "How old are you?" Naturally he asks, "Why?" And then I say, "Oh, I was just interested to see how long a man can live without brains." That's a good one, and he never says another word.

So, when you've got these two lines, the brains one and the intelligence one, you're quick-witted.

That particular time I had used the intelligence one. But it didn't seem to work, for the customer, who was under no obligation to do so, wanted to show he was quick-witted too—but the maitre d' intervened, and the manager, who happened to be there too, got three slaps in the face, but only one of them counted because the other two were meant for the maitre d'. But, by sheer accident, the two slaps which didn't count because they were meant for the maitre d' were so forceful that the manager lost four front teeth. The manager's wife, who saw it happen, was so frightened she had twins on the spot, and for a woman who's been married only a few weeks, that's embarrassing. And it all happened simply because I said, "I am the well-known writer." I'm not as well-known as all that. Naturally the manager was very angry because on my account he'd lost five front teeth—that's right! it was only four front teeth before . . . Sorry! you've got nothing better to do than keep track of my manager's front teeth? A lot I care about a manager's front teeth—because on my account he lost five front teeth and a customer. There wasn't much he could do about the teeth, but the customer had been a very good customer. Once he'd even ordered French fries. French fries is a very aristocratic thing. When the waiter asked, "Whadya want to go with 'em?" he said, "Baked potatoes!" Later it turned out I wasn't the reason the customer was staying away. I ran into him on the street once and asked him, "Why don't you ever come to the cabaret any more?" "I dun't care for that joint," he said; "the toothpicks are too sharp." I said, "There's nothing wrong with that; it's a good thing for toothpicks to be sharp." "Whasso good about it? You think it's good if I poke a hole through my eardrum?"

Our program at this cabaret was very good. First came a female lady, Fräulein Mitzi Vaselini. From this combination of the Viennese Mitzi and the Italian Vaselini, you can easily guess we're talk-

ing about a girl from Trieste. She sang lots of songs one after another. First the first one and then the second one; and if people let
her, a third one. But that never happened. The first one was the
lovely ballad "Let there be wine and for us don't pine." She sought
in the course of the performance to controvert the distressing fact
that wine can attain an older vintage than a seventeen-year-old
girl of at most twenty-eight by revealing she had consumed as
much wine as possible in the flower of her youth. Then she would
sing "Holloderodero!" and go home with a young man. But never
the same one.

An especially remarkable thing about her was a stunning pearl
necklace, a gift from a manager, on the occasion of a guest appearance in Gablonz. She wore so little clothing that I was always
worried that she would fall out on top. I'd say to her, "Just don't
make any moves; after all, you're standing out in the open!"

After this display of artistic strength, John Nebbish came on, a
German-American from Prussian Poland known as the King of
Ventriloquists. *Ventriloquist* comes from the Latin: *locus* means
"stomach," and *ventri* means "speech." It was a very good act, although the stomach was a little nervous. Sometimes it came out
with quite a misch-masch. Only his calling himself King of Ventriloquists was a scam. I mean it: every king is supposed to have a
crown, and yet at every performance he would come to me and ask
me to lend him a crown.

The star of our program was the tap dancer Amanda Sanscou-
lotti. A tap dancer is a dancer who the audience taps time to while
she dances. She was descended from an ancient French dynasty:
she was a granddaughter of Joan of Arc and Louis Quatorze the
Fourteenth. She once gave us quite a fright. One evening we
found her in the garden on a low bush with a man's suspenders
round her neck. Up top she was stone dead, but her legs were still
alive. The headwaiter suggested we should cut them off her—the
suspenders, not the legs—since she still hadn't paid for her dinner. Another guy put in his opinion: "Don't cut them off! Maybe
she knows what she's doing!"

We cut them off, although the suspenders were brand new. As
we were cutting them off, she was almost unconscious and came
to herself only when a friend of mine showed her a hundred-crown
note. So she not only came to herself, she even came to *him.*

But I'd rather not talk about my success. It would be presumptuous for me personally to say that I've done marvelously. I can't do something like that! Of course, I have done marvelously. The second day of my appearance in Graz, a Berlin manager who was passing through, a big manager—almost six feet tall—heard me and right away four days later wired me from Berlin to stay in Graz.

But I didn't do that; I came back to Vienna, because someone has to perform my stuff here. Besides, nobody's buying my books.

Let's Form a Corporation
(Wir gründen eine A.-G.)
1929
by
László Békeffi

CHARACTERS
Grünbaum
Békeffi

GRÜNBAUM: Next we present a sketch by Békeffi, in which we show you how to form a corporation.

BÉKEFFI (*comes on stage*): So, what's up?

GRÜNBAUM: Step this way, please.

BÉKEFFI: Well, whatd'you want?

GRÜNBAUM: Listen! I'd like to form a corporation, and I need you for it.

BÉKEFFI: A corporation? You've got that much money?

GRÜNBAUM: But my dear fellow, with money there's no art to it! Without money, however . . . without money! And we'll both show the audience how it can be done.

BÉKEFFI: I'm at your disposal.

GRÜNBAUM: Sit down. (*Békeffi sits down.*) The first thing to remember is that a corporation can inspire confidence only when it's backed by a factory, a product—in short, something of real value. Whenever the public hears about something like that, it takes the plunge. The only question is, what should we manufacture?

BÉKEFFI: Grünbaum, I've got a brilliant idea!

GRÜNBAUM: Out with it!

BÉKEFFI: We'll open a musical comedy factory!

GRÜNBAUM: Get out: who buys musical comedies today?

BÉKEFFI: Yes, you're right. Musical comedies aren't bought; they're stolen.

GRÜNBAUM: We have got to manufacture something that's cheap, quick-selling, in demand, and inexpensive to produce. I have another idea. Last summer I was in Hernals at fair time. You know what that's like. One booth on top of another, and people schlepping around buying all sorts of novelties. Their favorite buys are kazoos and harmonicas. You know what they look like? Here! (*He pulls out of his pocket a kazoo and a harmonica.*) They cost 20 or 30 cents, make a noise, people whoop it up, and everyone is delighted. Imagine how many country fairs there are in Austria, and how many kazoos and harmonicas people can buy. So we could form a corporation.

BÉKEFFI: A brilliant idea!

GRÜNBAUM: I solemnly declare the First Austrian Kazoo and Harmonica Works, Inc., to be founded. I'll be president and you can be chairman of the board.

BÉKEFFI: (*stands up*): Respected Herr President!

GRÜNBAUM: Oh, Herr Chairman of the Board!

BÉKEFFI: That'll be nice. But how are we going to build a factory?

GRÜNBAUM: What? Build a factory? Are you crazy? We've founded the factory; that doesn't mean we have to build it. It's very simple. Have you got two schillings?

BÉKEFFI: I should still have that much left.

GRÜNBAUM: And I've got two schillings. With these four schillings we buy a big piece of cardboard and a broomstick. On the cardboard we write in big letters: "First Austrian Kazoo and Harmonica Works, Inc., Factory Under Construction" and we nail it to the broomstick. And we get on the streetcar and ride out to the suburbs. There are big empty lots not far from the park, and there we plant our sign in the ground, steal a few bricks and a hod from a building site—there aren't any watchmen—and then whoever goes by will know about our building, and in 48 hours the news will spread through town like wildfire.

BÉKEFFI: I'm impressed! Congratulations!

GRÜNBAUM: The corporation will issue a preliminary 10,000

shares of stock at 100 schillings. When we've sold all 10,000 shares, we'll have 10 million, and then we're both made men.

BÉKEFFI: But how will we sell the shares?

GRÜNBAUM: Easy as pie. Do you know what a communiqué is?

BÉKEFFI: No.

GRÜNBAUM: A communiqué is an article inserted in the business section of a newspaper which we believe in good faith. You've certainly read articles in the paper that begin: "The General Stockholders' Meeting of the Oberhollabrunn Iron Foundry" or "The Board of Directors of Dried Fruit, Inc." You should be aware that these are paid announcements. So we'll insert a communiqué too—three of them, in fact. I'll dictate these three communiqués to you in a minute. The first communiqué we'll insert right away, the second in two weeks' time, and the third in four weeks, and I guarantee that after the three communiqués have appeared, all our shares will be sold. The most important thing is to phrase them so neatly that the public loses its senses of hearing and seeing.—Now take this down. Communiqué No. 1: "Financial circles are abuzz with the rumor that in the near future a factory complex is to be erected on several blocks of suburban land which will have great significance for the Austrian national economy. This is the First Austrian Kazoo and Harmonica Works, Inc. They are issuing 10,000 shares of stock with a face value of 100 schillings per share, 80% of which remain in the hands of the directors, and only 20% will be available to investors. Unfortunately, there has been so great an advance booking of this 20% that the general public will scarcely have a chance to invest its savings in this remunerative enterprise. As we have further learned, a powerful Dutch-American banking cartel stands behind this new undertaking, so that both the viability and the profitability of this enterprise is quite beyond question."

BÉKEFFI: That's fabulous, first rate!

GRÜNBAUM: You can just imagine how people will fight for our shares. They'll sell like hotcakes. So, let's get on with it. Communiqué No. 2: "Our correspondent informs us that the new construction of the First Austrian Kazoo and Harmonica Works, Inc., has made such progress that the administration building will be open for occupancy in the next few days. The first general stockholders' meeting will be held in three weeks' time in the banquet hall of the administration building. As announced, the board of directors will be conferring with other individuals, among them the following." (*To Békeffi.*) Now we have to find some good names, foreign ones too, so that the public can see what respectable people make up the board of directors. We could list any names you like; the public hasn't a clue who they are. For instance: "Baron Leopold Hohenau-Finkenstein of Seveningen Winemünde, Naval Fieldmarshal Lieutenant, General Director of the International Choral Society; Baron Ferdinand Bimsenstein von Wörthersee, von und zu Spiegelau, Lord High Candlebearer, President of Refuse Disposal, Inc., and Colonel of the Renovation Division; Baron Olaf Höringen Bjergersdorf Bjersterne, Royal Norwegian Fjord Inspector and Chief Commandant of United Geysers."

BÉKEFFI: We could use a few good exotic names as well.

GRÜNBAUM: You're right. So put down "Ali ben Saya Spahi ben Metzie Barmitzvoh Mehmed Bey, Imperial Turkish High Football Umpire and president of the Eunuchoid Super-arbitration Commission.—Della Spada Pellada de Granada Perspectiva, governor of the Spanish National Waxworks and paper-collar manufacturer."

BÉKEFFI: Now we should add a nice resounding Hungarian name. I know one.

GRÜNBAUM: Write it down.

BÉKEFFI: Count Janos Hunyadi.

GRÜNBAUM: Come on, that's the name of a laxative!

BÉKEFFI: So what? It sounds great: "Count Janos Hunyadi, Senior Hygiene Minister and Catharsis Inspector."

GRÜNBAUM: Let's get on with it. Communiqué No. 3: "We have learned from the best-informed financial sources that the First Austrian Kazoo . . ." (*hurriedly to Békeffi*) Wait—we don't need the whole name; we'll abbreviate it. For instance, the General Electric Co. is GE, so we'll call the First Austrian Kazoo and Harmonica Works, Inc., simply Kacaks, Inc. . . . Now, where did I leave off?

BÉKEFFI: "We have learned from the best-informed financial sources that Kacaks, Inc., is raising their share capital significantly, and each holder of an old share can obtain five new ones by sending a postcard to the directors at their office."

GRÜNBAUM: That way the few shares still on our hands will be literally torn out of them. We'll have 10 million and be made men.—Now I have 10 million in my pocket, the business is finished so far as I'm concerned. We go into bankruptcy. My brother-in-law will be the receiver of my estate.

BÉKEFFI: My brother-in-law will be the court's receiver.

GRÜNBAUM: And our affairs are in the best possible shape.

BÉKEFFI: But what will the investors do?

GRÜNBAUM: The investors? They have the kazoos; they can blow their brains out.

CURTAIN

Disarmament

(Arbrüstung)

1934

by

Peter Hammerschlag

Seven mousies tiny
Munched from their lunch-pails,
Silver coats all shiny,
Pink their little tails.

Seven coal-black kittens
Stalked them with their claws.
Who says it's forbidden?
Find that in the laws!

Mousies turned quite pallid,
Frightened almost dead:
"Ransom must be valid!
Take our cheese instead!"

Seven feline jawbones
Chomped and chewed and chuffed,
Till up to their craw bones
They were truly stuffed.

When the crumbs of cheese were gone—
"More!" the kitties blurt!
Then the seven settled on
Mousies for dessert.

Romeo and Juliet by August Strindberg
(Romeo und Julia von Strindberg)
1934
by
Hugo F. Koenigsgarten

(*In a half-darkened room Juliet sits and files her nails.*)

ROMEO (*paces restlessly back and forth*): It was the lark!

JULIET: It was the nightingale and not the lark!

ROMEO: It was—

JULIET: —the nightingale and not—

ROMEO: The lark! The lark! The lark! For twenty years now the same idiocy! I can't take it any more!

JULIET: Twenty years!

ROMEO: Ever since that time on the balcony!

JULIET: The balcony!

ROMEO: That time when I learned to hate you, Juliet!

JULIET (*triumphant*): And to love, Romeo!

ROMEO: It is the selfsame thing!—Be still!—Since that time you have sucked all the blood from my veins, sip by sip! I am going crazy!

JULIET: Just like your father—a real Montague!

ROMEO: That's what you'd like—you Capulet!

JULIET: Are you starting again?

(*The Nurse in ghostly garments enters from a concealed door.*)

NURSE: Lorenzo! Lorenzo!

ROMEO: Who is this mummy?

JULIET: My nurse. I killed her.

ROMEO: The way you kill everything.

NURSE: I cannot stand the fellow! I cannot stand the fellow!

ROMEO: What is she saying?

JULIET: She cannot stand you!—She thinks that she is a parrot—and in fact she really is!

NURSE: It's a pity about mankind. (*Slowly disappears.*)

ROMEO: Where does this door lead? I've never seen it before.

JULIET (*bursting out*): To the open sea!

ROMEO: Is that supposed to be a symbol?

JULIET: Imbecile! (*She files her nails again.*)

ROMEO (*pacing back and forth again*): It was the lark!

JULIET: It was the nightingale and not the lark.

ROMEO (*sinks into a chair*): I'm going stark raving mad!

JULIET (*leaps up, whirls around*): Thank God! The straitjacket! The straitjacket for my divorced husband!

CURTAIN

Translator's Note

Koenigsgarten has included allusions to several of Strindberg's works. The vampire references, the concealed door, and the parrot are from *The Ghost Sonata;* the line "It's a pity about mankind" is from *The Dream Play;* the straitjacket from *The Father;* and the general situation from *The Dance of Death*. By the Open Sea was a novel of Strindberg's.

CABARET CAME TO HUNGARY IN 1906 WITH THE OPENING OF the Bonbonnière and was rapidly embraced by urbane Budapest society. There, political satire was practiced by Endre Nagy, who sought to rehabilitate the Hungarian language in a city that, as part of the Austrian empire, was primarily German-speaking. He was aided by Vilma Medgyaszay, Hungary's first diseuse. Nagy's group was so influential that when it discredited the government of the time, the cabinet's downfall was attributed to the cabaret.

This group included Andor Gábor, Frigyes Karinthy, and the playwright Molnar. Gábor (1884–1953) enjoyed great success around World War I but in the 1920s moved to Germany to become co-founder of the Union of Proletarian-Revolutionary German Writers. Karinthy (1887–1938), polymath and publicist, displayed no ideological stripe; his criticism was not of parties but of human folly. His numerous sketches attack all sorts of foibles of everyday life and social conventions, though they rise on occasion to full-scale if bizarre attacks on war and other grand illusions. A translator of Swift, Mark Twain, and A. A. Milne, Karinthy seems to combine the savagery of the first two with the whimsicality of the last.

Another literary cabaret was the Modern Színház (Art Noveau Stage), opened in 1910 by Sándor Faludi, manager of a comedy theater; its conférencier was Ferenc Molnár (1878–1952), who has been described as "technically certainly not the most brilliant, yet an uncommonly witty, perhaps the most witty of Hungarian M.C.'s." The man who so described him was László Békeffi, who began his own career as conférencier in 1913 at the Ferenczy-Cabaret.

There were eighteen cabarets in operation in Budapest between 1916 and 1936, although the repressive right-wing Horty regime reduced their chance of acting as a loyal opposition. Nevertheless, specific politicians were satirized, and some ministers were disappointed if they failed to be mocked with any regularity. Békeffi remained a national celebrity: for years he was the leading light of

Wertheimer's literary cabaret on Andrássy Street, and in 1934 and 1935 served as conférencier at the Budapest Sziváváry (Rainbow), a kind of immense Magyar Blue Bird with a cast of eighty-two and acts grounded in ballet and folklore. On 5 September 1936, Békeffi opened his own cabaret, Podium, which his authority as vice-president of the Hungarian Stage-Authors' Union made an institution in short space. He offered tough commentary on politicians, aristocrats, and plutocrats, and when he animadverted on the financial stability of a famous bank, he was offered money by the bank's agents to desist. "What is a bank? A company that does business with the customers' money. If things go well, the customer gets a share of the profits; if things go badly, he can whistle for his money. . . . This money is the basis of all industry."

The Saltshaker
(Aztali sótartó)
1925
by
Andor Gábor

CHARACTERS
The Husband
The Wife
The Maid

THE WIFE (*lays the tablecloth; brings in plates, spoons, knives, forks, and a saltshaker too*): Now, we can serve lunch right away. As soon as Cuddles gets home . . .

THE HUSBAND (*enters in a good mood; rubs his hands together; sings*): "Lovely luncheon, don't be late. My tummy wants you on the plate!"

THE WIFE (*cheerfully*): Look, Cuddles, the table's already set. After all, I can't serve you your soup in the street.

THE HUSBAND: That's only a figure of speech: I can't serve it in the street . . . You can too. You can serve it outside or, in other words, out-of-doors. The high cost of living won't get any higher on that account, for it's high enough already, the devil hang it high. Simple working-class women serve lunch to their lords and masters out in the fields.

THE WIFE: If you went to the office in the fields, I'd serve you lunch there too.

THE HUSBAND: Till that time, however, I shall merely repeat: "Oh, lovely luncheon, don't be late. My tummy wants you on the plate." There: the greatest hits of operetta compiled, edited, and with an introduction by . . .

THE WIFE (*hurrying*): Don't rush me so, Cuddles, or I'll get all flustered.

THE HUSBAND: I'd never do that! Besides I'm in a very good mood today. Today you could use me as bait for sparrows. Shall I catch you a sparrow? Or would you prefer some other bird? For example: an eagle with two heads? You have but to command. But don't call me Cuddles. That name makes me too happy.

THE WIFE: Jesus! The saltshaker fell over!

THE HUSBAND: Why so alarmed, as if our wonderful social order had been overthrown?

THE WIFE: Because some salt spilled out.

THE HUSBAND: What do you expect to spill out? When a saltshaker topples, salt spills out. When a church topples, preachers spill out. And when the stock market topples, Jews spill out. There's nothing surprising about that.

THE WIFE: When a saltshaker falls over, a quarrel follows.

THE HUSBAND: Hahaha. Who says so?

THE WIFE: I do!

THE HUSBAND: And who else?

THE WIFE: Common belief.

THE HUSBAND: What belief? I don't believe Jewish belief, I don't believe Christian belief, and as a conservative freethinker I don't have to believe commoners, any more than I believe your *Lady's Home Companion* precepts, I believe . . .

THE WIFE: Public opinion says so! It says when a saltshaker falls over . . .

THE HUSBAND (*interrupting*): And who else?

THE WIFE: That's enough.

THE HUSBAND: For you. Not for me. If you cited authoritative sources, I might accept it. If you said, "Darwin in his work on the origin of species says: 'The fall of saltshakers is antecedent to the outbreak of a quarrel,' " I would accept it. Or if you said, "Immanuel Kant . . ."

THE WIFE: Ish!

THE HUSBAND: Not ish, im . . . Immanuel Kant. If he stated it in his work *The Critique of Pure Reason,* then I'd accept it. But you say the only ones who say so are you, whom I know, and common belief, whom I don't have the honor to know. That's not enough for me. By the way, if we're talking saltshakers, we ought to consult the Salt Tariff Board too.

THE WIFE: Well, it's so, anyway. When a saltshaker falls over, a quarrel follows. My mama said so too.

THE HUSBAND: Bravo! Your mama, may God prolong her life— somewhere other than in my house. Your mama is naturally an authority. The supreme court. The papal curia. But if I know your dear mama, the purple furia, she would describe the League of Nations Peace Conference as a quarrel too. Your mother calls it a quarrel when turtledoves kill and boo.

THE WIFE: Turtledoves bill and coo.

THE HUSBAND: Bill and coo then. But don't stray into the realm of anthropology; just stick to the domain of saltshakers and believe me, your wedded husband; when saltshakers fall over, nothing follows.

THE WIFE: Only a quarrel.

THE HUSBAND: Only? How can you say only? A quarrel is one of the ugliest things imaginable. I find it extraordinary and astonishing that you should refer to a quarrel only as "only."

THE WIFE: Only or not, the fact remains: if a saltshaker falls over, a quarrel follows.

THE HUSBAND: That's a superstition. Just like the fiction that you can catch sparrows more easily if you sprinkle salt on their tails.

THE WIFE: We're not talking about the salt you quarrel . . . no, sprinkle on a sparrow's tail, but about the salt that's in the saltshaker. Or at least was. Because it's spilled out of the saltshaker. And therefore a sprink—no, a quarrel will follow.

THE HUSBAND (*shakes his head*): All right, be stubborn. A quarrel means the breakup of blessed domestic calm. And a saltshaker is not blessed domestic calm; it can break in smithereens nice and quietly.

THE WIFE: That makes no sense, Cuddles.

THE HUSBAND (*stares at her*): Maybe you'll be so kind as to describe the causal relationship existing between a person's emotional life and a household utensil used as a saltshaker? My emotional life is cheerful—it is cheerful, you see that, don't you, it is cheerful—how it is supposed to alter through an accident, an accident, a utensil accidentally . . .

THE WIFE: It's no accident.

THE HUSBAND: What's no accident?

THE WIFE: That there's salt in a saltshaker. That's exactly why it's a saltshaker.

THE HUSBAND: Top marks! Bull's eye. But, forgive me, love, just as it contains salt, it could also contain a diamond.

THE WIFE: A diamond in a saltshaker? Fairy tales!

THE HUSBAND: Not a whit. If you put diamonds in a saltshaker, then it's got diamonds in it.

THE WIFE: Diamonds? (*Flatly.*) Impossible!

THE HUSBAND: Why so?

THE WIFE: Because nobody put any in.

THE HUSBAND: But what if, God forbid, somebody were to put one in?

THE WIFE (*Q.E.D.*): Then he's a fool!

THE HUSBAND: I grant you that! He *is* a fool! But there would be a diamond in the saltshaker! Right?

THE WIFE: No!

THE HUSBAND: Fine . . . So you won't make any concessions?

THE WIFE: No. Because the whole thing is hypothetical, make-believe, sophistry . . . I say: when the saltshaker falls over, a quarrel follows, and you bring up diamonds.

THE HUSBAND: My angel . . . a quarrel follows—*that's* hypothetical. Why should a quarrel ensue? Where are the grounds for a quarrel in this? You say a quarrel will follow; I say no quarrel will follow. Who would quarrel over this? Who would quarrel with whom? Maybe you would explain this to me as an interested party?

THE WIFE: I don't know. I only say . . .

THE HUSBAND: Then don't say it! All right?

THE WIFE: But even if I don't say it, that's the way it is.

THE HUSBAND: What is?

THE WIFE: When a saltshaker falls over . . .

THE HUSBAND: It falls over . . . Does this sentence have to be finished? Does this sentence have to be spoken at all? Can you do at least this much for me and not utter it? May I request this at least from the wife I led to the altar?

(*The Wife is about to reply.*)

THE HUSBAND (*drowning her with words*): Let's take it for granted that you are convinced . . . that the salt shaker . . . Ridiculous. I won't repeat such nonsense. You won't mind if I don't repeat it?

THE WIFE: I can do it myself: the saltshaker . . .

THE HUSBAND: Tell me, please, what century are we living in?

THE WIFE: I don't know.

THE HUSBAND (*gulps*): You know perfectly well that we live in the twentieth century, in the century of progress, and that it is a perfectly absurd delusion . . . this . . . whachamacallit . . . this thingumabob . . . this fairy tale . . . it's like saying the stork brings saltshakers.

THE WIFE: I didn't say that.

THE HUSBAND: Yes, you did.

THE WIFE: No, I didn't.

THE HUSBAND: Yes, you did. Because if you can say one thing, you can say the other.

THE WIFE: Listen you! I did not say it!

THE HUSBAND: Try and understand that you said it componentially.

THE WIFE: Impossible. I don't even know what "componentially" means, so I couldn't say it. I only said that when a saltshaker falls over, a quarrel follows.

THE HUSBAND: Don't say that. I implore you, connubial wife of my bosom, don't say that! It cannot be said.

THE WIFE: It can.

THE HUSBAND: It is the one thing that cannot be said.

THE WIFE: Anything can be said.

THE HUSBAND: No, anything but that.

THE WIFE: Why not, Cuddles?

THE HUSBAND: Because I forbid it. You heard me. I forbid it, and I'll stick to that prohibition.

THE WIFE: In other words, I'm not supposed to say that when the salt . . . ?

THE HUSBAND: I advise you not to. If you want, recite the five books of Moses, recite the sixth as well . . . the long and the short multiplication tables backwards and forwards, up and down . . . Recite *Faust,* recite all of Shakespeare's chronicle plays in the translations by Schlegel, Gundolf, or Hans Rothe, and, if you want, I'll have Shaw's translator translate them just for you . . . All those bloodthirsty tyrants can go to hell and good riddance, but as for this infamous slander that when the saltshaker . . . no, I won't say it, because it's disproved by the facts themselves.

THE WIFE: What facts?

THE HUSBAND: The facts that the saltshaker has fallen over, and even so, no quarrel followed.

THE WIFE: Oh really! No quarrel followed?

THE HUSBAND: No! No! No!

THE WIFE: All right, it didn't! But it will!

THE HUSBAND: It will not. I'll prove to you there'll be no quarrel. I'm not going to be browbeaten by a mere saltshaker. I'll show you, there'll be such calm here the rafters will bend and the walls will cave in! There will be such calm, no trace of a quarrel, that people will come running and ask (*he roars*) why it's so quiet here, why such order, such serenity, such bliss, such tranquillity prevails here! That's what'll happen, I guarantee you!

THE WIFE: Better and better. If it's calm, then the saltshaker is wrong.

THE HUSBAND: Forget the saltshaker! Get thee behind me, Satan! Strike that word from your vocabulary. How can a question of who is right arise even for a second? Me, who married you with all the legal authority of the state, or a renegade saltshaker that only cohabits with you, that even fell over whereas I never fall over, and even if I did fall over, it would never occur to me to make the hair-raising, foolhardy statement that a quarrel would ensue because of it?! And there will be no quarrel—why should there be, since there isn't the vaguest connection between me and this miserable saltshaker!

THE WIFE: And yet the atmosphere seems to suggest . . .

THE HUSBAND (*takes a knife from the table, lunges at his wife*): What atmosphere? I insist you tell me: what atmosphere? Is this not the mildest, most heavenly atmosphere? Does not the probable prospect prevail that the atmosphere will remain paradisiacally cheerful and unruffled to the furthest stretch of human existence? In spite of all the saltshakers in the world!?

THE WIFE: Well, the saltshaker knows what it's talking about!

THE HUSBAND: The saltshaker knows, but you don't . . .

THE WIFE: The saltshaker . . .

THE HUSBAND (*assaults his wife*): Back! Take back the saltshaker. The addressee declines delivery! Pocket the saltshaker! Bite it in half! But don't say a quarrel will follow . . . None will follow: I'd sooner break every bone in your body, I'd sooner strike you dead if I had to, calmly, with ice-cold composure, with tender love, with peaceful rapture . . . (*He sticks the knife in his pocket*).

THE MAID (*from outside*): I'm bringing in the soup, ma'am.

THE HUSBAND (*lets go of his wife, pants, pulls himself together*): Heh heh . . . she's bringing in the soup.

THE MAID (*entering*): Oh gosh! The saltshaker fell over. There's going to be a quarrel!

THE HUSBAND (*hastily lifts the saltshaker from the table, swings it around in a circle twice and hurls it at the back wall*: Watch out! Fire! I defy you, you wicked witches, there will be no quarrel here, even if it's raining saltshakers! And not then either!

CURTAIN

Same, Only Different

(Ugyanaz férfiben)

by

Frigyes Karinthy

CHARACTERS
Sándor
Bella
Fox

Scene: Sándor's room, part office, part lounge. Door left and right; large desk with telephone. Columns to the L and R of the door, small knick-knack tables.

SÁNDOR (*seated at the desk, on the phone*): Hello . . . Yes . . . Please send it on . . . I'll sign it . . . Right . . . Thanks! Hello . . . Good-bye. (*He replaces the receiver, looks at his watch. Five-thirty. Sighs.*) She'll be here any minute now. (*Picks up receiver.*) I don't want to be disturbed for a while. (*Hangs up receiver.*) I wish she'd get here . . . (*Picks up her framed photograph.*) Dearest . . . dearest . . . (*Puts it down.*) Never mind, everything's all right. (*Glances at his watch. Five-thirty. Turns off the light; listens for sounds outside, then tries out various poses at the desk. Settles on one effective posture, a negligent attitude expressive of brooding revery, eyes fixed dreamily on a distant point in space as if he'd been sitting like that for hours at least. Holds this position. Knock at the door.*)
SÁNDOR (*quietly*): Come in!
BELLA (*enters left; she wears a veil; an attractive, nervous woman, high-strung in gesture and voice; affected. One of those misunderstood types, fretful and complaining, a bit on the eccentric side*): Here I am . . .

SÁNDOR (*in the same position*): Thanks for coming . . .

BELLA: Is that all? You won't even get up? How long have you been sitting that way?

SÁNDOR: Hours and hours . . . Staring into space . . .

BELLA: Sándor . . . I hope you realize my coming up here means much more than it would for any other woman? Because if you don't, I . . .

SÁNDOR (*with deep emotion*): Why, Bella . . . You don't seriously imagine you have to tell me that? You still don't believe I understand you . . . I'm the only one who does understand you . . . Bella . . . you and your soul . . .

(From this point on, the gestures that accompany the dialogue are left to the discretion of the actors.)

BELLA: I do believe you . . . I hope—I know you understand me, Sándor . . . When you invite a lady to come up and see you, you don't regard it as the same common, silly adventure some vulgar man might.

SÁNDOR (*passionately*): Bella . . . you mustn't think I'm that sort of man. I just want to talk to you, Bella . . . to make an acquaintance with your mind via our conversation . . . to touch the sweet, affectionate mind I adore through words alone. You see, I've turned off the light, so that in this darkened room I won't be led into temptation by things that could breed coarse, indecent thoughts in me; so that I won't see you're a woman and I'm a man. Your body is the only feminine thing about you, Bella—your mind is a great, a remarkable mind—I'm in love with your mind, Bella, with your words . . . That's why I wanted to be alone with you. I've always despised those men who can be satisfied with a pretty face because it happens to belong to a woman. I fell in love with you at first sight. Remember? On Margaret Island. Our minds merged.

BELLA (*recollecting*): You may be right . . . I've often thought of things that way myself . . . Oh dear! I really don't know who I am. You see, sometimes I just stare into space without a thought in my head.

SÁNDOR: Bella! If you only knew how beautifully you put that . . . I must make a mental note of what you said, it is so profound, so true. Bella, tell me, how many people could appreciate what you said just now? (*He rises.*)

BELLA: Do you?

SÁNDOR: I do, Bella. I'm overwhelmed with admiration for your profound and beautiful mind.

BELLA: You may be right. Lots of time I don't understand myself.

SÁNDOR: I can't believe that, Bella. Please go on.

BELLA: Sometimes I have the feeling I'd like to be somewhere else.

SÁNDOR: Is that right? Please go on.

BELLA: I can't say where—anywhere, somewhere I've never been before.

SÁNDOR: Bella! How true, how insightful . . . How did you put that? Let me engrave it on the tablets of my mind . . . "Somewhere I've never been before."

BELLA: I don't think people are born to be what they turn into later on.

SÁNDOR: Bella! How very true! How exquisitely put. (*Bella manages an exaggerated sigh.*) Bella . . . you must tell me why you sighed!

BELLA: Who knows—I don't.

SÁNDOR: I do, Bella . . . it was in reply to my question. That reply makes our relationship crystal clear. I won't ask you any more questions. I feel I understand you and admire you. I don't want anything from you. (*Moves closer and closer to her.*)

BELLA (*drawing away*): No, Sándor, don't come any closer . . . I have to go now.

SÁNDOR (*distressed*): Must you go so soon, Bella?

BELLA: I must . . . I have other things to do! . . . And the present moment is so exquisitely lovely that we mustn't prolong it . . . (*Retreats.*)

SÁNDOR (*following her*): But, Bella . . . let me hope . . .

BELLA: Tomorrow . . . tomorrow at five-thirty. Till tomorrow.

SÁNDOR: Bella . . . Good-bye.

(*Bella knocks over one of the knick-knacks on her way out.*)

BELLA: Oh dear! It gave me quite a fright! I'm so clumsy!

SÁNDOR (*ardently*): Clumsy! Oh no, Bella . . . believe me, there was so much of you in that gesture, so much of your wonderful, dreamy self. I admire you for that gesture. (*Kisses her hand.*)

BELLA: Good-bye, Sándor!

SÁNDOR: Good-bye, Bella!

(They stand staring at each other for a little while. Bella suddenly withdraws her hand and hurries out. Sándor looks after her, sighs, returns to the desk, musing, turns on the light.)

SÁNDOR: All right, wake up! There's work to be done. *(Studying some papers.)* What the hell is this? Still here? Damn it! Still not filed! *(Sits down.)* Damn and blast! *(Shouts.)* Fox!! Fox!! Fox!! *(Enter Fox; a pale, weedy young man with a cowlick.)*

FOX: Yes, sir!

SÁNDOR: Lookit, Fox! Why haven't you filed this lousy rubber contract in the Krakower dossier?

FOX: I'm sorry sir; I completely forgot about it.

SÁNDOR: Complete forgot about it? What's your damned head stuffed with if a simple thing like this can slip out of it, huh? What do you think you're doing here all day on the money I pay you? Are you a nitwit? Or what?

FOX: Excuse me, sir. I don't know . . . sometimes I feel so strange.

SÁNDOR: Feel so strange? Got a bellyache, I suppose?

FOX: Oh no . . . but I don't know what it is . . . honestly, sir, sometimes I stare into space without a thought in my head.

SÁNDOR: Stare into space without a thought in your head? On my money? Then you'd better check into a madhouse—that's where they treat cases like you—but don't come to this office taking my money under false pretenses! This is ridiculous!

FOX: Don't lose your temper, sir . . . please believe me. I often feel like I'd rather be anywhere else.

SÁNDOR: Anywhere else? Would you indeed? Well, that's very interesting! Maybe you're not happy in the Rubber Department, you snivelling puppy! You'd like to be transferred to the Mucilage Department, wouldn't you, naturally, they only work mornings there. The snag is, my good man, they won't want you now that you've demonstrated your incompetence in this department.

FOX: I don't mean that, sir. I don't know where, anywhere, somewhere I've never been before.

SÁNDOR: The loony bin, man, the loony bin. That's where you belong.

FOX: Sir, I don't think people are born to be what they turn into later.

SÁNDOR: Do tell! You got more of that garbage? You should be ashamed of yourself, a grown-up man, talking drivel like that instead of apologizing for your stupidity!

(*Fox sighs.*)

SÁNDOR: What are you wheezing for? Trying to wheeze me out of here?

FOX: Who knows? I don't know myself.

SÁNDOR (*rising*): Who knows? You don't know yourself? You've got the nerve to say that to my face? You'll know soon enough, I promise you! (*He marches on him brandishing the files.*)

(*Fox retreats nervously and knocks over another knick-knack.*)

SÁNDOR: Idiot! Clumsy idiot! Are you blind? Isn't it bad enough you don't do a lick of work, you have to break things too! I'd like you to know you're fired, starting the first of the month. Get out of here! And take this junk with you! (*Throws the file after Fox.*) They send me these nincompoops just to get on my nerves!

CURTAIN

The Turtle, or Who's the Crazy Around Here?

(Teknosbéka, vagy ki az orült a csárdában)

by

Frigyes Karinthy

CHARACTERS
The Doctor
Sam
Male Nurse
Lunatic

It all takes place in an observation room in a mental hospital.

DOCTOR (*enters right, looks around and shouts*): Vandrak!

MALE NURSE (*enters from room left, a straitjacket over his arm*): You called, sir?

DOCTOR: Well, what's up? Did you remove his straitjacket?

MALE NURSE: Yes sir. He feels all right. He went to sleep.

DOCTOR: Fine. Was he restless with the straitjacket off?

MALE NURSE: Not much. But he wouldn't let go of the teeth.

DOCTOR: That figures. I expected that. Go back in; I'll be down later. I'm going up to the violent ward now. And be careful.

MALE NURSE: I will, sir. (*He puts the straitjacket on a chair and exits left.*)

DOCTOR (*mops his brow. A knock at the door right; he moves to it*): Come in! (*He opens the door.*)

SAM (*hesitates as he comes in*): Good afternoon . . . Excuse me. (*He looks around nervously.*) I'm looking for Dr. Haduva.

DOCTOR: I'm Dr. Haduva. Can I help you?

SAM: The doorman told me you'd be coming here from your office. Forgive me for following you. My name is Sam Sobersides, and I'm a third-year medical student.

DOCTOR (*shaking hands amiably*): Pleased to meet you, my dear sir. Your uncle the County Councillor told me you'd be paying us a visit. I'm delighted to see you. What can I do for you?

SAM (*offhandedly*): Maybe my uncle mentioned that lately I've taken an interest in . . . well, I'd like to look around a little.

DOCTOR: Yes, yes, I know. You want to see what a mental hospital's like. I'll be glad to show you around. Have you seen the park yet?

SAM: No, I came straight here from your office.

DOCTOR: Well then, let's plunge *in medias res.* Where we are now is one of the special observation rooms in the paranoia section where we're presently studying a most interesting case of dementia, who's been in isolation for a week now. A mild case of *dementia praecox.*

SAM (*superciliously*): Yes, yes, I know. *Dementia multiforma* . . . volume four, page nine. Obsessions, delusions of grandeur, persecution complexes . . .

DOCTOR: That's right. I can see you've been studying the data.

SAM: I should mention I've plowed through all five volumes on psychiatry on my own, though I won't be attending the lectures till next year. But I've never seen a living lunatic (*naively*), and I'm very curious.

DOCTOR (*smiles*): Well, you'll see more than your share here. Only you mustn't get upset. The first time it's liable to have a funny effect on the nerves.

SAM (*waves aside his warning*): Oh, please, you can count on me, I've read about how to deal with them and talk to them. As I said, I've read all the relevant literature.

DOCTOR: Well, then, we're all right. Shall we start down on the first floor? Or stay here?

SAM (*pointing to the door left, fascinated*): Here? Is the patient here?

DOCTOR: Yes. Well, shall we go in and see him?

SAM (*steps back alarmed, then nonchalantly*): Of course . . . why not . . . we're not disturbing him, are we?

DOCTOR: Certainly not. As I was saying, he's one of our milder cases. He was a little restless this afternoon, but he's feeling much better now.

SAM (*restless*): Restless, was he?

DOCTOR: Yes. He yanked out three of the nurse's teeth; then he put a tub on his back and crawled out on the roof on his hands and knees. But he's feeling much better now.

SAM: How's that again?

DOCTOR: A simple case, one you'll understand, my dear sir. There's been a lot written about this case history. He imagines he's a turtle. His dominant idea is that he is Moses, savior of the world, who picks nits out of people's heads, sometimes as an anteater, sometimes as a turtle.

SAM: Well . . . well . . . so he was a little restless.

DOCTOR: A simple case. He thinks everyone else is insane and their insanity is due to nits in their brain.

SAM: That makes sense—I mean, I understand. Only I can't quite see why he yanked out three of what's-his-name's teeth.

DOCTOR: To make it harder to discover.

SAM: Discover what?

DOCTOR: The turtle.

SAM: Oh, yes . . .

DOCTOR: The thing of it is, this patient . . . (*A knock at the door.*) Who's there?

VOICE: Doctor, come quickly, please. Sedlacsik has bitten off Bleyweiss's little finger!

DOCTOR (*hand to his head*): Good grief, I forgot all about it! He wanted to bite off Bleyweiss's head, and I got as far as making him concede that biting off his finger would do. I meant to talk him out of that this afternoon, but it's too late now! (*To Sam.*) Excuse me, I've got to run. Please wait; I'll be back in five minutes.

SAM (*looks at the door anxiously*): Listen, maybe I can come with you.

DOCTOR: There's no need. This is a surgical matter. I'll be back in a minute. (*He exits right, locking the door out of habit.*)

SAM: Doctor. (*He goes to the door and finds it's locked.*) Oh, no. He locked it. (*He rattles the door.*) Oh, for heaven's sake!

MALE NURSE (*meanwhile enters left, notices Sam, who doesn't see him*): Doctor . . . (*Aside.*) Who's that? The door's locked? Another one for this section? Thanks a lot; I've got my hands full with Moses as it is. (*Loudly.*) Hey, what's up?

SAM (*turns around. His hair stands on end. Aside*): The turtle. All right, Sam Sobersides, get a grip on yourself. (*Loudly, pretending to be cool and collected.*) Hello. Ah, yes, never mind. I was just having a look at the door. Well, how are you? Feeling all right?

MALE NURSE (*suspiciously*): I manage. Are you waiting for the doctor?

SAM (*alert, keeping a close watch on the nurse's every move*: Yes, yes. He'll be here in a minute, my colleague will. As a matter of fact I'm a professional too.

MALE NURSE (*suspecting something*): Really? Well, why don't you take a seat?

SAM (*quickly*): Thanks, I'm not tired.

MALE NURSE: I'm afraid you can't get out until he comes back.

SAM (*aside*): He talks so rationally . . . if I didn't know. I'll have to be careful when his psychosis surfaces. *Dementia praecox*, page four, paragraph five.

MALE NURSE (*aside*): Talking to himself. Must be a new patient. I'll keep an eye on him till they come to collect him.

SAM (*clears his throat, condescendingly*): Well, how do you like it here? No complaints about the sanatorium, I hope?

MALE NURSE (*shrugging*): No, no complaints. Food ain't bad. Wages could be higher, though.

SAM (*aside*): Wages? Of course. He doesn't realize he's in an asylum. No point arguing with him. His psychosis will surface any minute now . . . *Dementia praecox*, page four. (*Aloud.*) I'm sure you deserve a raise.

MALE NURSE: Another couple of crowns. Lot of work here, not to mention the danger.

SAM (*aside*): Crowns, coronation, delusions of grandeur, page fifty. No point in arguing with him. Turtle. (*Aloud, pleasantly.*) Well, yes, that's how things are in an aquarium.

MALE NURSE: In a what?

SAM: In an aquarium. In a whachamacallit, a stone-age aquarium, you know, one from the time of Moses. Which we're in.

MALE NURSE (*aside*): Oh, so he doesn't know where he is or how he got in here. (*Aloud.*) And why would you be thinking this is an aquarium?

SAM (*humoring him*): Well, turtles live in aquariums, don't they?

MALE NURSE (*aside*): He thinks he's a turtle. Lucky I found that out. (*Aloud.*) Of course, of course, that's the best place for turtles.

SAM: So tell me, do you like being a turtle?

MALE NURSE (*aside*): He thinks I'm a turtle too? Well, why argue? (*Aloud.*) Sure do. At least we're with our own kind.

SAM: Don't you get tired always crawling around on all fours, with that heavy tub on your back?

MALE NURSE: That's all right, go right ahead if you feel like it. It won't bother me.

SAM (*doesn't understand*): What?

MALE NURSE: I mean, go ahead, walk on all fours, the way you usually do.

SAM (*scared*): Me?

MALE NURSE: Of course. If you're a turtle, you ought to walk on all fours. You are a turtle, ain't you?

SAM (*aside*): Oh Lord, he's started. He wants to make me one too. Better not argue, or he'll yank my teeth out. (*Aloud.*) Well yes, actually, to be frank I find it more comfortable.

MALE NURSE (*with determination*): Then go ahead.

SAM (*scared*): All right, if you insist. (*He gets down on all fours.*)

MALE NURSE (*aside*): The fit's on him. I'd better be careful. (*He stands next to the chair with the straitjacket.*)

SAM (*on all fours, suspicious, watching the nurse's every move*): Well, please, feel free.

MALE NURSE (*doesn't understand him*): Beg pardon?

SAM: Go ahead, down on all fours, the way you feel most comfortable. (*Aside, mopping his brow.*) This is no joke. I wish they'd come; I'm really scared.

MALE NURSE (*humoring him*): Sure, sure. Of course. (*Aside.*) A tough case. He'll be hard to manage all alone. I wish Haduva would show up. (*He gets down on all fours, but with the straitjacket.*)

SAM (*suspicious*): Excuse me, what's that thing?

MALE NURSE: Nothing. A rag from the tub. I usually wash it in the tub.

SAM: Ah yes. Of course. Ha ha! (*As the nurse gets closer, he backs away fast. His voice oozes honey.*) This is really very pleasant. I just love to crawl around this way. (*He crawls.*)

MALE NURSE (*backs away, scared, gets the straitjacket ready*): Me too. It's the best thing for turtles.

SAM (*choked up with terror*): I can't stand it any more. I have to call for help. (*Relieved.*) Ah, there's a bell by the door. If only I can get that far. (*He jumps, turns and crawls to the door.*)

(The Male Nurse follows him cautiously, holding the straitjacket in front. When he catches up to him, he tries to throw it over him).

SAM *(near the door, turning suddenly and gnashing his teeth in a frightened manner)*: Bow wow. *(He leaps forward.)*

MALE NURSE *(leaps back)*: Grrr . . . What's wrong?

SAM: Let me be a turtle. I'm a turtle. Quark, quark.

MALE NURSE: Me too. Brek brek. But I'm the stronger turtle.

SAM: Quark, quark. I'm the stronger. If you touch me, I'll eat you up. *(He gnashes his teeth.)*

MALE NURSE *(aside)*: He's having his fit. Here goes. *(Aloud.)* We'll see about that. *(He tries to jump him, to get the straitjacket on him.)*

SAM *(slips out of the straitjacket, jumps up, runs around and screams mindlessly)*: Help, doctor, help, open the door, nurse, nurse! He's trying to throttle me.

(The Male Nurse also jumps up, holding up the straitjacket, and runs after him. They chase one another.)

(The Lunatic cautiously opens the door left, enters without being noticed, snatches the straitjacket from behind, and tosses it over the nurse's head. Catching it together at the back, he holds the nurse helpless.)

MALE NURSE: Help!

SAM *(sees the lunatic and calms down. He stops)*: Well, thank God, there's the nurse! *(He mops his brow.)* Goodness, I'm overheated. *(To the lunatic.)* Hold him tight, nurse! He's having an attack! He jumped me! Why do they leave people like this on their own?

MALE NURSE *(struggling to free himself)*: Help!

SAM: It's terrible. He's screaming. *(Once he notices that the nurse's hands are tied behind him, he gets braver.)* Can I help?

LUNATIC: Gag him with something so he can't scream. *(He holds the straitjacket tight at the back and pulls the nurse towards the chair.)*

SAM *(straightens up and mops his brow)*: Whew, what an adventure!

LUNATIC *(sarcastically, looking Sam up and down, arms folded)*: We were just a wee bit frightened, were we? If I hadn't shown up, there would have been trouble, wouldn't there?

SAM *(ashamed of his former fright)*: Oh dear, I wasn't as scared as all that. I'm not a layman. I know how to deal with lunatics. I was on my own, that was the trouble.

LUNATIC (*sarcastically*): Still, you feel safer now I'm here, don't you?

SAM (*laughs*): Well, as far as that goes, to tell the truth I do feel calmer. As a matter of fact, this is the first time I've run up against a real lunatic, and that's not the same as reading about it in a book, though I must say it was well described. I was able to diagnose the case correctly from the start. *Dementia praecox* . . . As a matter of fact, I . . . I beg your pardon, I should have introduced myself: Sam Sobersides, third-year medical student.

(The Lunatic nods with dignity. He does not reply.)

SAM (*nods toward the nurse*): A difficult case, isn't he?

LUNATIC (*shrugs with resignation*): Hopeless.

SAM (*sympathetically*): Really? I sensed that right away. You know, there's something about a lunatic that makes you nervous, even before you're aware anything's wrong with him. Some sort of emanation. There's been some debate recently about the scientific possibility of such a thing.

LUNATIC (*sarcastically*): Of course. Theories.

SAM: Naturally, I realize that practice is more important. Only someone like yourself who lives with them and makes them his business can really understand the insane. (*Respectfully, gesturing to the nurse.*) Have you been caring for this unfortunate creature long?

LUNATIC: Not very long. I was assigned a different one before. They took him away. This one's been here only two days.

SAM (*respectfully*): And you handle him so well already. That's practice, of course. You knew right away what his psychosis was, didn't you?

LUNATIC (*showing his superiority*): The very first instant.

SAM: He's dangerous, isn't he?

LUNATIC: One of the most dangerous lunatics I've ever seen here. And believe you me, this place is crawling with them.

SAM (*shudders*): Brr. The way he came in and looked at me. There's something awful in the eyes of lunatics like him. I must say it sent cold shivers down my spine, the way he looked at me. Look at him now, that awful way he has of rolling his eyes.

LUNATIC: I'm used to it. When you're always around lunatics, you get used to it.

SAM (*sympathetically and respectfully*): It must be very wearing to be around them all the time.

LUNATIC: Yes, it is. For the first time in months I'm talking to a sane man, someone who can understand me. For I believe you do understand me.

SAM (*flattered*): Oh yes, I do, I do. It must be awful having to deal with psychotics all the time. You need a lot of cunning, I'm sure.

LUNATIC (*getting warmed up*): As you can imagine. I see you do understand me. At long last a man who understands me and can grasp what I suffer here among all these lunatics. (*He shakes his hand.*) You're the first man who really understands me!

SAM (*visibly moved as he shakes hands*): After all, you practically saved my life: obviously I'd feel close to you! In a place like this the sane had better stick together and get along!

LUNATIC: Thank you. (*They stroke each other's hands.*)

SAM: Now tell me . . . (*He gestures at the nurse.*) What was that poor fellow getting at? How can you restrain him? What's his chief psychosis? Dr. Haduva was telling me about it, but he was called away in a hurry.

LUNATIC (*sarcastically*): Dr. Haduva? Which Dr. Haduva?

SAM: The one who was here, who showed me in. The one with the pinch-nose glasses.

(*The Lunatic laughs out loud.*)

SAM (*scared*): What's that for?

LUNATIC (*slapping him on the back*): You mean that fellow with the glasses who thinks he's a doctor?

SAM (*turning cold*): Good grief, isn't he?

LUNATIC (*slapping him on the back with paternal condescension*): He, my dear friend, is one of the most dangerous madmen in this place. His psychosis is to think he's a psychiatrist.

SAM (*throws up his hands*): Jesus Christ! And I was talking to him so calmly!

LUNATIC: Never mind. You can't tell right away. You need practice. I've known the poor fellow a long time. Much longer than this one. (*He turns to the nurse.*) They only assigned me this one two days ago.

SAM (*deflated*): But then how can you know for sure that someone

is crazy? After this experience I won't believe a word the text-
books say.

LUNATIC (*patronizingly*): You have to talk to them, my dear sir,
the way I do, you must observe them, and then you discover
their basic psychoses.

SAM (*turning to the nurse*): What about this one, what's his basic
psychosis, besides the . . .

LUNATIC: His? Water, dear sir. Cold showers, and water. That's
his psychosis.

SAM: Water?

LUNATIC (*winks*): Water. His psychosis is to make water gush
forth.

SAM (*the light dawns*): Oh yes, he thinks he's Moses and can make
water gush forth. That poor madman Dr. Haduva said something about that too, and you, nurse—excuse me, I mean Doctor—how did you discover that this was his basic psychosis?

LUNATIC: Elementary. If you have a minute, I'll explain. I can
see you're an educated man; let me clarify it for you. I observed
that this poor madman feels comfortable only when he is in the
company of madmen like himself. The moment a sane man of
sound mind comes anywhere near him, he rushes to the wall
and turns on the shower.

SAM: Terrible! And why does he do that?

LUNATIC: Ah, there's the crux. His psychosis is that a sane man
must be held under a shower to make him insane, so they can
understand him.

SAM (*claps his hands*): You're right. I noticed that too. At the very
beginning he tried to get me under the faucet.

LUNATIC (*proudly*): You see, just as I said.

SAM: Now tell me, how do you recognize, how do you distin-
guish the sane from the insane? After all, you need a degree of
judgement to do that.

LUNATIC: Elementary. By instinct. Judging by what a sane person says and does.

SAM: For instance?

LUNATIC: For instance, well, if I say something rational to him
or try to do something rational with him, he runs to the faucet
and does his best to hold me under the shower . . . That's his
psychosis.

SAM: And what triggers his psychosis?

LUNATIC: My not pretending to agree with what he thinks. Whenever, quite by accident, I would say anything rational to him, he would be overcome by his psychosis and try to choke me with water. After all, if I tell a sane person—you, for example—I am now going to gouge your eyes out and reach into your brain through the openings and pull out the nit, you don't turn violent; you let me do it. This wretched madman here had a fit and put me under the shower, just as he tried to do with you, because that's his psychosis.

SAM: Excuse me, I don't quite understand. In other words, he tried to gouge your eyes out?

LUNATIC: Of course not. Naturally, I tried to gouge out his eyes, just as I yanked the teeth out of his predecessor. In other words, I acted as any sane man would. Then he just attacked me.

SAM (*everything is spinning*): I'm sorry, my dear nurse, I mean Doctor, or rather Superintendent, I'm not quite sure who you're talking about.

LUNATIC: Who? This lunatic here.

SAM: The turtle?

LUNATIC (*quickly*): What turtle?

SAM (*pointing at the nurse*): This guy here who thinks he's a turtle.

LUNATIC (*conspiratorially seizing Sam's lapels*): He told you he was a turtle?

SAM: That's right.

LUNATIC (*laughs in alarm*): Ha, ha, ha! I told you he was stark raving mad! Ha, ha, ha ha!!

SAM (*nervous*): I don't follow.

LUNATIC (*conspiratorially*): He's not the turtle, and he can't be the turtle.

SAM: Why not?

LUNATIC (*holding onto his coat*): Because I am the turtle. But don't tell anyone. I am forced to go around in human shape so I can reach into your brain and pull the nit out of your head.

SAM (*trembling*): Whose head?

LUNATIC: Yours, of course. (*Speaking naturally.*) You will let me? I can do it right now. (*He reaches for Sam's eyes.*)

SAM (*retreats in terror, gets down on all fours, rushes to the door*): Help! Help! Help! Superintendent! Help!

(*The doctor hurries in R.*)

DOCTOR: What's this, what's this, what's going on here? (*To Sam.*) What are you doing? What's happened?

SAM (*retreats in terror*): The third lunatic, the one who thinks he's a psychiatrist.

DOCTOR (*sees the nurse*): Why, what did they do to you? (*He runs over, frees him, takes the handkerchief out of his mouth.*) What's going on here?

MALE NURSE (*flinging himself at Sam*): Quick, get hold of the other one while I grab this one. (*He holds Sam from behind.*)

SAM: Help! Let me go! I'm a turtle! I'm a doctor! . . . You lunatic!

LUNATIC (*holds onto the doctor*): Hold him! Help! He thinks he's a psychiatrist.

DOCTOR: We're in a nice mess. And I thought he was a colleague. True, his uncle did warn me he'd had some trouble; he asked me to examine him. He thinks he's an observer of madmen.

SAM: Not me. Hold him, that guy! His psychosis is that he's a psychiatrist, that he can cure insanity, that he can extract people's psychoses from their heads.

LUNATIC (*he is terrifying*): Ha, ha, ha! Ridiculous! Only I can do that. Only I can remove the nit. Because I am God.

SAM: That's not true. I am God.

DOCTOR: That's not true. I am.

MALE NURSE: Idiots. Of course I am God! Who else would it be?

DOCTOR (*listening intently, then suddenly*): Hold it, guys. Back to our cells. Here comes the Superintendent. (*All quickly leave right and left.*)

CURTAIN

English Musical Comedy
(Angol Operett)
1924
by
Ferenc Molnár

MANAGER: What've you got?

AGENT: A new English musical comedy. Something fantastic! Something that's never been done before!

MANAGER: An English original?

AGENT: As original as can be. If you like, I'll give you a brief plot synopsis.

MANAGER: Please do.

AGENT: The title is "Lord Bloom." This Lord Bloom is an old bachelor, who decides to take a steamer to Cairo. His aunt, who, for her part, is in love with a circus acrobat, is naturally against it.

MANAGER: Great.

AGENT: His friend, Lord Pilitz, wants to purloin his letter of credit in order to break the bank at Monte Carlo unimpeded.

MANAGER: The bank?

AGENT: I'm speaking clearly enough, aren't I? Count Pirnitzer, who has been standing behind the sofa throughout the scene, suddenly sends a message to the Major, who is, of course, beside himself with rage.

MANAGER: I'm beginning to understand.

AGENT: Dr. Morituri, the famous ophthalmologist, makes a third to their party, because he once agreed to forge a letter of credit on Lord Pilitz's bank . . . Do you follow me?

MANAGER: Of course.

AGENT: The second act comes next. The curtain goes up. We see a noisy, busy marketplace. Lord Bloom, disguised as a lady vegetable peddler, is chatting up Admiral Weissenstein. It later turns out that the admiral is none other than Count Pirnitzer. Naturally, his wife has followed him, and they sing a duet at this point. Lord Pilitz is furious, and so is Lilla.

MANAGER: Who's Lilla?

AGENT: During the second act she'll be let down on a rope from the grid. Naturally, the aunt enters in the wake of all this and swears vengeance on Lord Vogler.

MANAGER (*excited*): All right, and the third act?

AGENT: Can't you guess?

MANAGER: No.

AGENT: The third act is simply fantastic. Just imagine: Lord Pilitz comes back from Cairo, where Lord Bloom was unable to go, the young people embrace, the aunt slaps everybody, Count Pirnitzer cedes his rights to his brother, the ship's captain rushes in and shouts: "Lord Pilitz, hurry home; your wife has had a baby!" You can imagine how angry Lord Bloom gets at that. He tears up his will and tells them to stoke up the ship's boilers, but the engineer is nowhere to be found. What do you say to that wrinkle?

MANAGER: Splendid!

AGENT: The engineer, who is none other than Lilla in man's clothing, comes in upside-down, swallows the will, solves the mystery, whereupon the captain bursts in and shouts again: "Lord Pilitz, hurry home; your wife has had a baby!" At that point the orchestra chimes in, the ship sails away upstage, but Lord Bloom arrives too late, and the young folks manage to escape to Antwerp. Well?

MANAGER: First-rate. Only . . .

AGENT: Only . . . ?

MANAGER: I think the plot's a bit too obvious . . .

POSTWAR UNIFICATION AND INDEPENDENCE IN POLAND RE-
inforced the earlier taste for cabaret, and it may be said that Polish
poetry between the wars made its debut there. These years saw the
emergence of many miniature stages calling themselves "Überbrettl" or "Chat Noir." Of these, the most interesting was the Ka-
wiarnia Poetów Pod Pikadorem (Poets' Café at the Sign of the Picador), founded in Cracow in 1918. Its inspiration was neither
Wolzogen's Motley Stage nor Salis's *cabaret artistique,* but the Petrograd Poets' Café, created by the Russian futurists David Burliuk
and Vladimir Mayakovsky. The Picador was announced by
Tadeusz Raabe in a futurist-style manifesto, which called for new
concepts of poetry and life; this so-called Skamander movement
was headed by Jan Lechoń, Antoni Słonimski, and Julian Tuwim
(1894–1953). The material was often infused with misogyny, for,
like the prewar Green Balloon, the Picador was primarily a male
resort, the only woman in the group the radical writer Marja
Mirska. On the other hand, if the Balloon had always seemed an
aristocratic sanctum for initiates, the Picador came across as a
modest enterprise open to all, the audience serving as a public
forum. In general, however, political and artistic cabarets were far
fewer than burgeoning musical cabarets like the Black Cat and
Mirage.

Tuwim is considered one of the best Polish poets of the period:
he had a gift for both languid lyrics of urban life and topical trav-
esty. Much of his comic verse gains its effectiveness from the use
of colloquial idioms and doggerel rhymes. His skits, many created
for the Warsaw theater of miniatures Qui pro quo (1919–32), are
laconic: in a short space they can sketch the limits of human despair and limn a whole personality with a few pungent phrases. A
characteristic of Tuwim's sketches and those of Konrad Tom is
Jewish humor, which infused Polish comedy in this period.
Tom—a professional sketch-writer who supplied all the leading
cabarets and wrote and directed such Yiddish films as *Yidl mitn
Fidl* (1936)—created pithy monologues and scenes which, like

The Snag, became classics, known by heart by performers and audiences alike.

Qui pro quo was suspected of being too easy on the government of patriarchal Marshal Piłsudski, whose ministers enjoyed cabaret satire; but the cabaret strove to preserve a liberal, anticlerical, antinationalistic tone in the face of strong anti-Semitic and totalitarian trends. This benign liberalism collapsed under a censorship dominated by the Right and was replaced by the more militant pro-Communist cabaret Czerwona Latarnia (Red Lantern) of Stanisław Jerzy Lec, which performed agitprop in the streets. The last demonstration of this kind was a political agitation played by actors of the Cricot theater on stilts with giant masks designed by Jerzy Zaruba; it came a few days before the German invasion of 1939.

Something by Chopin

(Cokolwiek Szopena)

c. 1925

by

Julian Tuwim

CHARACTERS
A Young Man
A Young Lady

A provincial, lower-middle-class drawing room: plush furniture, blue artificial flowers, peacock feathers, "landscapes," yellowing photographs, lots of bric-à-brac, etc. The Young Lady is playing the piano. The Young Man stands contemplatively behind her.

YOUNG MAN: It's perfectly true—music hath powers. It ennobles a person and spurs him to action. Honestly, Miss Cesia, I'm very grateful to you . . . for this music and all the rest . . .

YOUNG LADY: What do you mean, all the rest? . . . you needn't be; it's nothing at all . . .

YOUNG MAN: No, dear lady, I'm quite serious. I'm most lucky to have made your acquaintance. Otherwise, I would have been bored to death in this small town. I've been here a full week, and the prevailing boredom is practically a sine qua non . . .

YOUNG LADY: Yes, an uninteresting little town . . . But you have your work here . . .

YOUNG MAN: I won't deny it . . . Working in a drugstore provides a certain internal modicum of brain food, but one's environment should also contribute potential. After Rzeszów, where I used to be, this place is awfully provincial.

YOUNG LADY: Is it pretty in Rzeszów? An ever-so-interesting life? Lots of company?

YOUNG MAN: Ah, what can I compare it with? The tempo of life. Vesti la giubba. Lots of intellectual goings-on, movies twice a week. The cosmetics counter at the drugstore. In short: vive le roi!

YOUNG LADY (*sighs*): Yes . . . of course, society has its attractions . . . Would you care for a little slice of cake? Mama sends her apologies; she had to go out . . . Have this one . . . there are more raisins in it . . . ever-so . . .

YOUNG MAN: Thanks, tout à vous. The important thing in a dump like this—excuse me—is to cultivate a certain intellectual contact with art. For instance: you play the piano; therefore you associate by means of sound . . . Some allegro, a smidgeon of capriccio, or a musical sapristi—and—the soul is somewhere else, creativity, and so on.

YOUNG LADY: Ever-so. Art by itself makes up for a good deal. Last summer there was even a landscape painter staying here . . . he painted our little woods. He kept his colors in these tubes and held his paintbrush . . . how can I put it? Just like Maxim Kolodont . . .

YOUNG MAN: Of course, painting too, but the smell is not high-class, and you get your hands dirty. Whereas music is clean; the keyboard—although some keys are black—never soils your fingers. Play something else, Miss Cesia. Any trifle at all, any little quantum . . . in the key of B . . . or C . . .

YOUNG LADY: I'm really embarrassed, Mr. Klemens, because it's . . . ever-so . . . it's only amateurish, so I'd rather not . . .

YOUNG MAN: Yes, I've been to concerts, honestly, real prima facie ones. The doctor's wife in Rzeszów gave a song recital,—as a matter of fact, it was flawless, sans souci, but even here the music produced by your dainty fingers can do wonders for the soul . . . Why don't you play something by Chopin?

YOUNG LADY: Oh, you've guessed it . . . I adore Chopin . . . If he was alive, I'd fall in love with him.

YOUNG MAN: Fall in love? What can you know of love, Miss Cesia?

YOUNG LADY: Why shouldn't I? I can ever-so . . . You've come here from the outside world, so you think hearts beat differently in the provinces? I could love with all my heart and soul, every bit . . . and I keep dreaming some prince will come and take me away with him and we'll live happily ever after . . . ever-so . . .

YOUNG MAN: My cousin wrote me that next spring there'll be an opening in a drugstore in Warsaw, Sliska Street, so I'll definitely be going there . . .

YOUNG LADY: Oh lord, Warsaw . . .

YOUNG MAN: That's real living, Miss Cesia. A flood of lights, hansom cabs with rubber tires, streetcars, autos, department stores, theaters, good pay, appreciation from high society. Wherever you show up, the whisper goes around: "Look, look, the assistant pharmacist." That's what I call living. Comme-ci comme-ça is not living.

YOUNG LADY (*dreamily*): So . . . you wanted to hear . . . something by Chopin?

YOUNG MAN: Après vous—with the greatest of pleasure.

YOUNG LADY: "Why is my heart so heavy?" (*Sits down at the piano and plays Chopin's "Why Is My Heart So Heavy?"*)

YOUNG MAN: You played that—honestly—with lots of feeling; a person can tell it comes from the heart, Miss Cesia . . . Or are you really that sad?

YOUNG LADY: Oh, awfully, Mr. Klemens. Since you've come here from the outside world, you must certainly have moved in aristocratic circles, but you have an artist's soul; you understand what it means to long for a wonderful life . . . for a life full of incident, beauty, and art, and . . . ever-so . . . and in general . . .

YOUNG MAN: I do understand . . . In a miserable dump like this it must be very hard . . . I feel it myself. Especially if one has no love object of one's own . . . Love means a lot. I'm lonely too now . . . But in the spring I'll move to Warsaw. There, I'm bound to come in contact with artists, because my cousin's brother-in-law knows a violinist who plays at the movies . . . that must be a beautiful life.

YOUNG LADY: You were saying you're lonely . . .

YOUNG MAN: Yes . . . But in love, Miss Cesia. (*He sits at the piano and plays a waltz.*)

YOUNG LADY: Mr. Klemens . . . I honestly don't know . . . Mama has gone out . . . Maybe another little slice of cake? You played that so . . . Tears in your eyes . . . ever-so . . . You say

. . . in love . . . Mr. Klemens. The moment I saw you, I felt that you were . . . And you guessed it . . . and asked for Chopin . . . And now . . . I honestly don't know . . . Mama has gone out . . . and a new life. Do you really love me?

YOUNG MAN: Hm . . . How can I explain this to you? Some sort of mix-up, I suppose. I am indeed in love—engaged, in fact— the wedding is set for May . . . in Warsaw too, and you thought I was referring to you . . . Excuse me for the misunderstanding . . . Everything's come out so tutti frutti, as a matter of fact . . . Pardon me. I had absolutely no intention . . .

YOUNG LADY (*disconcerted*): Ever-so? . . .

YOUNG MAN: And you thought très dommage that since it was something by Chopin . . . Please forgive me . . .

(The Young Lady goes back to the piano and begins to play "Why Is My Heart So Heavy?")

Interrogation
(*Dochodzenie*)
c. 1925
by
Julian Tuwim

Policemen bring a prisoner into a cell. The Prisoner sits on the plank bed. He is calm and serious. After a while the Examining Magistrate comes in. He sits at the table, takes papers out of his briefcase. The policemen leave the cell.

MAGISTRATE: I am the examining magistrate. I will be asking you some questions. Please answer me calmly.

PRISONER: I'm completely calm.

MAGISTRATE: Name?

PRISONER: Hyacinth Waterlilynski.

MAGISTRATE: Age?

PRISONER: Thirty-five.

MAGISTRATE: Occupation?

PRISONER: Technical engineer.

MAGISTRATE: Address?

PRISONER: 100 Krucha Street, at present Central Penitentiary.

MAGISTRATE: Do you admit that at ten o'clock this morning you murdered your wife Rose Waterlilynska, maiden name Lotus.

PRISONER: I do.

MAGISTRATE: How did it happen?

PRISONER: If I may, your honor. Yesterday, when my wife was out, I took a few boards out of the dining room floor, put a box filled with twenty-five kilos of dynamite underneath, fixed up an electric cord, ran it under the carpet, and plugged it in in the kitchen. Today, while my wife sat there eating her breakfast, I went into the kitchen, turned on the electricity, and detonated the dynamite. Is my wife alive?

MAGISTRATE: Nobody knows. So far there's not a trace of her. All the police found at the scene of the crime was a little pink, sweet-smelling ash. It may be your wife. (*He pulls out a sample of pink powder.*) Please tell me what led you to commit this gruesome crime.

PRISONER: Oh, that's a long story, your honor. My wife was awful!

MAGISTRATE: Bad-tempered?

PRISONER: Not bad-tempered. She was an idiot.

MAGISTRATE: Pretty?

PRISONER: Tastes differ. I didn't care for her.

MAGISTRATE: Was she unfaithful to you?

PRISONER: No. At least not so far as I know.

MAGISTRATE: Did she nag you?

PRISONER: On the contrary. She was always good to me. She fussed a lot over me, warned me not to catch cold . . . not to drink, not to smoke . . . to go to bed early.

MAGISTRATE: Then why did you murder her?

PRISONER: Partly because of that. The main reason was she was constantly cuddling me, coddling me, trying to make our life a so-called enchanted idyll, consisting of health, happiness, prosperity, thrift, and similar abominations . . . Your honor, picture yourself as a young man of thirty-five, sitting at the table with some old frump, eating burned soup and veal in an insipid sauce and hearing phrases like "Hubby dear, things are so boring . . . After supper we'll go to the movies, then to Ziemianska for a little coffee. Then we'll come back home, I'll sing something to my little hubby, and if my little hubby is real good, he'll get a little kiss." And yet Kazio Sztycki had phoned earlier for me and him to meet at the Adria at five, pick up that redhead Lidka, drive downtown for dinner, live it up, take the girl back to Kazio's, where our whole crazy gang would show up, and the fun would go on till the next morning! Well?

MAGISTRATE: And suppose you had gone there and given free rein to your—if I may—tempestuous temperament?

PRISONER: At home there'd be screaming fits, scenes, despair, sheer hell!

MAGISTRATE: So you denied yourself all indulgences, did you? And that was why you blew your young wife sky-high? How dreadful, Mr. Waterlilynski.

PRISONER: That's not all, your honor. For instance, she loved tidiness. For instance, I'd leave a mess on my desk when I went out, but I could make perfect sense out of that mess! And when I got back, everything had been made neat and tidy, so I couldn't find anything any more.

MAGISTRATE: Did she arrange your books in the bookcase according to a certain system?

PRISONER: Yes, but how did you know that?

MAGISTRATE: Did she buy you ties on your birthday, which you couldn't wear, and did she think these ties were gorgeous?

PRISONER: Naturally! She had remarkable intuition. For instance, she suggested I give up smoking and instead of cigarettes . . .

MAGISTRATE: Suck peppermint drops, right?

PRISONER: Exactly!

MAGISTRATE: And if you were downtown, you often couldn't get through on the telephone?

PRISONER: For hours at a time, your honor. Busy! Busy! Busy! And my business was extremely urgent!

MAGISTRATE: While this female was chatting with some bosom friend, right? Gossiping for hours on end about other women, and how hideously they dressed, right? How many pairs of shoes do you own, Mr. Waterlilynski?

PRISONER: Two pairs.

MAGISTRATE: And how many did she have?

PRISONER: Fourteen!

MAGISTRATE: How much time do you spend at the hairdresser's?

PRISONER: I shave myself, and a haircut lasts at most fifteen minutes.

MAGISTRATE: Did the deceased ever spend less than two hours there?

PRISONER: Never. Three and four hours!

MAGISTRATE: Where did she go in the summer?

PRISONER: Krynica.

MAGISTRATE: Figures! And in winter to Zakopane?

PRISONER: That's right.

MAGISTRATE: And before every trip a whole dozen new dresses?

PRISONER: But she "never had anything to wear"!

MAGISTRATE: She would also say: "Other men, they . . ." Always the same thing—in her opinion other men were always better, right?

PRISONER: Always. But I'd be slaving away ten and twelve hours a day.

MAGISTRATE: A maid?

PRISONER: One held out for ten days, but that was a miracle.

MAGISTRATE: Stewed fruit?

PRISONER: Applesauce. All year long. (*They both sigh deeply.*)

MAGISTRATE: Mr. Waterlilynski . . . Might you have a little of that dynamite left. I would . . .

PRISONER: Unfortunately, the dynamite's all gone, but . . . (*He pulls a rather large packet out of his overcoat*) . . . I don't know whether the judge's lady, I mean your wife, might respond to cyanide . . .

Wedding Night

(*Noc Póslubna*)

c. 1925

by

Julian Tuwim

(Characters: Husband and Wife. A modest but festally clean bedroom in a lower-middle-class flat. Empty for a moment, then the Wife enters in a veil and white gown, followed by an embarrassed Husband.)

WIFE: Here's our little nest, Isaac dear. God grant we'll be happy here.

HUSBAND: Why not? God grant it. (*Sits down at the table with his hat on; stares motionless into space.*)

WIFE: Why are you so sad, Isaac?

HUSBAND: Sad? No. Why sad? A little tired, a little drunk.

WIFE: But you won't drink any more, will you, Isaac? Come on, promise me?

HUSBAND: I can live without a drink. Why not? Please sit down.

WIFE: And we'll just sit?

HUSBAND: You can sit, you can walk around. What difference does it make?

WIFE: Those little peepers. That darling nose. All mine. Do you love your little Dotty?

HUSBAND (*smiles, embarrassed*): What kind of a question is that? Naturally. Why not?

WIFE: You know what? I think we'll make a wonderful life for ourselves. After all, I'm not short on brains; if I wanted, I could even get you interested in higher things.

HUSBAND: Why not? If I got the time . . . Tomorrow I can't. I have to finish the tails for Samuelson . . . for the guy across the street, press some pants . . .

WIFE: Darling. I love you for your frankness. Kiss your bride. Harder. Harder than that. You're walking away already?

HUSBAND: I'm not leaving. I live here.

WIFE: But give me a hug. After all, this is our wedding night. Our nuptials.

HUSBAND (*tries to get up*): With club soda or straight?

WIFE: No. Not *cocktails*. Our *nuptial* rites, I'm saying.

HUSBAND: And I've got to get to Shpitzveig's by eight to measure . . .

WIFE: You're no good, Isaac. You might stop thinking about things like that for one day.

HUSBAND: What for? What am I supposed to think about? I'm a tailor—it's my profession—and Shpitzveig is a customer.

WIFE: You know, I once read this masterpiece—*Love and Nature*. This awesome power was described in it. It described the coming together of the flesh . . . a mystery, they called it.

HUSBAND: What do I know from mysteries? I have to sew to live. If your papa hands over a couple thousand zlotys, I can buy a few pieces merchandise and pay off my debt to Zuckerstein. What else do I know?

WIFE: You don't know what it means to love?

HUSBAND: Why shouldn't I know? I know. I like to make love.

WIFE: Come on then. Come. Take me in your arms.

HUSBAND: And your papa also said he'd give us an apartment on Solna Street—the workroom could be enlarged. Then I could take on two assistants . . . why not? Right away more orders and what comes with it.

WIFE: Stop it, Isaac, stop it. Make love to me here, here in our little nest. Don't trust Papa. You don't know Papa. There won't be any apartment on Solna Street. Come on, kiss me on the lips; you're my one and only.

HUSBAND: That can't be, there's got to be something on Solna Street. Your papa promised. And since I gave up my tailor's workroom to be our bedroom, I'd have to sew in the kitchen . . . I can't do that.

WIFE: Kiss me. But no . . . wait, Isaac . . . I have to confess something . . . I'm too honest not to confess . . . Hubby, listen . . .

HUSBAND: What'll I do with myself in the kitchen? Why? I proposed to a woman of forty-one, so why should I be in the
kitchen?

WIFE: Isaac, don't break my heart with this chronology. I want
to admit something to you—I was seduced once . . . but it
was, it was against my will . . . it was a brutal rape, Isaac . . .
But you'll forgive me.

HUSBAND: Why not? I can forgive, but it's no fun. Who was it,
Dotty?

WIFE: I don't know, Isaac. Papa is looking for him. He's caught
three already. Forgive me.

HUSBAND: Them your papa's looking for. But when he was supposed to give me five hundred zlotys in advance, he lied. But
that two thousand he'll give me. He promised. Then I buy a
few pieces merchandise and pay off Zuckerstein . . .

WIFE: Don't worry, don't be upset, my one and only. We'll start
a new beautiful life . . . Do you like children, Isaac?

HUSBAND: Why not? Without children it's no fun. "The laughter of children is the happiness of a home."

WIFE: Then listen to your wife, darling. Kids will be coming.
Now that we have our own little nest, we'll be together with
the kids . . . I'll write . . .

HUSBAND: What kids, Dotty?

WIFE: You did forgive me for not being a virgin. Now drink your
cup of bitterness to the dregs—my kids are at my aunt's, three
girls, Isaac, and one little boy.

HUSBAND: Why not? Let them come. But it's not a good thing;
in fact, it's a bad thing. So we'll have kids here? And who's
gonna feed 'em?

WIFE: If the two of us can manage, Isaac, we'll make things
stretch for all six . . .

HUSBAND: Maybe we will and maybe we won't. How do I know?
But it's not a nice thing that I'll be working in the kitchen and
four kids are on their way. Not only did I propose to a forty-
one-year-old dame; I got to slave for somebody else's kids?
Tough luck, Dotty. What're we gonna do?

WIFE: And now what's mine is yours. Kiss me, caress me, take
me, Isaac.

HUSBAND: Why not? I can take. When your papa hands over the
two thousand and I pay off Zuckerstein and buy the merchan-

dise, things'll be easier. The kids need stuff too. And when's your papa gonna hand it over, Dotty?

WIFE: Don't talk about it—I'm all yours—I'm burning up with passion—and you're talking about money. Stop thinking about it. You don't know Papa. He promised, but he won't come across. Don't count on it, Isaac. The night is ours. Come.

HUSBAND (*stunned, after a pause*): He won't come across? Why won't he come across? I proposed to a forty-one-year-old dame . . . and there's no apartment on Solna Street . . . And I have to sew in the kitchen . . . and four kids are on the way . . . and he won't come across with the two thousand? I won't pay off Zuckerstein? I won't buy the merchandise? Then what am I gonna do, Dotty? (*He weeps.*)

WIFE: You're going to come here, Isaac . . . Kiss . . . hug, hold . . . we'll start a new, beautiful life . . . Come . . .

HUSBAND (*takes off the tuxedo and formal shirt, keeps his hat on, goes on undressing and says, sobbing*): Why not? Coming right away. Only remember—wake me before seven . . . I gotta iron the pants for across the street and be at Shpitzveig's by eight.

The Snag
(Sęk)
by
Konrad Tom

CHARACTERS
Rapaport
Goldberg

RAPAPORT: Hello! Long-distance operator, please. This is number 3 and 3 and 3 speaking. Yes, Lubartów please, number 33. Hello! Please miss, please miss, it's an urgent call. Yes. Hello! Yes, I did book this call in advance—Hello! Hello! . . .

GOLDBERG (*in the audience*): Hello . . .

RAPAPORT: Hello . . .

GOLDBERG: Hello . . . Who's that? Who's that? Who is that?! . . .

RAPAPORT: Jake?

GOLDBERG: Who's that?

RAPAPORT: Is that Jake?

GOLDBERG: Who's that?

RAPAPORT: If that's not Jake, my name won't mean anything, sir. Is that Jake?

GOLDBERG: Jake who . . . ?

RAPAPORT: Goldberg . . .

GOLDBERG: And if this is Jake, who's that?

RAPAPORT: Rapaport . . .

GOLDBERG: Benny? . . .

RAPAPORT: Yes.

GOLDBERG: This is Jake.

RAPAPORT: Goldberg?

GOLDBERG: Yes. What's up?

RAPAPORT: I've got a deal cooking . . .

GOLDBERG: A deal!

RAPAPORT: Yes.

GOLDBERG: How much can I lose?

RAPAPORT: Why do we have to lose? . . . Ask me how much we can make!

RAPAPORT: What we'll make we'll make. I'm asking how much I got to cover, in case we do lose.

RAPAPORT: Small potatoes—you got two, three thousand?

GOLDBERG: I suppose so . . . What's up?

RAPAPORT: It's like this: Friedman is holding an auction, because of Shapiro's I.O.U. with Glass's endorsement and Balunstein is the legal owner. He's offering fifty percent free and clear. The goods are at Lutzman's, but Honigman has a lien on the goods because of Roitberg's I.O.U. For that I.O.U. you can get a guarantee from Roitberg's father-in-law Rosenzweig. Mrs. Rosenzweig is ill.

GOLDBERG: What's she got?

RAPAPORT: Whatever it is, we inherit her forty percent. Only Honigman has to be sure that Roitberg will let him out, once Rosenzweig pays, if Mrs. Rosenzweig snuffs it today, and then Malvina Feinstein will have nothing against it. Lipshits has to get five hundred dollars. No, just half in cash and the rest as your disclaimer. That much is clear . . .

GOLDBERG: I understand that part. But what makes you so sure Mrs. Rosenzweig is gonna kick the bucket?

RAPAPORT: That's the snag.

GOLDBERG: The what?

RAPAPORT: The snag!

GOLDBERG: Who?

RAPAPORT: The snag!

GOLDBERG: I don't understand!

RAPAPORT: The snag. Like you snag your coat on a branch.

GOLDBERG: What branch?

RAPAPORT: On a tree. A snag on a branch on a tree in a wood.

GOLDBERG: Who's got the wood. Lutzman?

RAPAPORT: What Lutzman? Lutzman's in textiles. Wood like in a forest. Trees, like you cut into boards, and if they cut the board rough, you can get snagged there too.

GOLDBERG: Wait, wait, where is this forest?

RAPAPORT: What forest?

GOLDBERG: You mentioned . . .

RAPAPORT: What do you care all of a sudden . . . It doesn't matter. "This is the forest primeval," so in the forest there's a wood, in the wood there's trees, they cut down the trees, they saw them into boards, on the board you get snagged . . .

GOLDBERG: And who owns this forest?

RAPAPORT: What do you care? . . . Nobody . . .

GOLDBERG: Can I buy it?

RAPAPORT: The textiles?

GOLDBERG: No, the sawmill . . .

RAPAPORT: What sawmill, for crying out loud . . .

GOLDBERG: The forest you cut down and saw up!

RAPAPORT: We're worried about Mrs. Rosenzweig: will she hold out till the auction . . .

GOLDBERG: Will she sell?

RAPAPORT: What . . . what?

GOLDBERG: The sawmill?

RAPAPORT: But she doesn't own . . . What sawmill?

GOLDBERG: But you said it yourself . . . this forest . . .

RAPAPORT: Goldberg! . . . Why the hell did I say snag? . . . I take back that snag . . . I take back all the snags in the world, understand?

GOLDBERG: What?

RAPAPORT: The snag.

GOLDBERG: Which one?

RAPAPORT: The one that got its picture in the papers—that's the snag I take back.

GOLDBERG: The papers! There was an ad?

RAPAPORT: What ad?

GOLDBERG: That she's selling . . .

RAPAPORT: Who?

GOLDBERG: Only I'd keep the sawmill for myself.

RAPAPORT: Listen, Jake . . . why do you need a sawmill? Drop this sawmill.

GOLDBERG: You know, Rapaport, I don't understand you—you wake me up in the middle of the night, for half an hour you talk me into buying a forest, and now you won't let me have the sawmill . . . What kind of deal is that?

RAPAPORT: Jake, sweetheart!

GOLDBERG: Wait, don't interrupt—let's say I pay two thousand for the forest, sure, somebody else'll get the sawmill, he'll dictate the prices, I'll let him make a profit cutting my wood, so where's the logic? . . . So I'd rather buy the sawmill, am I right?

RAPAPORT: Theoretically yes . . . Only, Jake, silly me, I thought I'd use an old expression, I said "That's the snag," meaning the business with Lutzman might fall through unless Mrs. Rosenzweig rolls over and plays dead like a dog.

GOLDBERG: A dog? What breed?

RAPAPORT: Oh, go to hell!

GOLDBERG: Mrs. Rosenzweig has a dog for sale? I'll buy it for my kid. He's always asking for one—but what breed?

RAPAPORT: What breed . . . Pedigreed Aryan!

GOLDBERG: But two thousand for a dog . . . I can offer five zlotys. Is it a big doggy?

RAPAPORT: Listen, Jake . . . Hello! Yes, we're still on the line. Listen, Jake, this conversation is going to cost me a fortune!

GOLDBERG: What difference does that make when a person's buying a forest and a sawmill and a dog!

RAPAPORT: Take the sawmill for free.

GOLDBERG: And the forest?

RAPAPORT: Take the damned forest for free.

GOLDBERG: And the dog?

RAPAPORT: And the dog can lick your ugly kisser!

THE OCTOBER REVOLUTION CHANGED THE COURSE OF CAB-
aret's development in Russia. The Crooked Mirror closed in 1918,
and the Bat followed suit two years later, reorganizing in Paris as
the Chauve Souris. Another poets' cabaret, the Bibabo, founded
in Petrograd in 1917 by the Georgian director Mardzhanov and
the so-called "Bohemian Poet," Nikolay Agnivtsev, moved to
Kiev during the Civil War. There, many former cabaretists—including Evreinov, Kugel, Averchenko, Teffi, and Baliev—took
refuge. The Bibabo changed its name to Krivoy Dzhimmi
(Crooked Jimmy) in 1919, when its format became that of a political satirical revue. Agnivtsev left for Berlin to work for the
Blue Bird, and Mardzhanov returned to Petrograd, where he
opened Khromoy Dzho (Limping Joe), a short-lived enterprise
that presented everything from gypsy ballads to futurist plays.

In 1922, under the New Economic Policy, Crooked Jimmy was
reorganized in Moscow as a theater collective presenting "Jim-
miads." Essentially the style and content were those of the old
Crooked Mirror, with Evreinov as artistic director for a few
months. He rewrote *School for Stars* (see *Cabaret Performance*, vol.
1). Another major success was an updated variation on his *Inspector
General*, which had been presented as if staged by five different
directors: this time it was Gogol's *Getting Married* presented in
fourteen different ways! One of the directors parodied was the constructivist Foregger, who had condemned cabaret as Western decadence at the same time he praised the red-blooded music hall.
Jimmy's conférencier was Aleksey Grigorevich Alekseev (Lifshits,
b. 1887), whose monocle and evening dress were clearly a throwback to pre-Revolutionary days. When Evreinov emigrated to
Paris, Agnivtsev returned from Berlin and planned some exciting
novelties, but in 1924 Crooked Jimmy's company was absorbed
into the Moscow Theater of Satire.

Essentially, the cabaret format was redirected to serve the goals
of the Communist party. During the Civil War, performance bri-
gades were sent to the front to instruct soldiers in new policies.
The Theater of Revolutionary Satire, opened in 1919, played in

clubs, on railway platforms, and in any likely hall, directing its shafts at class enemies and upholders of the old régime. A natural offshoot of this kind of agitprop was the Sinyaya Bluza, or Blue Blouse, movement. The first troupe was formed in 1923 by Boris Yuzhanin, an instructor at the Moscow Institute for Journalism, as a "living newspaper" which could work under any conditions in any form. Using the principle of "biomechanics" as elaborated by the director Meyerhold, the Blouses (so-called from their factory-worker smocks) presented stage pictures that used human bodies as components of a machine. Little by little the Blouses proliferated until there were 5,000 troupes, both amateur and professional, throughout Russia, with a membership of 100,000. Their acts, they proclaimed, comprised "parade-entrée-exercises, contact with spectators, avant-garde oratory (mass action), international newspaper columns, skits from everyday life, dialogue, monologue, revue, doggerel, etc." The favorite seems to have been comic doubles-acts. Cabaret format and material were thus applied to the cause of public education; every routine bore a message. The butts included emigrés, bourgeois aspirations, careerism, and the inability to adjust to the new Soviet society. The sketch translated here, *Jogging the Memory,* a plea to workers to buy a state-manufactured notepad, was based on a playlet by Arkady Averchenko (1881–1925), a prolific pre-Revolutionary humorist whom Prince Mirsky characterized as a member of the "Anglo-American school of comic writing"—in other words, funny in a rapid-fire, cartoony way.

The journalistic base of cabaret-style performance in Russia is evident as well in the work of Nikolay Pavlovich Smirnov-Sokolsky (1898–1962). A reporter who wrote material for variety performers, he made his own stage debut in 1915, and from 1920 was a star of the Soviet cabaret. He created the type of the satirical news-column, delivered as if improvised and with emotional oratorical flourishes. The viewpoint was that of the Soviet man in the street, but the colloquial, rhythmic language resembled the spiels of the "granddads," the pre-Revolutionary fairground pitchmen. Invariably costumed in a black velvet jacket and a floppy white tie, Smirnov-Sokolsky used trick scenery, puppets, slides, and film clips to enhance his routines. His parody of Kerensky's report on the Soviet Union is an interesting update of the slide gimmick Teffi had already exploited (see *Cabaret Performance,* vol. 1).

With the growing consolidation of Stalinist power, the Blue

Blouses were called to order and merged into the less vital TRAM movement. The *estrada,* or variety stage, became purely an entertainment form, often enlivened by jazz (L. O. Utyosov had organized a jazz orchestra in 1928). Only the Theater of Miniatures of the clown Arkady Raikin carried on the cabaret tradition; and it was essentially a one-man show, specializing in lightning-quick changes, with the rest of the company reduced to walk-ons.

"Getting Married" Almost According to Gogol

(from Seryoznoe i smeshnoe, 1972)

by

A. G. Alekseev

In those days every Moscow theater tried as much as possible to have its own sharply defined artistic profile, sometimes even to the detriment of common sense. This enabled us to show maliciously and merrily the same play as it might be treated by different theaters in an inexhaustible variety, emphasizing and ridiculing each director's tendency to stage the play as differently as possible from his colleagues, and often, alas, not as its author wrote it.

In one evening we would perform just the first two scenes from *Getting Married:* in them Podkolyosin, a minor official, dreams about getting married; indolently, slowly, and circumstantially he interrogates and cross-examines his servant Stepan as to whether the matchmaker came, whether his dress-coat is ready, whether the cloth is good. . . .

Bear in mind that this fragment had to be treated so that it could be repeated fourteen times in one evening! For we showed it the original way, then slightly distorted, then totally unlike itself, then versified—depending on the style of director parodied.

Before each new parody I would facetiously describe the staging principles of the specific theater and director. And by the end of the performance the audience was incapacitated with laughter. . . . These parodies were always created collectively: I made some notes, came up with the form and basic idea, and the others fleshed it out and polished it in rehearsals. . . .

The first parody was *Getting Married* as done at the Moscow Art Theater. "An Utterly Improbable Incident," Gogol called it, but

our actor, speaking the text of the comedy in its inviolable origi-
nality, played a tragedy, a tragedy of the troubled soul of the
spineless Russian intellectual; and the lines from beginning to end
were submerged in true-to-life details. Podkolyosin snored, the
furniture creaked, frogs croaked, the wind whistled . . . All of it
in lyrically muffled tones. Then Podkolyosin awoke, smoked,
yawned, and teased a caged canary to make it sing; somewhere in
the distance a dog barked; and finally against the background of
this sonic symphony Podkolyosin's soliloquy began: the actor recited it as a tragic prologue to an approaching catastrophe in a
man's life, with tears in his breaking voice. . . .

Then I offered the audience a production as done at a "theater
of miniatures," all three nightly shows. . . .

From behind the curtain of this theater came a cheeky conférencier with an enormous chrysanthemum in the buttonhole of his
rusty tuxedo. He addressed the audience familiarly: "Hi there, hi
there! We are now going to show you a sketch by the famous humorist Vasily Nikolaevich Gogol."

And with an insinuating smirk, winking to the audience, he
added: "As another humorist, Aleksandr Aleksandrovich Pushkin,
once said, we all got married to somebody sometime somehow.
Ha ha ha!"

He vanished. The first show began: everything went "as at the
MAT," but . . . in contrast, everything at the same time: Stepan
held the jug upside-down, but Podkolyosin angrily washed and
snorted, then teased the canary, and it barked . . . The curtain
came down. The second session began. Again the conférencier appeared, and in an obvious rush, so as not to detain the audience
arriving for the next show, shouted: "Gogol's Getting Married!
We all got married somehow sometime to somebody. Ha ha
ha!"—and vanished. The whole second show, as they say, "flashed
by." Podkolyosin rattled through his soliloquy; Stepan rushed in
and answered his questions without letting him finish them.

PODKOLYOSIN: Did the . . .
STEPAN: No way.
PODKOLYOSIN: Did you go . . .
STEPAN: I did.
PODKOLYOSIN: What did he . . .
STEPAN: Dress-coat.
PODKOLYOSIN: And did he ask . . .

STEPAN: No.
PODKOLYOSIN: Maybe . . .
STEPAN: No.
PODKOLYOSIN: But didn't he get around to . . .
STEPAN: No.
PODKOLYOSIN: Good, now go away.

The curtain came down, and the third show started. The conférencier stuck his head in, cried "Gogol's Getting Married," the curtain opened, Stepan ran in and answered Podkolyosin's first question, "Just you wait"—and then at terrific speed "zoomed through" without commas or periods: "The matchmaker didn't come I was at the tailor's he's saving the dress-coat already tacked on the button-holes—didn't ask anything first-class cloth says he'll do his best. That's all." Curtain.

A great theatrical celebrity of the time, the ingenious director Nikolay Mikhailovich Foregger . . . had very few good actors, but they were all, young lads and lasses alike, dancers and acrobats and eccentric comics and athletes. That's all he wanted: his theater was essentially a somewhat "sovieticized" music hall: in his productions gymnastics and dance on extremely risqué subjects were mixed with intelligent and very witty pamphleteering. So that the whole production turned into a kind of conglomeration of circus and variety with a pinch of eroticism and . . . politics.

So in our parody I reduced this medley to absurdity. In the Foregger-style *Getting Married,* against a backdrop that was a decorative hodgepodge of bright posterlike futurism and music-hall topicality, Podkolyosin and Stepan in clown costumes fly out to meet one another, swinging on trapezes overhead, and in such poses, soaring across the stage, they recite their lines. Here's how it opened:

PODKOLYOSIN:
Swinging, swinging, then things go awry . . .
The lovely floor beckons my soul . . .
This fleeting world so quickly floats by . . .
Stepan! Where you headed?
STEPAN: The Komsomol!

. . . I regularly parodied Meyerhold's productions [which] at that period impressed me in this way: the director would concoct something extravagant, which excited the throng of connoisseurs and astounded the public, and then he would wonder: "What next? How can I 'outspit' myself in the next production?"

. . . So, our curtain rose. The set represented something in the nature of a chicken coop: wooden cages heaped up next to each other; the actors spoke the dialogue as they laboriously climbed from one cage to another. This created a series of parodic *mises-en-scène*. And through the bars, as through a wringer, emerged the crowd of suitors [as in Meyerhold's constructivist slat-set for *The Magnanimous Cuckold*]. . . .

. . . The creator of the Chamber Theater, Aleksander Yakov-levich Tairov, was a brilliant and very idiosyncratic director. Char-acteristic of productions at his theater were fantastical costumes, singsong speech, and mannered gesticulation by the actors—in short, emphatic, deliberate "theatricality." All this we "laid on" in our parody.

Podkolyosin in the guise of an Egyptian priest was sitting cross-legged on a very high pedestal, reciting his soliloquy to the sounds of a musical cacophony. Stepan entered in the costume of a Pierrot and kept changing poses that had nothing to do with the script, in alogical sequence; in extremely bombastic tones he spoke of the dress coat, the buttonholes, and other everyday things as if some mysterious priestly rite had transpired.

The most farcical version was *Getting Married* as performed in the sticks. It might seem an incredible caricature nowadays, but at the time. . . . Barn-storming theaters flourished in remote little burgs. . . . What we played was almost a photograph of such a theater and roused a vivid response in the spectator. . . . The leading role was played not by Podkolyosin or Stepan but by the prompter. In the middle of stage stood a sofa, near it a sort of potted palm. Podkolyosin sat on the sofa, staring straight at the prompter's box, and word for word repeated his soliloquy after the prompter, and if he didn't catch a line, asked for it out of the corner of his mouth—and then garbled it. Then Stepan came in. He was hilariously played as the kind of impudent, shameless ac-tor who doesn't give a damn.

Here's how the dialogue began!

PROMPTER: The matchmaker's come?

PODKOLYOSIN (*after the prompter, grieving*): The matchmaker's come!

PROMPTER: It's a question! You're asking!

PODKOLYOSIN: I got a little question for you! The matchmaker's come?

STEPAN: Yes, she's come.

PROMPTER (*shouts*): Oh no! No! She hasn't!

STEPAN: Oh, you mean the matchmaker? The matchmaker hasn't come!

PROMPTER: You go to the tailor?

PODKOLYOSIN: You go to the tailor!

PROMPTER: It's another question! You're asking him: you go to the tailor?

PODKOLYOSIN: Stepa, I'm peppering you with questions! You go to the tailor?

STEPAN: No I didn't.

PROMPTER (*in despair*): You did! you did!

STEPAN: I did, I did.

PROMPTER (*to Podkolyosin*): So, is he sewing the dress coat?

PODKOLYOSIN (*in a whisper*): What? What?

PROMPTER (*one word at a time*): So.

PODKOLYOSIN: So.

PROMPTER: Is he sewing.

PODKOLYOSIN: Is he sewing.

PROMPTER: The dress coat.

PODKOLYOSIN: The dress coat. The dress coat!

STEPAN: Yes, he's got lots of dress coats . . . Hanging on a rack . . .

PROMPTER: But is the cloth on them, I'll bet, not as good as mine?

PODKOLYOSIN (*to Prompter*): I didn't get that.

PROMPTER: But is the cloth on them . . .

PODKOLYOSIN: But is there cloth on them?

STEPAN: He says yes. There's only the lining left to do, and then it'll be finished!

PROMPTER (*to the actor*): Quiet, what are you improvising! But is the cloth on them . . .

PODKOLYOSIN: I said that already!

PROMPTER: I bet, not as good as mine?

PODKOLYOSIN (*very surprised*): Bed? What bed?

PROMPTER: Never you mind! Just say it! I bet, not as good as mine!

PODKOLYOSIN (*shrugging*): Say, Stepa, is their bed not as good as mine?

STEPAN: What bed, there was a cot!

PROMPTER (*in horror*): Quiiiiet!!! Yes, yours'll be a lot better-looking . . .

STEPAN (*quietly, to the prompter*): What are you improvising there? (*Puts the palm right in front of the prompter's box and leans on it, listening.*)

PROMPTER: Yes, it'll be a-lot-bet-ter-look-ing . . .

STEPAN: Yes, it'll be a lot of bird dropping . . .

Whereupon even Podkolyosin couldn't help it and burst out laughing. A similar muddle continued to the end. This was a hard act to follow, so we always put this excerpt before the intermission.

Jogging the Memory
(Not v obikhode)
1927
from A. Averchenko
by
The Blue Blouses Troupe

ONE: So, tomorrow morning you'll phone me up?

TWO: Yes, yes, sure. By the way, what's your phone number?

ONE: It's a good thing you remembered to ask—it's unlisted. Make a note of it: five-four-two-six.

TWO: Why should I make a note? I'll remember it as is. What did you say it was?

ONE: Five-four-two-six, fifty-four twenty-six.

TWO: That's a lot for one man.

ONE: Don't forget.

TWO: What's there to forget? It's simple: sixty-four, twenty-six.

ONE: Not sixty-four—fifty-four.

TWO: Aha. Fifty-four . . . In other words, the first half is fifty-four, the second is twenty-six. Which means, the first half is double the second half.

ONE: What are you talking about? The second half times two makes only fifty-two, not fifty-four.

TWO: Aha. Then it's simple. In other words, multiply the second half by two and add another two to the product.

ONE: By your system my number could be twenty-six twenty.

TWO: What do you mean? How so?

ONE: It would come out the same: the second half times two and add two to the product.

TWO: Oh hell, you're right . . . What did you say your number was?

ONE: Fifty-four, twenty-six.

TWO: Right. Which means the first thing to do is get the second half firmly memorized and go on from there. The second half is—what?

ONE: Twenty-six. You can't remember it that way. You'd better work it out by percentages.

TWO: That'll do it. So, in other words, one percent of twenty-six is two-point-six . . . Hm . . . How do you remember six-tenths?

ONE: Very simple. Add the first six to October tenth, the anniversary of the Revolution, and there you have it.

TWO: That won't work. The number is twenty-six. How can I remember it? Let's say I've got twenty digits on my hands and feet . . . Then add six. But how am I going to remember six?

ONE: Remember that six is nine turned on its head.

TWO: You think so? No, that won't work: if six is nine upside down, then nine is six upside down.

ONE: You know what? I've got the perfect solution. Take a pencil, a piece of paper, and write it down.

TWO: No, why should I? I can remember it as is. Look how simple it is: to find the first half of the number, you have to multiply the second half by two and add another two. So the real problem is: how do you remember the second half? . . . Hm . . . Let's say, two ten-ruble notes, one five-ruble note and one silver ruble . . . Which makes twenty-six.

ONE: Too complicated. How old are you?

TWO: Thirty-two.

ONE: Thirty-two? All right, all right . . . Which means, if we subtract twenty-six from thirty-two, we get . . . six. See? Which means, by subtracting six from the number of your age, you get the second half you're looking for.

TWO: That's not bad, I gotta admit, but how am I going to remember the six?

ONE: Listen . . . you're never going to remember a detail like that.

TWO: Sure I will, but why six, why not eight or five?

ONE: Well, you might remember it this way: you've got five fingers on one hand and . . . and another silver ruble.

TWO: No, no, give me a break; you're getting me confused—

thirty-two years, five fingers, and a ruble. How am I supposed to connect five fingers with my age? Ridiculous.

ONE: No, we'd better discard that system.

TWO: Let's approach it from another angle. What's your telephone number?

ONE: Fifty-four twenty-six.

TWO: My father died at the age of fifty-seven, and my elder sister at twenty-one. Fifty-seven twenty-one . . . Which means, my father died three years after the telephone, and my sister didn't make it to the second half of your telephone by five years.

ONE: Why dig up the dead? And how can your sister "not make it to my telephone by five years"? No, we can make this a lot easier: add the numbers in fifty-four and you get nine; add the numbers in twenty-six and you get eight.

TWO: So?

ONE: Add eight and nine and you get seventeen.

TWO: So what?

ONE: Add the numerals in seventeen and you get . . . eight.

TWO: The result of which is?

ONE: Well, eight . . . Remember the number eight. Five and three . . . or four and four.

TWO: So what about it?

ONE: I can't work it out if you keep giving me that sarcastic look. You're making me nervous . . . Just figure it out for yourself.

TWO: Do me a favor. Now I've got it; it's real simple. Fifty-four, twenty-six, you say? Well, look, before the half-price sale, an overcoat at (*name of firm*) cost fifty rubles, but now it costs twenty-five. In the first case, we have a surplus of four over fifty, and in the second, a surplus of one over twenty-five. Hm . . . how am I going to remember that?

ONE: There's nothing simpler about that. Before the half-price sale you wore this overcoat for four years, and after the sale you only managed to hang on to it for a year.

TWO: You aren't even close! And just now when there's a campaign for quality on!

ONE: In that case I give it up. Work it out for yourself.

TWO: So I shall. What year was Perekop captured?

ONE: 920.

TWO: There you are. And how long is the new industrialization plan supposed to last?

ONE: Five years.

TWO: Twenty plus five makes twenty-five. We just have to add a
one. What have you got that's only one?

ONE: One nose, one mouth, one chin . . .

TWO: Not that. There's no way to connect Perekop and a chin.
Make it something else. Is there a one in the government?

ONE: Hm . . . there are lots of committees. Aha. ARCEC is one.

TWO: There we are . . . So, the second number is equal to Perekop plus the five-year industrialization plan plus the All-
Russian Central Executive Committee.

ONE: Fine. Now what about the first half?

TWO: The first half . . . It's coming . . . Hm . . . the first . . .
Ha! a stroke of genius. What's the temperature today?

ONE: Twenty degrees Réamur.

TWO: Hm . . . Twenty plus three, minus six Perekops . . .

ONE: Good grief, he's having sunstroke . . .

TWO (*mutters*): ARCEC plus five-year plan, add twenty degrees
plus industrialization with rationalization and five sunstrokes
. . . that makes . . . that makes . . . the answer is . . . It's
coming.

ONE: My dear fellow . . . wait a minute . . . Right now . . .
right now . . . right now I'm going to write it down for you
. . . don't fall apart. Now look, I'm taking a pencil, and here's
a piece of paper and I'll write . . . You see . . . Hold on . . .
Just a minute . . . (*tragically*) I forgot . . . I forgot my telephone number. Citizens, how can a thing like this happen: a
man forgets his own telephone number? This damned wild
goose chase put me out. How am I going to phone home now?
I haven't got it written down anywhere.

TWO: Hold on . . . Hold on, my friend. We'll go right now and
phone Pyotr Stepanovich. He'll know your telephone number.

ONE: Oof-f . . . Luckily he does . . .

TWO: Well, then, we'll ask him for your number, and then we'll
both write it down on a NOT notepad. Then we're saved.

ONE: Then we've saved. All that's left is to point the moral.

TWO: And so we shall. All right, let's do a little moralizing.

ONE: Let's. (*Sings*)

> The moral isn't long, you see,
> This lesson can be learned by rote:
> You don't need an elephant's memory:
> If it's important make a note.

A detail may prove the foundation
For work, and life too, we might add,
So take this down from our dictation:—
You need to get a NOT notepad.

Translator's Note

NOT, the Scientific Organization of Labor, introduced "Fordism," assembly
lines, and efficiency to Soviet factories and theaters.

Kerensky's Report on the U.S.S.R. (Excerpts)
(Doklad Kerenskogo ob SSSR)
1931
by
N. P. Smirnov-Sokolsky

. . . Miracles do happen in this country. And the greatest miracle, the most miraculous thing, in my opinion, is that here in Russia once a certain Aleksandr Fyodorovich Kerensky considered himself a sort of hero of the people. . . . He wouldn't be worth remembering, except that not so long ago he, along with Pal Nikolaevich Milyukov, decided to make a complete report about our Soviet Republic to the socialist faction of the French parliament.

Now I am going to repeat this very report to you. As you will understand, I myself need more than the mere words or expressions of the "unforgettable" Aleksandr Fyodorovich Kerensky. Which is why, feeling myself unequal to the task, I have called film to my aid, and assisted by this "great silent presence," I shall try to deliver the report of this "great communicator." . . .

The picture I shall show you is, of course, considerably weaker than those pictures our film directors have shown you—this is entirely understandable; I am probably a million times less talented than they, but it comforts me to know that I cost the government that much less in proportion. . . . Let's have screen, lights, action . . .

First, there'll be a title, as on any self-respecting picture. Usually it's the best thing: it's where our film directors are most successful.

(*On screen the title "Report on the USSR by A. F. Kerensky"*)

Of course, Aleksandr Fyodorovich Kerensky was speaking in person—the former Supreme Commander-in-Chief, the former president of the Council of Ministries and, in general, unfortunately, a former Russian here in Russia. . . .

(*On screen: the puppet Petrushka*)

Even now he is considered abroad to be a great public speaker on political subjects.

(*On screen: a Victrola*)

We ourselves remember how well he used to speak.

(*On screen: a balalaika*)

His speech to Parliament was full of substance.

(*On screen: water poured into a bucket*)

Pal Nikolaevich Milyukov, full of ardent love for dear Mother Russia, was only a yes-man to him.

(*On screen: a dog barking*)

All the information which I impart to you, said Aleksandr Fyodorovich, we have collected from the most reliable sources.

(*On screen: two gossiping old biddies*)

We have at our disposal a series of original documents, discrediting the activities of the Bolshevist Comintern abroad.

(*On screen: a forge*)

A good deal of truth has been conveyed to us by the former general counsel of the Bolshevist Embassy, who has come over to our side, Mr. Besedovsky, whose relationship to his motherland seems to be uniquely noble.

(*On screen: a pig*)

The country is burning down. The ruins of our former Russian government are quietly smouldering.

(*On screen: factory chimneys smoking*)

Transportation is a wreck, the trains have stopped. . . .

(*On screen: a railway station, with a train waiting*)

The peasants have forgotten how to till the soil; they have thrown away the plow and ride around in automobiles seized from the bourgeoisie.

(*On screen: tractors at work*)

The unsown fields, devoid of any vegetation whatever, present a dismal, unforgettable picture . . .

(*On screen: a bald head*)

The dastardly robber chieftain Stenka Razin stands at the head of the so-called government.

(*On screen: a portrait of M. I. Kalinin*)

Agriculture is in ruins. Unfed horses, released by their owners, prowl the city streets in wild herds.

(*On screen: sportsmen riding on horseback*)

Hard times have befallen the citizens of the so-called Soviet Republic. On their weak shoulders they bear a burden too heavy for their strength—a bitter [*gorky*] burden.

(*On screen: the arrival of Gorky in Moscow*)

Among the intelligentsia there are frequent outbreaks of mass insanity. People go out of their minds.

(*On screen: people dancing the foxtrot*)

Citizens shed bitter tears over the brilliant past.

(*On screen: a baby crying*). . . .

The country is impoverished; people go about shoeless, ill-clad, without the wherewithal to hide their nakedness.

(*On screen: chorus girls at a music hall*)

Moscow has died; eerie and deserted are the streets of the once noisy metropolis . . .

(*On screen: a populous street in Moscow*)

The Bolsheviks have destroyed everything that we held dearest in that land.

(*On screen: a demijohn is smashed*)

The times of Ivan the Terrible have revived. People are racked and tormented with medieval tortures.

(*On screen: people listening to the radio*)

The population rob and steal right in the streets. "Your money or your life!" is heard on the lips of highway robbers.

(*On screen: a patrolman imposing a fine*)

At night one can hear wretched victims wildly screaming for help.

(*On screen: a soprano sings a gipsy ballad*)

Some citizens walk the streets in strange costumes.

(*On screen: a nude baby*)

Others, brutalized by terror, leap on one another like wild beasts.

(*On screen: a couple kissing*)

Sometimes they go to extremes, throw themselves headlong into rivers, perform forced labor, and are chained to wheelbarrows.

(*On screen: young people getting marriage licenses at a registry office*)

Foreseeing the awful hour of retribution, long lines of people rush to prostrate themselves before God for their transgressions.

(*On screen: queueing up at the IRS*)

All talk that the country is achieving socialism is, of course, rubbish. Enriched private entrepreneurs insolently ride around the city in luxurious carriages.

(*On screen: "first aid" ambulance*)

And at the very moment when all civilized nations are preparing to help this wretched land . . .

(*On screen: weapons aimed at the audience*)

when the Bolsheviks themselves timidly plead for mercy on their knees,

(*On screen: the Red Army on guard*)

with nowhere to look to for support and no one in whom to invest hope,

(*On screen: sections of the Red Army, Budyonny, Voroshilov*)

Litvinov is ready to make any concessions.

(*On screen: a hand making the "up yours" gesture*)

And I believe that the white emigrés can expect a bright future.

(*On screen: a cemetery*)

Thus spake Aleksandr Fyodorovich Kerensky. The golden content of his wise speech has reached even to us, diffusing the subtle aroma of this great man's glorious political activities.

(*On screen: a string of sewage-disposal carts*). . . .

Translator's Notes

Aleksandr F. Kerensky (1881–1970), prime minister of the coalition government before the Bolshevik takeover, lived in Paris till 1940. The Soviets always portrayed him as an impotent tool of the aristocracy. His foreign minister had been *Pavel N. Milyukov,* who also lived in Paris.

Mikhail I. Kalinin, a supporter of Stalin, was the popular, benign-looking chairman of the Central Executive Committee of Soviets.

The writer *Maksim Gorky* had first attacked the Communist government, but in 1928 returned to Russia from Capri and became an important propagandist for Stalin.

Semyon M. Budyonny was a legendary cavalry officer, who, with *Kliment E. Voroshilov* as his political commissar, achieved some of the Bolsheviks' earliest military victories. By 1930 Budyonny was a marshal and Voroshilov commissar of Defense.

Maksim Litvinov was commissar and Soviet representative at the League of Nations, later ambassador to the United States.

AS CONSTITUENTS OF THE AUSTRO-HUNGARIAN EMPIRE, BO-
hemia, Moravia, and Slovakia were not encouraged to promote
their native cultures. But Prague was home to so-called *šantans*
(*chantants*), where folksingers could perform in Czech rather than
in official German. In 1910, an artists' cabaret called Lucerna (the
Lantern) was formed by the novelist Eduard Bass, the opera librettist Jaroslav Kvapil, the popular singer Karel Hašler, the expert in macabre humor Emil Longen, and Longen's wife, Xena,
who specialized in playing prostitutes. A leading light was the
gregarious journalist Jaroslav Hašek, not yet the author of *The
Good Soldier Švejk,* who wrote the cabaret's first sketch, *A Glass of
Black Coffee,* and occasionally played dame roles. The targets of
satire included Alfons Mucha's *art nouveau* style and the theft
of the Mona Lisa from the Louvre. Half the performances were in
German and half in Czech, the latter comprising ghetto songs
translated from Yiddish.

The next year a wine bar, the Montmartre, opened with a Chat
Noir room featuring apache dances. Under the leadership of the
singer Josef Waltner, it became the "Simpl of the Moldau," with a
repertory of songs in Czech, Yiddish, and German. Franz Kafka
was an habitué, as was Hašek, who improvised stories; but Hašek
proved to be an unreliable performer, cadging drinks and obstre-
perously breaking up the show. The Tango Argentina was first
performed in Prague at the Montmartre by a dancer known as
Emka Revoluce (i.e., Revolution) and a waiter who, because of his
past, was called Hamlet.

The same year, 1911, also saw the formation of the *Červená
semda,* or Red Seven, a student cabaret of scenes, songs, and parodies. Three years later it went professional, offering satirical
solos, organized by the librettist Dr. Jiři Červený. When Bass became the conférencier, it turned into a focal point for antimilitarist, anti-Habsburg sentiments; and when a Czech Republic was
declared in 1918, the cabaret criticized the seamy side of that government. Such comedians as Vlasta Burian and Ferenc Futurista

were members of the ensemble, and after Hašek returned from his five years in Bolshevik Russia, he was asked to spin yarns about his experiences. By this time he had become, in his biographer Cecil Parrott's words, "like Professor Unrath in *The Blue Angel*," and to Bass's consternation, he read *How I Met the Author of My Obituary* in return for a liter of beer. The Red Seven closed in 1922, succumbing to the pressures of economic inflation.

The cabaret tradition found its best development in the Osvobozené Divadlo, or Liberated Theater, which spoke for a generation during its existence from 1925 to 1938. Its founders, former law students Jiří Voskovec (Wachsmann, 1904–81) and Jan Werich (1905–80), wrote, directed, designed, and acted in some twenty-five full-scale shows, which they called "jazz revues." Tin-Pan Alley and American silent film comedy had an influence on "V + W" as they were known, but they were also molded by Hašek's carefree poetry, Apollinaire's protosurrealism, and the Italo-French clowns Les Fratellini. V + W themselves functioned as a white-face clown team, Voskovec the less aggressive, more pedantic, Werich the more impulsive and earthy.

In the 1,000-seat Liberated Theater, a company of fifty presented richly satiric scenarios, poetic yet political, with improvisation around preplanned points. The shows took particular notice of fascism as it burgeoned in Europe. *Caesar* (1932) attacked Mussolini, while *Ass and Shadow* (1933) moved beyond this to a broader assault on totalitarianism and demagoguery. *World Behind Bars* (1933), written with the left-wing cartoonist Adolf Hoffmeister (b. 1902), used Prohibition-era America as a metaphor for capitalism: the images of gangsters, political corruption, and bootlegging borrowed from movies and comic strips became emblematic of a world in which freedom was contingent on money. The effect is reminiscent of Brecht's Neverland America in his *Jungle of Cities, St. Joan of the Stockyards,* and *Happy End.*

How I Met the Author of My Obituary
(Jak jsem se setkal s autorem svého nekrologa)
1921
by
Jaroslav Hašek

During the five or six years I stayed in Russia I was killed and liquidated several times by various organizations and individuals.

When I returned to my own country I learned that I had been thrice hanged, twice shot, and once drawn and quartered by savage Kirghiz insurgents in the vicinity of Lake Kale-Yshel.

Finally, I was definitively stabbed to death in a wild brawl with drunken sailors in a low dive in Odessa. This version strikes me as the most likely.

It also seemed most likely to my dear friend Kolman, who, having found an eyewitness to my ignominious yet heroic death, wrote a whole article for his paper about this event which had ended so unfortunately for me.

He did not limit himself to a small filler. His kind heart led him to write my obituary, which I read soon after my return to Prague.

Convinced that the dead do not rise from the grave, he had vilified me most elegantly in this obituary.

To persuade him that I was alive, I went looking for him,— and that's how this story came to be.

Even Edgar Poe, master of nightmares and horrors, couldn't have dreamed up a more ghastly subject.

I found the author of my obituary in a certain Prague wine bar, at midnight on the dot, when according to a certain Imperial and Royal decree of 18 April 1836, wine bars are supposed to close.

He was staring at the ceiling. They were stripping stained tableclothes from the tables. I sat down at his table and quietly asked:

"Do you mind? Is this seat taken?"

He went on observing the spot on the ceiling which he found so engrossing and replied with perfect logic:

"Go ahead. I think they're ready to close, so what do you care if it's taken or not."

I took him by the arm and swivelled him around to face me. He stared at me in silence for a moment and finally whispered:

"Excuse me, weren't you in Russia?"

I started to laugh:

"So you finally recognize me? I was killed in Russia in a filthy dive in a wild brawl with drunken sailors."

He turned pale.

"You're . . . you're . . ."

"Yes," I said emphatically, "I was killed by sailors in a tavern in Odessa, and you devoted an obituary to me."

He murmured barely audibly:

"You read what I wrote about you?"

"Well, of course; it's a very interesting obituary, except for a few paltry misinterpretations. And a pretty long-winded one too. Not even His Imperial Majesty the Emperor got as many lines when he died. Your paper devoted 152 lines to him, and 186 to me, at thirty-three hellers a line,—what niggardly pay journalists used to get!—which came to fifty-five crowns fifteen hellers in all."

"What exactly do you want from me?" he asked in alarm. "Do you want me to turn those fifty-five crowns fifteen hellers over to you?"

"You can keep your earnings," I replied. "Dead men don't accept fees for their own obituaries."

He turned even paler.

"You know what?" I asked nonchalantly, "let's pay up and go somewhere else. I'd like to spend this night with you."

"Couldn't we put it off till tomorrow?"

I glared fixedly at him.

"Check!" shouted my companion.

Having hailed a cab at the corner, I suggested that the author of my obituary get in and in a sepulchral voice ordered the driver:

"Drive us to Olšany Cemetery!"

The author of my obituary made the sign of the cross.

For a long time an embarrassing silence prevailed, broken only by the crack of the whip and the snorting of the horses.

I leaned over to my companion.

"Have you noticed that somewhere down in the streets of Žižkov, the dogs have started to howl?"

He began to tremble, drew himself up, and stammered a question:

"Were you really in Russia?"

"I was killed in a low dive in Odessa in a brawl with drunken sailors," I answered drily.

"Jesus Maria," my companion responded, "this is more gruesome than *The Specter's Bride* by Erben."

And again there was an embarrassing silence. . . . Somewhere dogs actually started to howl.

When we reached Strašnická Highway, I suggested that my companion pay the cabdriver. We stood in the shadows of Strašnická Highway.

"Say, isn't there a restaurant around here?" the author of my obituary asked me in a hopeless and pitiful tone.

"A restaurant?" I started to laugh. "Now we'll climb over the cemetery wall, and on a gravestone somewhere we'll have a little talk about that obituary. You climb first and lend me a hand."

Silently he gave me his hand, and we jumped down into the cemetery. Beneath our feet cypress twigs crackled. The wind wailed mournfully through the crosses.

"I'm not going any farther!" my friend blurted out. "Where are you trying to drag me?"

"Today," I said cheerily, maintaining my grip on him, "we're going to have a look at the crypt of that old Prague family of aristocrats, the Bonepianis. A totally derelict crypt in section one, row six, by the wall. Derelict from the time they buried the last descendant, who was brought in 1874 from Odessa, where he was killed by sailors in a low dive during a brawl."

My companion made the sign of the cross again.

When we were settled on the slab that covered the crypt laden with the dust of the last descendants of the Prague citizens Bonepiani, I carefully took the author of my obituary by the arm and stated quietly:

"Dear friend! In high school our teachers taught us the beautiful, noble adage 'Speak no ill of the dead!' You ventured, though, to write all kinds of nasty things about me, a dead man. If I had had to write my own obituary, I would have written that no death left such a heavy impression as the death of Mr. So-and-so! I would have written: 'The late writer's greatest merit was his genuine love for virtue, for everything held sacred by pure souls.' But you wrote that I died a scoundrel and a buffoon! Stop crying! A time comes when the heart boils with desire to describe what was most beautiful about the lives of the dead. But you . . . wrote that the deceased was an alcoholic."

The author of my obituary wept all the more loudly; his doleful sobs echoed through the quiet cemetery and faded away somewhere far off near the Jewish Furnaces.

"Dear friend," I said resolutely, "stop crying, you can't put it right now. . . ."

So saying, I leaped over the cemetery wall, ran down to the gatekeeper's shack, rang his bell, and explained that while returning from some moonlighting work, I had heard crying behind the cemetery wall in section one.

"Probably some widower who's had a drop too much," the gatekeeper replied cynically; "we'll see he's arrested."

I waited at the corner. About ten minutes later nightwatchmen were escorting the author of my obituary out of the cemetery to the police station.

He was resisting and shouting:

"Is this a dream or reality? Gentlemen, do you know *The Specter's Bride* by Erben?"

Translator's Notes

Hašek had spent two weeks in Russia as a Bolshevik commissar, and rumors about his death were frequent in Prague. A slanderous obituary entitled "Traitor," written by a so-called friend, Jaroslav Kolman-Kassius, appeared in January 1919.

The Specter's Bride. A ballad in which a dead man appears to the bride.

Jewish Furnaces. A reference to a Prague neighborhood.

World Behind Bars (Excerpts)
(Svet za mřížemi)
1933
by
Jiři Voskovec, Jan Werich, and Adolf Hoffmeister

ACT ONE, SCENE TWO

[*Act One opens with a nocturnal panorama of Kork City on the backdrop. A street with Hector Litter's brewery. The noise of a demonstration can be heard. In this scene, the poet Rum, in love with Litter's daughter Miami, argues with the brewer about the upcoming referendum on prohibition.*]

LITTER (*coming out of his house*): I won't have you corrupting my daughter, sir, much less in my own house.

RUM: Mr. Industrialist . . .

LITTER: Industrial Magnate to you . . .

RUM: What difference does a word make?

LITTER: A great deal. That word puts my daughter out of the reach of the likes of you.

RUM: We'll see about that once you've talked to me!

LITTER: I don't need to talk to poets! I own land, real estate, securities, stocks, and bonds. I have a position in society. I don't read poets, and I'm certainly not going to talk to them.

RUM (*waving a piece of paper under Litter's nose*): Wait and see: you'll talk to me.

LITTER: Pamphlets, sir, don't concern me. I support prohibition out of conviction; beer may have made me a wealthy man, but I am channelling my wealth into ideals. I don't want the world to be drunk, not even on my beer. Eliminating alcohol means eliminating the petty demon of the people. Down with poison, up with vitamins! Temperance!

RUM:

What bare-faced impudence!
You're planning thievery
And speak of temperance!

LITTER: How dare you speak to me that way?

RUM:

I'll speak to you the way I should:
Lip-service ideals are no good,
When in your hip-pocket you stash
A wallet bulging with cold cash.

LITTER: You cad! You call yourself a poet? A member of the literati, an intellectual? And you address a poor businessman that way?

RUM: Mr. Industrial Magnate!

LITTER: What do you want? . . . And don't waste my time.

RUM: If there's nothing to drink, there's an end to imagination!!

LITTER: Won't that be a pity!

RUM: It'll spell death to the old toast: Long live libation-lovers!

LITTER: Fairy tales!

RUM: Mr. Factory Owner, once your prohibition law passes, what will wedding guests pour in their glasses?

LITTER (*sings*): We'll make tea, herb tea, hot chocolate, black coffee! (*Speaks*) Soda, lemonade, fruit juice, grenadine . . . Get lost!

RUM: I'm off to the last preelection meeting of the "wets." And I'll unmask your scheme. A brewery owner campaigns for prohibition just so he can sell bootleg beer at higher prices.

LITTER: Hogwash!

RUM: You've corrupted the political process, you bloodsucker! Beer wasn't profitable enough but now you can sell it under the counter for fantastic prices! You organized the underworld to help you smuggle alcohol the minute prohibition is declared.

LITTER: Lies and slander!

RUM: I have proof. (*He waves some papers under Litter's nose.*) Take a look: photographs of your contract with Wu-Fang, the underworld boss. It'll be in all the evening papers.

LITTER: I'll buy that photo!

RUM: Withdraw the prohibition bill.

LITTER: Half a million!

RUM: I'm off to see the editor!

LITTER: One million!

RUM: Goodbye! A good strong drink is worth more than you think.

LITTER (*bellows*): I've never harmed a downy little chick in my life, but you I'll shoot if you don't hand over that photo. (*He draws a revolver.*)

RUM: If drink is gone, imagination's dead!

LITTER (*bellows*): Hand it over, or I'll shoot!

RUM: It'll spell death to the old toast: Long live libation-lovers! (*A hand holding a revolver comes around the corner. A shot is fired. Rum staggers.*)

LITTER (*stares at his revolver*): Gosh, what happened?

RUM (*collapses*):
>   Mr. Factory Owner, if your dry law does pass,
>   Place on my grave a well-filled wine glass.

CURTAIN

ACT ONE, SCENE TWELVE

[*As election day ends, Heave and Ho appear, climbing out of a manhole. Heave lives by scavenging for valuables in the city sewers. Ho always wears a tuxedo, so he can gate-crash weddings as an uninvited guest, lose himself in the crowd, and feast to his heart's content. The referendum vote is tied, and these two now represent the deciding votes.*

Wu-Fang, the gang leader; Litter and his son-in-law Colt Bulldogg; and a Reporter are already on stage.]

HEAVE: You know, clean work it ain't, but a guy's got to make a living somehow . . .

(*Ho notices the Reporter and Wu-Fang.*)

HEAVE: . . . When this blows over, we'll climb out again.

WU-FANG: Hold it right there!

REPORTER: Who are you?

HO: We won't disturb you, gentlemen. (*Starts to leave.*)

COLT: As you were!

HEAVE: In the sewer, you mean?

WU-FANG (*to the Reporter*): Do you know this man?

HEAVE (*to Ho*): We probably got the manholes mixed up and wound up in a nuthouse . . .

WU-FANG: No talking!

HO: What's going on here, anyway?

LITTER: Are you trying to kill us? Who hired you?

HEAVE: Now, gentlemen, don't lose your heads. We clean drain-pipes . . .

HO: . . . we've been working all night . . .

HEAVE: . . . And we'd really like to wash up!

REPORTER: And when did you crawl in there?

HO: We've been in there since last night.

COLT: And did you vote?

HEAVE: What a stupid question! Do you think there are ballot boxes down there?

LITTER: They didn't vote!

WU-FANG: Gentlemen, the factory owner's bathroom is at your disposal . . .

REPORTER: Come to the public baths as my guest . . .

LITTER: Come to my place and make yourselves at home.

COLT: You must be hungry, gentlemen . . .

REPORTER: Don't listen to them!

LITTER: That man's not with us. We'll take good care of you.

WU-FANG: C'mon along now . . .

HEAVE: Gentlemen, aren't you confusing us with someone else?

HO: Don't let my outfit fool you; I'm not Prince Walesky.

REPORTER: But you haven't voted!

HEAVE: We can prove that we just didn't have the chance . . .

WU-FANG: Are you sure you didn't vote?

HO: Yes, but we have an alibi . . .

LITTER: We aren't interested in alibis . . .

HEAVE: But any court will grant . . .

HO: There's still five minutes left, though. Don't keep us.

WU-FANG: You can vote right here!

COLT: All we need is a policeman as witness. (*Exits.*)

REPORTER: Come with me to the newspaper office!

LITTER: You stay right here and vote for prohibition!

HEAVE: Well, how do you know how we're going to vote?

WU-FANG: You're for the people's welfare, aren't you?

REPORTER: In vino veritas, the people's welfare lies in beer . . .

WU-FANG: It all depends on you.

REPORTER: Your votes will determine the outcome of the election . . .

LITTER: So vote . . .

REPORTER: . . . Against prohibition . . .

WU-FANG: . . . No, for prohibition!

LITTER: You'll be the heroes of the day!

HO: Enough already! One way or the other we'll be heroes of the day. But . . . how can I put it . . .

HEAVE: . . . If I'm not mistaken, my friend wants to say . . . we'd all like to move up in the world . . .

WU-FANG: But of course, your every wish will be granted.

REPORTER: Vote against, and the press will make you famous . . .

LITTER: . . . we'll find you a position . . .

REPORTER: . . . I'll write your biographies . . .

HO: You know, we are but simple folk . . .

LITTER: But you can end up noblemen!

HEAVE: That's exactly the point . . . anything'll change people's opinions under the right conditions!

REPORTER: Bribery!

HO: You stay out of this, you pup! We're lowly sewer experts . . .

HEAVE: . . . and if we were to become supervisors . . .

WU-FANG: With the factory owner's connections, it's a sure thing!

HO: Suppose we wanted to become supervisors of sewer workers . . .

LITTER: By all means. You can count on it.

HO: Or . . . well, you're a civil servant, you know how it is. What if some kind of cushy job were dreamed up for us? Say . . . officers in the secret police?

WU-FANG: Then that's what you'll be, gentlemen.

REPORTER: Come with me and you'll get in all the history books!

HO: Wait a minute. Maybe if they erected a monument to us . . .

REPORTER: It'll happen. You'll be famous!

HEAVE: And will they raise money for this monument through subscriptions?

REPORTER: Of course!

HO: And when enough money's been subscribed, someone will make off with it and that's an end to the monument.

REPORTER: That won't happen this time.

HEAVE (*to Litter and Wu-Fang*)*:* You know, gentlemen, you are offering us material benefits, but the other side is offering material benefits as well, so we're of two minds, as it were.

ACT TWO, SCENE TWELVE

[*Prohibition has passed. Ex-brewer Litter and Wu-Fang, now an engineer, are running a bootleg operation. Heave and Ho, now with the secret police, are in charge of upholding the new liquor laws. After breaking into Wu-Fang's headquarters, they discover bootleg cognac and get drunk sampling the evidence. The Honest Policeman, who was recently promoted to Inspector, arrives on the scene.*]

LITTER: Inspector, these men were caught trespassing. I demand an investigation!

HEAVE: Ooooh, trespassing! What about that cognac?

POLICEMAN: Quiet, I heard the word "cognac!" What about it?

HO: It's been smuggled in here.

WU-FANG: Inspector, I'll give you . . .

POLICEMAN: Where is this cognac?

HEAVE: It was here, in these bottles. But somebody's emptied them.

POLICEMAN: It is most important to ascertain the contents of those bottles. What do you have to say, Mr. Engineer?

WU-FANG: That is quite simple, Inspector. I am the proprietor of a laundry and dry-cleaning establishment. (*He opens a small door which reveals a conveyor belt carrying clothes.*) The bottles contained samples of a new cleaning fluid we're using.

HO: Get a doctor! We drank that stuff!

HEAVE: We've got to get our stomachs pumped! Man the pumps!

LITTER: I may be here merely as a visitor, Inspector, but I am nonetheless shocked by the behavior of your men!

WU-FANG: Incredible! They break in here without a warrant, drink my samples, and to make matters worse, point an accusing finger at me. I demand satisfaction.

POLICEMAN (*subdued*)*:* I'll take care of it right away, gentlemen.

LITTER: The sooner the better, Inspector. (*Exits.*)

WU-FANG: I expect an appropriate apology, Inspector. Good day. (*Exits.*)

HEAVE: Inspector . . .

POLICEMAN: Quiet, you impudent . . .

HO: But that's not a laundry!

HEAVE: And that cleaning fluid tasted awful good!

POLICEMAN: Against my explicit orders, you broke into this building, drank the evidence, and made a mockery of justice. You are beneath contempt. What's more, you're not only demoted; you're fired!

HO: We meant well.

POLICEMAN: As an inspector, I beg to differ. As a private individual, I advise you to remember: excess of zeal is harmful. (*Exits.*)

HEAVE: There you have it. The engineer stores his cognac here, the factory owner comes to collect it, the policeman gets promoted, and who bears the brunt of it all?

HO: Jan Q. Public.

EPILOGUE

(*On stage is a pub in a cage. Outside the bars stands a statue of Liberty and a cluster of signs: No Spitting. No Smoking. Off Limits to the Unemployed. Don't Talk to the Driver. Do Not Lean Out the Window. Curb Your Dog. Do Not Touch. No Parking. Do Not Enter. Do Not Pick the Flowers. Keep Off the Grass. Don't Let Us Die . . . etc. On stage behind the bars are an orchestra, Litter, Wu-Fang, the Dishonest Civilian, Polly, Miami, and Bulldogg, all in striped prison uniforms of elegant cut. Outside the bars stands the Honest Policeman.*

The curtain rises on a lively scene. Music is playing. Litter, in knickerbockers, lounges in an easy chair. Baby Polly and Miami play gin rummy. The Dishonest Civilian sips grenadine through a straw. Bulldogg reads the newspaper, and Wu-Fang toys with a yo-yo.)

HONEST POLICEMAN: Hey, convicts! (*The music stops.*) Prisoner Colt Bulldogg, Prisoner Ludmila Nasavrková a.k.a. Baby Polly, Miami Bulldogg née Litter, shall prepare to be released, for their sentences will be up in five minutes, and they will be set free!

THE AFORENAMED: Already? How time flies! Let us stay here! What did we ever do to you?

MIAMI: Just on the day when Papa serves tea!

COLT: And we can have target practice on the clay pigeons in the prison yard!

LITTER: I'll appeal for my children's sentences to be extended as an act of clemency.

POLLY: We won't get to see the police dog show!

POLICEMAN: Put on your civvies; you are to be set free.

POLLY: But what for, this suits me so well . . .

MIAMI: . . . It makes us look younger.

LITTER: Don't go; the food is terrible out there!

WU-FANG: And expensive! Here the state foots the bill.

POLICEMAN: Quiet in the cell! The law is giving you back your liberty; show some respect!

CIVILIAN: Go free quietly, prisoners. One minor offense can always put you back inside.

(Miami, Colt, and Polly leave the cell.)

LITTER *(to Wu-Fang and the Civilian):* Well, guys, we're lucky we got life sentences. Hey, guards, champagne, let's drink to a speedy reunion with the released.

(Heave and Ho enter, ragged and downcast. They notice the Policeman.)

HEAVE: Hurrah! Saved at last. Officer, let us out.

POLICEMAN: Of where?

HO: Let us go free!

POLICEMAN: But you're already free!

HEAVE: What do you mean? After all, we're behind bars.

POLICEMAN: But bars have two sides!

CIVILIAN: That's the point, it depends on how you figure which side is prison and which is freedom!

HO: Hang on! We're free; I've figured it out, hurray!

CIVILIAN: I would like to know how you figured it out.

POLICEMAN: . . . from the statue . . .

HO: . . . no, from the fact that everything is forbidden!

HEAVE: And from a certain feeling . . .

POLICEMAN: . . . from a certain feeling in the heart . . .

HO: . . . no! in the stomach—emptiness!

Caricature of Richard Hutter by Egon Sternfeld on the title page of one of Hutter's collections of "Plaudereien," or "Prattle."

Caricature of László Békeffi.

Caricature of Peter Hammerschlag by Bil (Willi Spira).

Art Nouveau Theater, Budapest.

Caricature of Endre Nagy.

Cover of the program for the Black Cat cabaret, Warsaw.

A. G. Alekseev at the Grotesque Theater in 1918. A caricature by A. Voronetsky.

The Blue Blouses in the sketch Fordizm i NOT, *which dealt with assembly-line procedures and education of the proletariat.*

Blue Blouses in the act "Physical Attraction."

Caricature of Smirnov-Sokolsky, by Kukrinitsy.

Caricature of Jaroslav Hašek, by Josef Lada, illustrator of his Good Soldier Švejk.

Voskovec and Werich as Jumpinmeados and Eatnobreados in The Ass and the Shadow.

IV

CABARET IN WESTERN AND NORTHERN EUROPE

1925–1937

DESPITE PUBLIC DEMONSTRATIONS AND SCANDALS STAGED by the Surrealists, postwar Paris failed to maintain the tradition of the bohemian *cabaret artistique*. Instead, the variety aesthetic reverted to the music hall, particularly in the *tour de chant,* a medley of songs sung by a single performer. Fréhel, Maurice Chevalier, and Edith Piaf mastered this mode and passed it on to such later *chansonniers* as Charles Aznavour, Jacques Brel, and Georges Brassens.

The indestructible Yvette Guilbert continued to perform in the 1920s and '30s, introducing new old material—that is, songs of the Middle Ages, Renaissance, and eighteenth century. Just as she had discovered Léon Xanrof's poems in a bookstall (see the previous volume), so in 1925 she accidentally came upon the verses of Fagus (Georges Faillet, 1872–1933). Grand guignolesque, morbid, they hymned the sins of the flesh: "All modern putridity is in them," said one critic. For Guilbert, it was a vivid throwback to her *Divan japonais* period, and she lost no time in getting the reclusive poet's permission to perform his poetry publicly. Fagus had commenced his career as an anarchist but turned into a hard-bitten royalist and ultra-Catholic. He was run over by a truck a year before Guilbert made a stage success of his syphilitic *Modern Dandy* and chlorotic *Lady of the Camellias.*

The revue tradition was an old one in France, and in the twentieth century it burgeoned as the *revue à grand spectacle,* featuring lavish staircases, troupes of nudes in acres of plumes and sequins, and athletic dance routines. The comic cabaret sketch survived, however, assimilated to the fleshy sumptuousness of the rest of the show, and with a diminution of satiric content. Typical is the Folies Bergère piece about taxes by the humorist Bernard Gervaise.

The Modern Dandy

(Le Dandy moderne)

1925

by

Fagus

Venus's venom erodes me at leisure,
An obstinate dying man who dieth not.
All through my body disease takes its pleasure,
Still living, I watch myself cunningly rot!
Rinse out the glass where I have drunk!

Somewhat pallid but attractive,
   Much as if I had T. B.,
On my walks—I still keep active—
   Women turn around to see
The way I hold my head erect,
   The way my moustache curls,
Those who don't know, don't suspect,
   Envy my success with girls! . . .
Rinse out the glass . . . where I have drunk.

And yet my skin is flaking,
   My forehead peels in scales,
My teeth are wobbling, aching,
   My memory dims and fails.
My marrow—I can hear it!—
   Crumbles in my vertebrae,
My shattered nerves can't bear it,
   As ataxia has its way!
Rinse out the glass . . . where I have drunk . . .

The moment I can sense it's here,
  The strongest force in all creation,
I shall put forward, have no fear,
  The date of my disintegration.
A bullet serves to force the door—
  Good night!—or else I'll lick
That bitter almond, arsenic . . .
Rinse out the glass where I have drunk!

Deep in the Heart of Taxes

(A vos rangs—fisc!)

(1933)

by

Bernard Gervaise

CHARACTERS

Monsieur IRS, the master of ceremonies

The Queen of Queens, the mistress of ceremonies

Various taxpayers of lesser importance

A PUBLIC SQUARE ON MID-LENTEN CARNIVAL DAY

(As the curtain rises, a man with a vulturine nose and fingers like talons enters right. At the same time a lady with a coronet on her head and a royal mantle on her shoulders comes forward from the left. As he walks, the hook-nosed gentleman stares intently in every direction. When they reach center stage, the two characters bump into one another.)

THE GENTLEMAN: Oh, excuse me! Madame! . . . *(Removing his hat.)* I am Monsieur IRS, at your service!

THE LADY: Thank you! . . . Were you looking for something?

MONSIEUR IRS: Yes, I'm looking for something to tax, something new. You can't imagine how hard it is to find! However, it is indispensable: I need another twelve billion to patch up my budget. I absolutely have to lay my hands on that trifling sum by the end of the month! . . . Now what could I slap a new tax on? I've already slapped a special duty on phonographs, radios, the flip side of records, billiards, yo-yos, ping-pong and skating, dogs, cats, children and goldfish, marriage, divorce, births and burials, silk stockings, cotton stockings, cotton nightcaps, subway tickets, permanent waves, baldness, corns, face powder, love, headcolds, heat, cold, water, gas and electricity . . . I'm just about to put a surtax on shows, movies, theater, boxing matches, scenes thrown in private, meetings of Parliament, and Punch-and-Judy in the Luxembourg Gardens. Then I'll pass a special tax on dance halls . . .

THE LADY: Tax-i dances!

MONSIEUR IRS: Beg pardon?

THE LADY: Never mind, it was a pun.

MONSIEUR IRS: Good idea, I'll tax puns!

THE LADY: But we'll be ruined, Monsieur IRS!

MONSIEUR IRS: Precisely what's needed! Are we not entering the long-foretold era of restrictions, deflation, Serious Austerity! . . . Besides, the taxpayer is not as poor as he pretends to be. What if I told you that you can still see certain individuals indulging in superfluous expenditure, such as slurping aperitifs and puffing pipes! . . .

THE LADY: Instead of coughing up.

MONSIEUR IRS: You said it! . . . But I realize, Madame, I have forgot to ask with whom I have the great honor of speaking.

THE LADY *(with a pretty curtsey)*: I am the Queen of Queens.

MONSIEUR IRS *(greedily surveying the Queen's robes and jewels)*: The Queen of Queens! I should have suspected it, with such a cloak, so dazzling a coronet! . . . *(He extends his talons to seize these valuable items.)*

THE QUEEN OF QUEENS: Draw in your claws! I've paid at the office! Which is why this is all paste!

MONSIEUR IRS: Never mind about that; we have also put a tax on paste! . . . Would it be indiscreet to ask what you're doing here, dear lady?

THE QUEEN OF QUEENS: I am waiting for my subjects . . . And here they come now!

(The classical troupe of Shrovetide mummers—Pierrots, Harlequins, Columbines, musketeers, odalisques, etc.—enters.)

MONSIEUR IRS *(with a sigh of regret)*: To think that I forgot to tax masquerade costumes! . . . Oh well, I'll do it next year! *(Pointing out a young woman dressed as Folly.)* What's she supposed to be?

THE QUEEN OF QUEENS: She's Folly, Monsieur IRS; you see her cap ornamented with silver ding-dongs.

MONSIEUR IRS (*beside himself*): Silver! Why, that's folly with bells on indeed! (*He leaps on Folly, grabs her bells, and stuffs them in his pocket. Indicating another, very short young woman, in a very abbreviated costume.*) All right now, that's a more sensible outfit!

THE QUEEN OF QUEENS: It's a contemporary costume, Monsieur IRS, the Forty-hour Week.

MONSIEUR IRS: The forty . . .

THE QUEEN OF QUEENS: -hour week. It's the latest invention of prominent economists to fight unemployment. If this reform is adopted, workers will work only forty hours a week.

MONSIEUR IRS: And the rest of the time?

THE QUEEN OF QUEENS: The rest of the time—I don't know. They won't do anything, I suppose.

MONSIEUR IRS: I see; we're talking about a homeopathic remedy. They're curing unemployment with unemployment . . . And do you happen to know when it goes into force, this wonderful forty-hour week?

THE QUEEN OF QUEENS: Yes. Directly following a month of Sundays!

(*Enter a naked gentleman.*)

MONSIEUR IRS: Now what in the world is that? . . . (*To the naked man.*) And what are you got up to be, my good man?

THE NAKED MAN: A multimillionaire.

MONSIEUR IRS: A multimillionaire.

THE NAKED MAN: Yes, when I left home just now, I was wearing magnificent clothes, superb jewels, gold rings, gold-rimmed eyeglasses, gold teeth. Unfortunately, I decided to stop by the tax-collector's and pay what I owe! That's why I'm costumed as Father Adam!

THE QUEEN OF QUEENS (*examining the naked man with interest*): Your costume seems incomplete. Father Adam used to wear a fig leaf!

THE NAKED MAN: Alas! They're impossible to find; it's not the right season. Besides, the article seems to be much in demand. You have no idea how many people dress like Father Adam these days.

MONSIEUR IRS (*moved to compassion*): There, there, my good

man, I haven't got a fig leaf on me, but this can take its place. (*He hands him a sheet of paper, a green sheet with the inscription: "Audit less costs." To the Queen of Queens.*) Now, tell me, dear lady, what are all these people doing here? They seem to be waiting for something.

THE QUEEN OF QUEENS: Indeed they are, Monsieur IRS. They are waiting for the parade which is organized every year by the Public Authorities on the occasion of Mid-Lenten carnival.

MONSIEUR IRS (*suddenly furious*): A parade! But there's not going to be a parade! If you think I've got money to waste on nonsense like that! . . . Besides, there's been a miscalculation; today is not Mid-Lent.

THE QUEEN OF QUEENS: Come, come, Monsieur IRS, you're out of your mind; today is March 23rd. All the calendars will tell you that . . .

MONSIEUR IRS: The calendars are wrong. Mid-Lent should be celebrated not on March 23rd but on June 30th . . . In 1933, Lent will last all year long! . . .

CABARET IN THE STRICT SENSE WAS NOT A VIABLE FORM IN Italy during the 1920s and '30s, partly because the Mussolini régime relegated nonconformist theater to private stages, partly because there was no audience large enough to support it. On the variety stage Ettore Petrolini carried on his ribald comedy, and the futurist spirit was perpetuated in the Teatro degli Indipendenti. (For Petrolini and the Futurists, see the first volume of *Cabaret Performance.*)

This theater was founded in 1922 by Anton Giulio Bragaglia, whom the Futurists counted as a fellow-traveler. He had already forestalled Léger's *Ballet mécanique* by a year with his *Ballo meccanico futurista,* and conceived a cabaretic dance-drama form called the *sintesi visive,* which he explained as "the scenic portrayal of the dominant and essential ideas of a musical excerpt." His theater was set up in a Palladian bath, where he intended to revive the "marvelous," especially "comic art." With an aesthetic of "theater for theater's sake," Bragaglia presented nearly two hundred ballets and comedies by such modernists as Pirandello and Evreinov.

One of the Teatro's house authors was Achille Campanile (b. 1902), who came to public notice in 1924 and 1925 with his one-act farces *Tragedy in Two Strokes* and *The Inventor of the Horse,* which are forerunners of postwar absurdism. His brief sketch *The Kiss,* on the other hand, has close counterparts in such earlier cabaret explorations of illusion versus reality as the works of Boris Geyer and Nikolay Evreinov. (Evreinov enjoyed a certain popularity in Italy in the 1920s, perhaps because of the parallel that could be drawn between him and Pirandello.)

The Kiss

(Il bacio)

1925

by

Achille Campanile

CHARACTERS

He and She

Lonely street, evening. A couple of lovers enter and slowly walk down it. They stop.

HE: What an enchanting evening, what a moon, what stillness in this lonely street! (*About to embrace her.*)

SHE: Don't take advantage. Somebody might come by.

HE: There's no one here. Just one kiss, I entreat you. One of those long-drawn-out kisses in which our souls melt in a single sigh and almost yearn to die, slowly, sweetly, in an ecstasy of bliss. (*Embraces her.*)

The two join their mouths in a prolonged kiss. A short pause, during which, as they stand with their mouths joined in the prolonged kiss, the light turns violet and suggestive background music begins—for instance, the slow waltz by Moskovsky—and simultaneously we can hear their thoughts, which their recorded voices utter over a loudspeaker, lest we confuse them with their spoken remarks. Naturally, neither one is supposed to hear the other's thoughts.

HE (*thoughts*): How strange life is! You'd think these things would be divine, but they disintegrate from the very start. These long, long kisses aren't what they're cracked up to be, after all. A sort of shiver goes down your spine when the lips come together, but then it becomes habit. Like now, I don't feel a very intense emotion; in fact, I don't feel any emotion. I can look around . . . (*his mouth still attached to hers, he tries to cast his eyes round furtively and goes on*) . . . be distracted, think of other things. Oh, right, I've got to remember, tomorrow, to get a haircut. (*He runs his free hand over his long hair*) . . . On the other hand, I don't want to be the first one to pull away. She thinks I'm in ecstasy . . . (*scratches his calf*) . . . and I have to preserve her illusions. I don't understand why women have such a craving for these interminable kisses. They consider them to be really important. What's more, my hat's about to fall off. I wonder what time it is? . . . (*Tries to read the time on the wristwatch he is wearing on the arm that embraces Her. And goes on.*) . . . You can't see a blasted thing here. But she might make up her mind to pull away, any minute now. My God, I can't stand here like this for eternity. If only a cop would come by, or a patrolman, or another pair of lovers, or a pedestrian . . . (*As before, peers into the shadows.*) But no, not even a dog. We are alone and undisturbed. And the situation is becoming untenable.

SHE (*thoughts*): How different we are from men, we women! We feel a vicarious pleasure. We enjoy the joy we give. Because if I were to say that this long, long kiss makes me ecstatic, I would be insincere. In fact, once the first moment was over, I must confess I felt nothing. And yet I don't want to be the first to pull away. He imagines I feel the same emotions he does, and he would be displeased if I disillusioned him. Let's wait till he pulls away. But in the meantime he doesn't, and I can't go ahead of him. My goodness, how thirsty he is for my lips! Unfortunately not a living soul comes by. I'd like a pretext for pulling away. Oh, it's starting to rain! (*Furtively, still in the embrace, she puts a hand on his shoulder to feel if it's raining. And goes on.*) . . . Oh dear! It's only a bright moonbeam, my mistake.

During the two soliloquies tiny, furtive movements by the two lovers, still joined in the interminable kiss. He settles his hat which is beginning to fall off; she brushes back a lock of hair; ad libitum. When their soliloquies are over, the two remain a moment in the embarrassing situation, listening hard, in the hope of hearing a passerby come in; finally, at the sound of a falling leaf, they hurriedly pull apart, pretending to believe that someone is coming.

HE (*tottering*): Ah . . .

SHE (*in a muffled voice, hand to her brow*): You'll be the death of
me! . . .

CURTAIN

THE GREATEST INNOVATOR OF THE DUTCH CABARET WAS Louis Davids (1883–1939). Born Simon David in Rotterdam, as a child he performed with his indigent parents at fairs and taverns. An ardent autodidact, he hungered for money, fame, and power, competing rabidly even after he had achieved them.

Davids, like his predecessors Eduard Jacobs and Jean-Louis Pisuisse (see *Cabaret Performance,* vol. 1), was a skirt-chaser, whose most enduring relationship was with the English music-hall singer Margie Morris. She wrote the music for many of his works, and when she left him in 1922, he bought up her copyrights. Davids thought of everything: he rehearsed very carefully in order to give the impression of casual, understated melancholy, and exploited modern mass media, appearing in films from 1906 on. His best movie, *Op Stap* (*Step Right Up,* 1935), features him singing "If You've Been Born for a Dime," his most personal statement.

Mother Is Dancing
(Moeder is dansen)
1927
by
Louis Davids

Crying for your mother, baby?
Baby, give it up.
Mother needs her daily whoopee,
You will have to trust to pappy,
Dad will croon a lullaby
For his son left all alone;
Mommy craves that mean ol' banjo
And the saxophone.

FIRST REFRAIN:
    Mommy is dancing, baby, please don't cry,
    Mommy's gone to a nightclub to get high . . .
    Mommy's on her twentieth blues.
    Dad puts on your jammies warm,
    Mommy charlestons up a storm;
    Mommy's flirting with the boys in the band,
    Daddy stays at home and
    When she comes back, whenever that is,
    You'll get a great big cocktail kiss.
    Mommy is dancing, my boy.

    Germans got their Republik,
    Mother is dancing,
    And their Hohenzollern clique,

Mother is dancing.
The Yanks make Europe one bum check,
The Romanoffs get it in the neck,
The League of Nations ain't worth heck,
Mother is dancing.

FIRST REFRAIN:
    Mommy is dancing, etc.

When you're grown up, darling baby,
You can go along.
When you want your first long trousers,
Wear the tux pants of your mother's.
When you pass your bar exam
And quote Wherefore, whereas,
Mom'll listen to Paul Whiteman,
Digging all that jazz.

SECOND REFRAIN:
    Mommy is dancing, baby, please don't cry,
    Mommy's gone to a nightclub to get high.
    Mommy's dress weighs under a pound.
    With whitewash Mommy's face is laved,
    Up to the scalp her neck is shaved;
    Mommy is dancing,
    Daddy's mommy now.
    Go to sleep somehow.
    Or ma'll have a royal fit,
    Belt us with her make-up kit,
    Mommy is dancing, sweet boy.

Industry's on the decline,
Mother is dancing,
No more jobs, join the breadline,
Mother is dancing.
Trouble from Rooskis and Chinese,
Europe they would like to seize,
Kiss good-bye to the Dutch Indies.
Mother is dancing.

SECOND REFRAIN:
    Mommy is dancing, etc.

Don't cry, baby, for your mother.
That's all out of date.
You're no longer her concern,
Mommy's got the stomp to learn,
The season's in full swing by now.
Hush now, little cupid,
Keeping up her reputation
Makes her act so stupid.

THIRD REFRAIN:
Sleep, li'l fella, try to sleep,
Mother is dancing,
'Cause your father is a sheep,
Mother is dancing.
He'll sing about where he was born,
His happy home, ere he got shorn,
Mommy foxtrots until morn,
Mother is dancing.

Mother is dancing, please, babe, don't cry,
On chic dancehalls has Mom spent the rent,
Daddy sits without one lousy cent,
Daddy can't express his despair,
Mother's decided to bob her hair;
Mommy is dancing,
Mom chases clarinets,
Dad's out of cigarettes,
Ma safeguards her silhouette,
Pa has got to babyset.
Mother is dancing, my child.

If You've Been Born for a Dime
(Als je voor een dubbetjle geboren bent)
1935
by
Louis Davids

There are folks who won't believe their fate's already set,
They scramble and they hustle till at last they drop down dead.
My firm opinion is: it makes no diff'rence what you do,
"What will be will be" goes for both me and you.

CHORUS:
If fate decrees you've been born for a dime,
You'll never make a quarter.
So you know a Greek tag or a classical rhyme,
No matter, life's a thwarter.
You're sure it's you that's pulling all the strings,
Too bad, life's planning other things. Don't get sore.
If fate decrees you've been born for a dime,
You'll not make a nickel more.

Damned few folks can puzzle out what is life's real meaning,
You could be so happy if you simply stopped your scheming.
Why search for happiness as if it were against the law?
What was under your nose you never saw.

CHORUS:
If fate decrees you've been born for a dime, etc.

[*Spoken*] That's just the way it is. You can even stand on your
head, but it won't change a thing. If you were born to wear a
shabby coat, you'll never have a mink. And if you were

meant for day-old bread, you'll never choke on caviar. Why don't you stop trying so hard; get smart, 'cause that's the way it'll always be. That's the way it is.

If fate decrees you've been born for a dime,
You'll not make a nickel more.

ALTHOUGH THE FIRST SCANDINAVIAN CABARET APPEARED IN Norway, its founder was a Dane. Herman Bang, the Danish poet and critic, who had staged plays at the Théâtre de l'Oeuvre in Paris, forestalled Wolzogen's Überbrettl by a year when in the Tivoli of the Norse capital Christiania (now Oslo) he opened a short-lived Literære Variété on New Year's Day, 1892. The program was a familiar one of recitations, songs, and a Christmas Eve topical revue. But Christiania was a straitlaced city: in 1902 a novel about the local bohemians was banned and its author, Hans Henrik Jæger, jailed. An Oslo Chat Noir appeared in 1912, animated by Bokken Lasson, who sang her own songs to lute accompaniment. Her motto was "The Norwegian cabaret must be bold and daring. The mirth-maker must be a horse thief, sly as Holberg's [comic servant] Henrik." But throughout Scandinavia, the popular revue format was more palatable to the general public than the more audacious cabaret, and by the mid-1920s, the Chat Noir had become a revue theater.

In Denmark, Nørrebro summer revues had been popular fare since the 1840s, and they were invigorated with cabaretlike wit by Holger Drachmann and Frederick Jensen. In 1908, a true cabaret, Edderkoppen (The Spider), was opened in Copenhagen by Bokken Lasson; Drachmann's sister-in-law, the caricaturist Storm P. Pederson; and the journalist Christian Gottschalk. It was not until Brecht, fleeing the Nazis in 1933, came to Denmark and staged his own *Roundheads and Peakheads* with Danish actors that pungent political satire influenced the lighthearted revues. During the Nazi Occupation, the café Lille Kongensgade (Little King Street), founded by Lulu Ziegler, carried on the tradition. Despite the Quislings, the Occupation failed to muzzle the Chat Noir, which put on a version of *Orpheus in the Underworld* that alluded to the presence of the Norwegian intelligentsia in concentration camps.

In Sweden, which had no political cabaret before the Nazi incursion, the function was again filled by the revue. The master of the form was Kurt Gerhard (1891–1964), who has been called the Noël Coward of Stockholm. His best show was *Oss greker emellan* (*Between Us Greeks*, 1933), an updated version of *Lysistrata*, in which Gerhard as Aristophanes served as conférencier and sang several of his own songs. Lysistrata was enacted by the pop-singer Zarah Leander, who did her famous Garbo impersonation (she later became a superstar under the Nazis). Recent happenings in Germany were mocked in a trio for Hindenburg, Hitler, and Goering sung in German-Swedish macaronics, and the scene curtain was a map of Sweden with the cities bearing Greek names (Göteborg = Sparta, Stockholm = Athens, and so on). The revue's title song, given here, is a good example of Gerhard's use of topical and local satire.

Another prolific sketch writer was Kar de Muma, or Cardamom (Erik Harald Zetterström, b. 1904), who penned columns for a Stockholm daily from 1931. He wrote dozens of revues for the Folkteatern, Södra Teatern, and Blanchteatern, including sketches for Kurt Gerhard, and adapted operettas for other theaters. His skits are characteristically mild and morality-tinged in their commentary on everyday behavior.

Between Us Greeks
(Oss greker emellan)
1933
by
Kurt Gerhard

Of pungent Attic salt I offer you a pinch or two.
I'm beautiful, so listen and don't say, "Who gives a Σkpou?"
But handsome guys like you shouldn't find my act distressing
Since I don't waste material upon my flimsy dressing
      between us Greeks, between us Greeks.

In the movies I saw Nero, who was in one of those moods,
Getting manicured and massaged by a bevy of cute nudes.
His generals were flirting under cover with the queen.
This stuff comes from the hist'ry books; you can't call it obscene
      between us Greeks, between us Greeks.

The actor Gösta Ekman thought he'd try a lit'ry mode.
He turned into a poet, took his act upon the road.
On stage he improvised a lot of rhetoric melodious,
And no one dared suggest his odes were positively odious
      between us Greeks, between us Greeks.

The other day I met Professor Almkvist in the thicket
Where my aesthetic senses thought his nudity not cricket.
If you look like an Apollo, then you needn't wear a thing,
But he lacks those firm attractions to which we maidens cling
      between us Greeks, between us Greeks.

Mr. G held court in Sweden, court in this case meaning tennis,
But he found Pettersson-Sweden was a reg'lar royal menace.

When Pete hit back a real hard-handed volley in the set,
The King said, "It's a lucky thing I cannot jump the net"
between us Greeks, between us Greeks.

Ståhl's and Hellberg's names are mentioned in all the smart
revues
Because they're known for coming up with savory menus.
They enhance with a French title ev'ry dish they have in stock;
Though *they* may call it *poulet,* what you're gnawing on is cock
between us Greeks, between us Greeks.

In Germany when Hitler laid a boycott on the Jews,
The Bonnier clan and Josef Sachs reacted to the news
With a toast: "Despite the boycott and threats to do us harm
I think our bank accounts'll safely weather out this storm"
between us Greeks, between us Greeks.

Translator's Note

. *Nero.* Charles Laughton played Nero in the film *The Sign of the Cross.* Gerhard took every opportunity to mock films, which he considered unfair competition for the theater.

Gösta Ekman, Sweden's most illustrious Shakespearean actor, had just played a poet on tour; he was a favorite butt of Gerhard's satire.

Johan Almkvist, a specialist in venereal diseases, was a leading proponent of nudism for health reasons; he was in his sixties at this time.

Mr. G was King Gustav V, a tennis enthusiast who often played with the professional tennis champion Carl-Erik Pettersson, alias Pettersson-Sweden.

The two Svens, *Ståhl* and *Hellberg,* were half-brothers. The former was a theater critic; the latter ran a famous restaurant.

Bonnier was Sweden's leading book publisher; *Josef Sachs* owned the department store Nordiska Kompaniet: both magnates were Jewish.

Bridge

(*Bridge*)

1937

by

Kar de Muma

Two tables of bridge. Four gentlemen seated at one. At the other, four women, played by Mimi Pollak, Birgit Rosengren, Carin Svensson, and Margit Lüning.

The four gentlemen begin their game and play three rounds. Then one says, "This isn't easy," whereupon another one gets up and says, "Really, if you're going to keep talking all the time, I won't play any more!"

MIMI: Who's supposed to start?

BIRGIT: You are, Mimi.

CARIN: No, Margie is. Aren't you, Margie?

MARGIT: No, it *is* Mimi—she was dealer.

CARIN: Oh, goodness, I always get such dreadful cards.

BIRGIT: Yes, Mimi, you start! Honestly, what a cute jumper! Did you get it at Beckman's? Is it silk or a wool blend?

CARIN: Oh, start already, Mimi!

MIMI: Oh dear, what a hand, not one face card! I pass!

BIRGIT: I think I'll bid one little spade, that's what I'll do.

MARGIT: Spades . . . well, now, let's see what I should bid . . .!

CARIN: For heavens' sake—I've only got eleven cards! Isn't that something! How many do the rest of you have?

BIRGIT: So that's why! I thought I had too many cards.— eleven—twelve—thirteen—fourteen—fifteen. Take one of mine—for goodness sake, don't take the ace of hearts.

MIMI: No, this trim is from Persson's, next to Sturebad, you know!

BIRGIT: Well, yesterday I saw a hat at Edman and Andersson's, Mary Stuart style, but turned under at the back . . .

MARGIT: It's your turn!

MIMI: Yes, what was just bid?

BIRGIT: I bid clubs . . . no, spades.

MIMI: Hey, take a look at this queen—she looks like Myrna Loy.

CARIN: Oh, let me see!

MARGIT: Let me see!

MIMI: No—don't look, don't look! Don't you dare peek at my cards—don't look!

CARIN: Mimi, put on a record! You know the one I mean . . . (*Sings.*)

BIRGIT: I think she looks more like Greta Garbo.

MIMI: Last week, believe me, all I did was play bridge. At Putte Lindqvist's. With Peppy and Tottie and Ruthie and Jeannie. They said I had talent . . .

CARIN: At playing cards . . . ?

MIMI: Don't be silly! No, now it's your turn . . .

MARGIT: I bid . . . hearts, that's my bid.

CARIN: You have to bid two hearts—Birgit bid spades.

MARGIT: Oh, I—that's right . . . no, then I'd rather bid two diamonds.

CARIN: Just think: Mamma and Poppa had an awful fight at breakfast yesterday.

MIMI: Does anybody care?

BIRGIT: Don't be funny!

CARIN: Yeah, because Mamma woke Poppa up at four o'clock in the morning and said, "If you hadn't held onto the knave of clubs and kept the eight instead, at Göransson's day before yesterday, we wouldn't have lost."

BIRGIT: She woke him up just for that?

MIMI: Don't be silly! What else would she wake him up for? Not what you're thinking.

BIRGIT: I bid three clubs. (*To Margit.*) You should have seen the awfully cute pullover that cow Ann-Katherine bought herself!

MIMI: I pass.

BIRGIT: I bid five spades.

MARGIT: Mimi's holding three queens—I just saw them.

MIMI: It's mean of you to tell. But that's just like you. Who was it said I should go to *The Charge of the Light Brigade* on my date with Åke?

CARIN: Oh, keep still for a bit—it's your turn!

MIMI: It happens to be *your* turn.

CARIN: I pass.

MARGIT: Pass.

MIMI: Pass. Well, play cards!

BIRGIT: Wait a minute—I'm just going to put on a record first.

CARIN: Put on a tango! This one . . . (*Sings.*)

MIMI (*gets up*): No, honestly—this is too boring and tiresome. I suggest we stop, that way we can sit and talk instead.

Typical revue sketch from a Parisian "follies" of the late 1920s, this one depicting the temptation of St. Anthony (and his pig).

Louis Davids and Margie Morris in
He, She, and Piano. *Photograph by
Gerard Jacob, c. 1916.*

The drop curtain for Gerhard's Between Us Greeks.

Zarah Leander doing her Garbo imitation in Between Us Greeks.

V

ANTI-NAZI AND EXILE CABARET

1931–1941

TUCHOLSKY WAS NOT ALONE IN REGARDING THE NAZIS AS too contemptuous to be worth ridiculing. When they and their doctrines were spoofed in most cabarets, the attitude was supercilious, for it was easy to dismiss galumphing Brown Shirts, bigoted burghers, and their Chaplinesque leader. Friedrich Hollaender's song "The Jews Are All to Blame for It," sung by Annemarie Hase in the cabaret revue *Star Villa Is Haunted* (1931), is typical in its lighthearted mockery of Nazi anti-Semitism. It builds on a joke of the early twenties which goes: "Everything's the fault of the Jews and the bicyclists." "Why the bicyclists?" "Why the Jews?"

Proletarian agitprop cabarets and revues which aimed to go beyond mere mockery and to change society came into being in Germany under the influence of two distinct phenomena. The first major impetus was given by the *Revue Roter Rummel* (*Red Rumpus Revue*) of 1924, staged by Erwin Piscator and Felix Gasbarra for the German Communist party on the eve of the November national elections. In it hundreds of amateurs performed in all the usual genres of commercial revue: "Music, song, acrobatics, paper-cutting, sports, projections, film, statistics, dramatic scenes, speeches." "The revue coincided aptly with the formal disintegration of the bourgeois drama," Piscator was to write in *The Political Theater,* and he replaced the traditional master and mistress of ceremonies with a team of proletarian and bourgeois to provide running commentary.

Three years later, the Blue Blouses toured Germany with great success, spawning an indigenous Red Blouses in Berlin under the artistic command of the film critic Béla Balász. Between 1926 and 1933 there were nearly 200 agitprop groups working in Germany, almost all of them on the left. Many of these troupes, whose stage material ranged from abortion rights to election reform, promoted political discourse between the Communist party and the people; but despite the overt antifascism of their politics, they also put up resistance to the universal dictates issued by Moscow and the Comintern.

The most famous of these troupes were the Red Rats (Rote Ratten) of Dresden, a socialist group founded in 1926; the Red Blacksmiths (Rote Schmiede) of Halle, founded in 1928; and the Red Megaphone (Rote Sprachrohr) of Berlin, also founded in 1928. The Red Rats admitted their debt to Piscator, using the title of his *Despite It All* for one of their shows. Beginning with 50-some participants, by 1932 they had a disciplined ensemble of 150 members, split into four troupes. There were no names given in the program and no curtain calls, since the performers regarded themselves not as actors, but as harbingers of political enlightenment. Clarity and concreteness were touchstones of their work, and they used masks and masklike makeups, designed by Reinhold Langner, to achieve this effect. In their last program, given shortly before the Nazis seized power, Langner played a police official who came through the auditorium to inspect the show, and successfully convinced the audience that he was the real thing.

The Jews Are All to Blame for It

(An allem sind die Juden schuld)

1931

by

Friedrich Hollaender

To be sung to the Habañera from *Carmen*

Is it raining, is it snowing, are you dry or are you wet,
Is there thunder, is there lightning, do you shiver, do you
  sweat,
Is the sun out, is it cloudy, are you melting, do you freeze,
Is it raw out, does it thaw out, do you cough or do you sneeze:
    The Jews are all to blame for it!
    To blame, to blame, to blame for it!
    Why so, why are the Jews to blame?
    My child, don't ask, they're just to blame!
    Your problems too, go blame the Jew!
    Believe you me, they are to blame,
    To blame for all, to blame for all. Olé!

If the telephone is busy, if your bathtub springs a leak,
If receipts don't tally up right, if your lager tastes too weak,
If the cake runs out on Sunday, if the Prince of Wales is gay,
If the bedstead creaks at nighttime, if your poodle's stool is
  gray:
    The Jews are all to blame for it, etc.

If Herr Dietrich raises taxes, if Miss Dietrich's angel's blue,
If the gift shop hikes its prices, if a virgin says, "I do,"

If there's crisis in the Balkans or a comic fails to please,
If a talkie soundtrack pops or Garbo's teeth have cavities:
    The Jews are all to blame for it, etc.

That the snow is so damned snowy, and it dances in the breeze,
That the fire is so damned fiery, and the woods are full of trees,
That the roses bear no rosebuds and the chopped meat smells of
    rot,
That Heine's poems are pretty good and Einstein knows a lot.
    The Jews are all to blame for it,
    To blame, to blame, to blame for it, etc.

Translator's Note

Hermann Dietrich was finance minister; *Marlene Dietrich* had just made a sensation in Von Sternberg's film *The Blue Angel*.

Despite It All (Excerpts)
(Trotz Alledem)
1932
from
The Red Rats Revue, Dresden

THERE'S A DRAFT

Chairs, table, two gentlemen at their beer glasses (Fat and Thin, that is to say Bank Manager and Worker).

THIN: There's a draft . . . Do you mind if I shut the window?

FAT: You call that a draft? A little fresh air will do you good, won't it?

THIN: Well, this is getting to be more than a little fresh air. There's a draft thick as pea soup.

FAT: It's remarkable how effeminate city-dwellers are.

THIN: What do you mean effeminate? If I catch something, you aren't the one who has to pay the doctor bills.

FAT: Pay your doctor bills, I should say not! Although why not! It's the fashion nowadays to live at other people's expense!

THIN: Actually, that's long been the fashion. I only have to look at certain well-fed gentlemen, who clearly didn't make their money by the sweat of their brow.

FAT: Some nice expressions you've got there. But that figures: you don't know a thing about the national economy, so you talk real big.

THIN: What you call national economy is exploitation by the managerial class.

FAT: In any case, I do not mean that the cost of living should be shifted onto the state.

THIN: It's only the managerial class that dares shift its costs onto the state and fill its belly with fat subsidies. But just you wait! There's going to be a turnaround! We've put up with this swinish behavior long enough!

FAT: Those absurd slogans of yours won't get a rise out of anybody these days. The wind has shifted.

THIN: You don't seem to be in the picture about the way things stand. Today Germany is freeing itself from its chains!

FAT: It certainly is freeing itself. From the chains the proletariat have clamped on it.

THIN: It's freeing itself from the chains of capitalism.

FAT: Have you ever heard of Adolf Hitler?

THIN: That's just what I was going to ask you!!

FAT: You were, were you? I can give you proof positive: I'm a National Socialist!

THIN: You're a National Socialist? You can't convince me just like that. I'm a National Socialist! Have you ever heard Hitler speak? Hitler is the spokesman of the underprivileged!

FAT: You're talking rot. I've heard Hitler speak more times than you have! He is the spokesman for economic common sense. He is mindful of the concerns of the managerial class, for only a sound economy, freed from its chains, can provide the cure.

THIN: You talk like a Jewish banker! Heil Hitler!

FAT: And you talk like a Marxist! Heil Hitler!

THIN: Don't try and tell me about National Socialism. I'm a squad leader from Pieschen. We Pieschners have a good sense of what Hitler wants. He lives and dies for the proletariat!

FAT: You're a squad leader? I happen to be a squad leader myself, in Blasewitz. Of course Hitler is on the side of the proletariat, but he knows that the only way to provide bread for the German worker is to nurture the managerial class and dismantle the welfare state. He lives and dies for a sound improvement in private property.

THIN: I will move that you be expelled from the party. Whatever you stand for, it's not Hitler.

FAT: No, you must go! You stand for the Reds.

THIN: Why should I sit here and listen to this nonsense about

Hitler? There's a draft and I want to close the window. (*He goes to the window.*)

FAT: It is stuffy in this room, and the window will remain open. (*He follows the thin gentleman to the window.*)

THIN: The window will be closed!

FAT: It will remain open! (*The window breaks into smithereens.*)

THIN: Now you've broken the window.

FAT: You broke it. You smashed it with your hand.

THIN: You opened it too quickly.

LANDLADY (*appears*): What's going on here?

FAT: This gentleman broke your window.

THIN: Not a bit of it; this gentleman broke it.

LANDLADY: But gentlemen! Who did break it?

FAT: This gentleman tore it out of my hand.

THIN: Quite the contrary: this gentleman opened it too abruptly.

LANDLADY: If you can't agree, then you'll both have to pay.

FAT: I should think not. I have no intention of paying for this gentleman's mistakes.

THIN: I don't intend to take responsibility for this gentleman.

LANDLADY: So maybe you think I should pay for the window? Business is rotten enough as it is. I can't let the joint be smashed up for a lousy beer. You do the damage and you should cough up the cost of it! That's only right! This is probably just a prearranged scheme to shift the blame from one to the other.

FAT: I insist that you refrain from such insinuations.

LANDLADY: Who can trust anybody these days? There's no more law in Germany! A sense of responsibility is a thing of the past. But I can tell you this, my good sirs: things will be very different soon! Hitler will see to that.

THIN: What has Hitler got to do with your broken glass?

LANDLADY: People won't dare to make so bold, and everything will go a lot better for the middle class. Today, when we're crushed between the big shots on the right and the arrogance of the workers on the left, life's not worth living any more.

THIN: What a shameless booze-peddler you must be to talk that way about the arrogance of the workers! You haven't a clue what National Socialism means!

FAT: It's particularly shameless to talk that way about big shots on the right. What's that supposed to mean? What do you mean by such vulgarity?

LANDLADY: Hitler is a spokesman for the Tavern-Keeper's Friendly Association and related branches, if you must know! He'll put an end to the sales tax and the beer tax. I heard it from his own lips, when he spoke here once. He lives and dies for the middle class. How could you kid me about National Socialism when my own husband's a squad leader?

FAT: A squad leader . . . Your husband? But I don't need to listen to any more of your ridiculous nonsense about our sacred movement. My train leaves in ten minutes. Here's the money for the beer.

THIN: You don't have the foggiest idea about Hitler's intentions. I'm paying too.

LANDLADY: And where's the money for the broken window?

FAT: Address yourself to this gentleman!

THIN: When will you stop acting so disgracefully!

LANDLADY: I think you're both to blame. I'll call the police.

FAT: You can whistle for it. Heil Hitler! (*He leaves.*)

THIN: Heil Hitler! That man's a scoundrel, a boor and a swindler!

LANDLADY: You're no better!

THIN: You C-clamp! You spinach quail! You octagonal dormer-window ghost, you've got your nerve! Heil Hitler! (*He goes.*)

LANDLADY: Heil Hitler! . . . (*after a short pause, casting insults at them.*) You dung sparrow, you loafer, you son of a bitch, you storm goat! Just you wait till we get the Third Reich!

LOST—ONE SMALL RUSSET DACHSHUND!

DAUGHTER: Well, mother, do you think we'll ever see our Hexy again?

MOTHER: I should think so! We've put an ad in all the papers and in big letters on all the bulletin boards: "Lost—One small russet dachshund. Answers to the name 'Hexy.' Whoever returns her gets a big reward."

DAUGHTER: But what if the dogcatcher picked her up?

MOTHER: He won't hurt the dog—not if there's a reward offered.

DAUGHTER: Or maybe an unemployed man will trap her! They're supposed to eat dogs and cats.

MOTHER: How can that be? There's plenty of beef, veal, and pork around. That tastes much better. Not that I mean I've ever eaten a dog—but I imagine it must.

DAUGHTER: If only Hexy weren't so fat! If she were melted down, there'd be a lovely pot of grease!

MOTHER: Stop that!—Our poor Hexy!

DAUGHTER: And maybe they'll make a handbag out of her coat. With a swastika. Because Hexy is pure Hitler brown.

MOTHER: I'm telling you to keep quiet! You're breaking my heart.

DAUGHTER: Well, we've got to be prepared for the worst these days when the world is so wicked.

(Son enters, excited. Hitler uniform. Revolver in hand, very upset.)

MOTHER: What's wrong, Eugene?

SON: Aah, nothing! I just had to bump off a Red swine.

MOTHER: For heaven's sake, was there any danger?

SON: Not on your life! The guy never even noticed me taking aim. Had his back to me the whole time.

MOTHER *(breathing more easily)*: Well, I hope you don't get into any trouble on that score!

SON: Chivalry is alive and well in Germany!

(The telephone rings in the next room.)

MOTHER: That must be about you!

DAUGHTER: They'll arrest you!

SON: What bull! *(Exits.)*

(Telephone conversation in the next room. A worried Mother and Daughter eavesdrop.)

MOTHER: Oh dear, oh dear, oh dear, oh dear!

DAUGHTER: They're going to arrest him!

SON *(returns)*: Don't be silly!

MOTHER: Who was it then?

SON: The police!

DAUGHTER: Are you going to get in hot water because of the killing?

SON: Hot water?—Me?—Crap!—Oh, you mean because of . . . *(Gestures a shooting.)* Nah, that's all been settled! Nobody gives two hoots in hell about that! But you know what? We're supposed to pay a fine. Because our Hexy was picked up on the streets without a muzzle and a dog tag. Five marks' fine! But I gave the guy a piece of my mind! They won't get a penny!

MOTHER: Our Hexy is all right!

DAUGHTER: Let's go right now and pick her up.

MOTHER: But what if they won't give her back to you?

SON: Then our SA will storm the police station! Not give her back! We'll see about that!

MOTHER: But what if they insist on the five marks first? We ought to pay in the end; that's what von Papen says in Lausanne.

SON: Forget von Papen! Goebbels has forbidden us to.—Anyway: let the workers fork over the three billion.—But: five marks! Never will we pay it!—(*To his sister.*) You hear me, not a penny! (*Barking in the next room.*)

MOTHER: That's Hexy!

DAUGHTER: That's her voice!

SON: Five marks! We've got a system again. Five marks!—In the Third Reich, thank God, everything'll be different. (*Looks at his hands.*) I'll go wash my hands now. That guy fell over like a clay pigeon in a shooting gallery.

CURTAIN

Translator's Notes

SA. Sturmabteilung, or Storm Troopers, Hitler's bully boys who had been banned from the streets by the Weimar Republic. With the rising popularity of the Nazi party, the SA returned to terrorize its opponents; Hitler himself grew to distrust it and used the SS to purge it on the Night of the Long Knives, 30 June 1934.

Von Papen. Franz von Papen, "smooth, gaunt, manipulative, reactionary Centrist," was Chancellor of the Republic in 1932 under von Hindenburg. Refusal to pay the European powers the reparations stipulated by the Treaty of Versailles was one of the planks of the Nazi platform, and the Lausanne Agreement of 1932 eventually relieved Germany of reparations charges.

THE NAZI SEIZURE OF POWER IN 1933 ALTERED THE FACE OF European cabaret drastically. The most vital cabarets were politically to the left or full of Jewish talent or both. (Artists of Jewish background represented in these two volumes include Jacobs, Hirschfeld, Szyfman, Reinhardt, Mynona, Bernauer, Gert, Tucholsky, Mehring, Grünbaum, Tuwim, Tom, Alekseev, Hollaender, Friedell, Koenigsgarten, Davids, Voskovec, Hammerschlag, and Soyfer.) Immediately many of the most important figures in German cabaret emigrated, first to German-speaking countries like Austria and Switzerland, and then, as Nazi power spread, to France, Holland, England, and the Americas. Of the Berlin cabarets, only the Katakombe under Werner Finck, the Tingeltangel-Theater, and the Kabarett der Komiker carried on. Adolf Gondrell took over the last in 1938 and ran it till it was bombed out in 1944.

The roll call of exiles is instructive.

Richard Huelsenbeck had already been living in New York for some years, practicing as a Jungian psychiatrist under the name Charles R. Hulbeck.

Kurt Schwitters fled to Norway, and then in 1940 escaped to England, where he was interned for months. His house in Hanover, containing his famous two-story painted plastic collage, the MERZ-structure, was destroyed in an air raid in 1943.

Raoul Hausmann emigrated to Spain in 1933 and, on the outbreak of the Civil War there, worked on two newspapers in Barcelona.

Rudolf Bernauer emigrated to England in 1933 and remained there after the war.

Paul Nikolaus emigrated to Switzerland in 1933 and there wrote a farewell note, reading in part: "I cannot live in Berlin any more, but I cannot live outside Berlin—so I'm going . . . Laugh when you think of me; that would be the best act of piety." Then he took poison and slashed his wrists.

Kurt Tucholsky moved to Sweden, where he took poison in

1935, leaving a note asking merely not to be disturbed. The Nazis made a public bonfire of his books.

Walter Mehring was living in Paris in 1935 when the Nazis revoked his German citizenship. He departed Marseilles for New York, where he stayed from 1942 to 1949.

Max Reinhardt, Bert Brecht, and Friedrich Hollaender eventually wound up in Hollywood, though only Hollaender successfully adapted to the movie world. His work there included "The Boys in the Backroom" for Dietrich in *Destry Rides Again.*

Hugo F. Koenigsgarten emigrated to London in 1938, where he wrote for the exile cabaret Laterndl. He got a Ph.D. from Oxford and for the rest of his life taught German and theater history in England.

Egon Friedell was in Vienna when the Anschluss of 1938 occurred. As he saw the Gestapo heading for his house, he killed himself by jumping out a window.

Fritz Grünbaum returned to his native Vienna, where he continued to perform. After the Anschluss, he was arrested for his sketch *Suffrage,* in which a dozen men in frock coats stand around listening to a Führer-figure with a toothbrush moustache and a forelock. The Führer makes a speech: "My party members! We are about to take a vote on an act conferring power on me! All those in favor, stand up, all those against, sit down!" The men look around, see no chairs, so remain standing. Pause. The Führer shouts at the top of his lungs: "Party members! The act is passed unanimously." Grünbaum was sent to Dachau, where, despite his ill health, he staged a New Year's cabaret, his act beginning, "Please, not Fritz Grünbaum speaks to you, but number——, offering you a little joy on the last day of the year." His comedy won him a hard roll and a "Jew, get some rest" from the Kapo on duty. He died in the camp in 1941 of intestinal tuberculosis.

Those who stayed in Germany faced a very sour music. Marcellus Schiffer killed himself in 1932, a few months before the Nazi takeover. Joachim Ringelnatz and his work were classified as "undesirable" in 1933; he died of tuberculosis the following year. Claire Waldoff was forbidden to appear on stage and retired to provincial obscurity. Wilhelm Bendow remained popular with the Nazis until 1944, when a remark deemed to be politically offensive caused him to spend the last months of the war in a labor camp. Karl Valentin imposed his own ban on performing, making only occasional radio appearances: he mocked the compulsory Nazi theater parties with, "Why so many empty theaters? Only because the audiences stay away."

In Holland, Louis Davids had long been convinced that he topped the Nazi list of those to be liquidated. But a martyr to asthma, he died two months before the war broke out.

In Hungary, the Nazis had often been assailed in cabarets despite government approval of fascism. László Vadnay (who later emigrated and became a Hollywood director) had created the characters of the dim-witted Hacsek and the explainer Sajo whose question-and-answer routines cast aspersions on Hitler, Mussolini, the invasion of Ethiopia, and the Nuremberg laws. The elegant and influential László Békeffi kept up the fight. His show *Turn Over the Documents* (1939) attacked the snooping into racial origins that had now spread beyond Germany. When the Germans occupied Hungary, he had recourse to wordplay and camouflaged innuendo. To the question "Who is our worst enemy?" he would answer, "The one who puts a gun to our head—a serious creditor." The Hungarian for "creditor" is *hitelezö,* which sounds very much like "Hitler." One night when the curtain failed to rise because of a "technical hitch," Békeffi came onto the apron and said, "Don't worry, it won't last long; soon they'll all be hanging the way they should." Three days later he was arrested and deported to Dachau, but unlike his partner Grünbaum, he managed to survive the war.

In Prague in 1938, the government resuscitated a law passed by Metternich in 1830 and used it to close several cabarets, including the Liberated Theater. Voskovec and Werich emigrated to the United States, where they worked for the Czech Broadcasting Unit. After the war, Werich returned to Prague permanently, but his partner preferred the States, where, as George Voskovec, he enjoyed a successful career as a character actor.

ERIKA MANN (1905–69), DAUGHTER OF THE NOVELIST Thomas Mann, had been an actress for some years before she decided to launch a cabaret. With her brother Klaus, his fiancée, Pamela (daughter of Frank Wedekind), and Erika's husband of the time, Gustaf Gründgens, she had founded a theater ensemble in 1925, which staged Klaus's play *Anja and Esther* and a four-handed revue.

It was an act of courage to open a satirical political cabaret in Hitler's bastion, Munich, on New Year's Day 1933. Die Pfeffermühle (Peppermill) played at the old Bonbonnière, with songs and sketches written by Erika and Klaus. The cast of eight included Therese Giehse, who would later be the first actress to play Mother Courage.

The lives of the Manns were not safe in Germany, so in March part of the troupe moved to the Hirschen Hotel in Zurich, the cast now including the grotesque dancer Lotte Goslar and Walter Mehring, who recited his "Emigrés' Chorale." As Klaus recalled, "Erika was mistress of ceremonies, manager, organizer; Erika sang, agitated, cajoled, inspired, in short, was the soul of the whole affair." The first program included her songs "The Prince of Liarland," an attack on Hitler's foreign policy, and "Mrs. X," sung "in poster style" by Giehse. One critic wrote that as Giehse performed it, it would "make a sweat of fear burst from your pores."

The attacks on the Third Reich were garbed in allegory and fable for political as well as artistic reasons. Zurich was no longer the innocuous Swiss haven of the First World War, where the Dadaists could provoke with impunity. Despite the Pfeffermühle's initial success, which led to a tour of Switzerland, a Zurich performance in the spring of 1934 was interrupted by stink bombs hurled by members of the Swiss Nazi party. As Giehse recalled, "Each of us took to carrying a rubber truncheon in her pocket." The German Embassy lodged a complaint against the troupe, and they were banned from certain cantons; ultimately, the so-called

"Lex Pfeffermühle" was passed, forbidding foreigners from staging political texts in Zurich.

The ensemble spent 1935 and 1936 on the road, performing in the Benelux countries and Czechoslovakia, but it was clear that Europe was too hot to hold them. In January 1937, the cabaret reopened in New York as the Peppermill, but flopped in barely a month's time. Somehow the satire failed to work in English to a politically apathetic audience. Still, the Peppermill had racked up 1,034 performances in seven countries. Erika Mann, now married to W. H. Auden, spent the war in the United States lecturing, agitating, and working as a journalist.

Mrs. X

(Frau X)

1934

by

Erika Mann

My name is X, a shopkeeper by trade,
I deal in some of this and that and t'other.
I wouldn't harm a soul; that's how I'm made.
Me and my husband's well-liked, give no bother.

Weekdays are filled with lying and with cheating,—
There's wine and chicken on the day of rest.
In these bad times it's simply self-defeating
To talk of honor, truth, and nobleness.

No cock will crow for that,
No cock will crow for that,
The chickens don't say boo,
The cat could not care less,
For we all know it's true:
Each cleans up his own mess.

My husband sleeps around; I always know it.
Many's the night I've cheated on him too.
He even takes a rented room to do it—
Me and my friend laugh at that till we're blue.

My friend betrayed me with my youngest daughter;
She lied to me—she's clever at survival.
Yes, yes, I know, the first time that he caught her
Was Whitsun; that's when she became my rival.

No cock will crow for that,
No cock will crow for that,
The chickens don't say boo,
The cat could not care less,
For we all know it's true:
Each cleans up his own mess.

And if war comes, it's got to be supported,—
It isn't just the military's show;
The growth of industry must not be thwarted.
Me and my husband learned that long ago.

When we're at home we listen to the wireless,
They broadcast what goes on in other lands,—
And other people seem to be quite fearless,—
Though Austria has trembling of the hands:

No cock will crow for that,
No cock will crow for that,
The chickens don't say boo.
The cat could not care less,
For we all know it's true:
Each cleans up his own mess.

If we don't stop it, we're the first to perish,—
The ostrich is the statesman we adore.
His buried head's an image that we cherish,
As he chirps dully, "I'm against the war!"

At last the world's in ruins and in rubble,
Though we worked shrewd and hard for its upkeep—
Through our best rooms the poison gases bubble—
Me and my husband, we don't make a peep.

Now all the cocks do crow
By the dawn's blood-red light.
The chickens weep boo-hoo.
Too late the cat's distress,
For now we know it's true:
Each cleans up his own mess.

The Peppermill
(Über die Pfeffermühle)
1957
by
Erika Mann

Naturally the question arises when a person has over 1,000 performances of this sort of thing behind her, what sense is there in a
show like this? Was this enormous exertion worth the effort? One
often wonders, and for the most part there is no answer to such a
question. I personally have been lucky enough to get at least a
partial answer. And that was in London in 1940, when the German troops were ready to invade everywhere, and London was full
of exiled governments and a great many fugitives from these countries, and these people—quite without my ever having had such
an idea—would say to me: "You know why we fled?" I would say,
"Because the Nazis occupied your country." And then they'd explain, "Yes, of course, that's why. But we fled at the right time.
Because we went to your Peppermill every year, and because no
newspaper and no report made it so vivid, clear and expressive to
us what it meant to live under the Nazi regime."

ONE OF THE RESIDUAL EFFECTS OF THE PEPPERMILL'S STAY in Zurich was to encourage the emerging Swiss cabaret. The first truly Swiss operation, the Cabaret Cornichon (Pickled Gherkin) had been opened by Walter Lesch and Otto Weissert in St. Peter's Hotel on 30 December 1933. Originally inspired by the folk tradition of the Basel Fastnacht and its satiric improvised verses, the Cornichon learned from Erika Mann the uses of political allegory. When the Peppermill went on tour, the Cornichon moved into its 208-seat space in the Hirschen Hotel, and Max Werner Lenz (1887–1973) was hired to be author, director, performer, and conférencier. Lenz had worked as an actor in Germany and Romania before returning to his native Switzerland in 1931, and he reworked the Cornichon's rather corny, provincial material into five-minute sketches with sharp, satiric point. His use of dialect retained the cabaret's folksy note, and songs such as "Man without a Passport" made poignant comment on the status of refugees from Nazi aggression.

Man without a Passport
(Mensch ohne Pass)
1935
by
Max Werner Lenz

I've been expelled so often I can't stand it.
"Refugee swine!" they call me right out loud.
"You should have stayed at home!" they say (they're candid).
But I had to be different from the crowd.
I'd say "Good day," not "Heil." Such provocation!
For that they swore in jail I'd end my days.
But as a martyr I have no vocation!
I ran—out of the fry-pan to the blaze.
  So now in the records my life's unclassified;
  No passport have I got.
  My place is outside; I must stand here outside.—
  Civil servants hate me a lot.

Such slogans on their shields have nations graven! (*turns to France:*)
This one says: "Men are equal, free, and brothers."
(*turns to Switzerland:*)
And this land wants to be praised as a haven.
But I'm arrested one place and the other.
For I'm illegal: that's how I am rated.
I meet no violence; they're civilized.
Yet, though my body isn't violated,
They persecute my soul, without disguise.
  Because in the records my life's unclassified;

No passport have I got.
My place is outside; I must stand here outside.—
Civil servants hate me a lot.

And now special committees have been founded,
Well-meaning ones to deal with us, I've heard;
An end to our disruption is propounded,
Yet civil servants still have the last word!
And so until they draft the newest orders,
Which takes a while, my status worsens more.
I'm smuggled secretly 'cross foreign borders
Till I drop dead—according to the law.
    Then in the records my life'll be unclassified;
    No passport will I need.
    My place will be inside; I can come in from outside,
    From borders and hatred forever freed.

MANY VIENNESE CABARETS WERE VIRTUALLY CAFÉ MINI-theaters presenting a characteristic form called the *Mittelstück*. This was a twenty- to forty-minute play made up of a number of episodes and songs, to be enjoyed in the time it took a customer to order, consume, and pay for a cup of coffee. It attempted to surpass ordinary cabaret material to achieve a kind of dramatic legitimacy.

A master of this form was Jura Soyfer (1912–39), the child of Russian-Jewish fugitives who had fled the Bolshevik revolution. He had already displayed his satiric verve as a Viennese schoolboy and became a collaborator on the radical papers the *Arbeiter-Zeitung* and the *Tag* and in several workers' cabarets. As a socialist, Soyfer made sure that all his cabaret material conveyed a message, but after 1934 there were state restrictions on socialist assemblies. Soyfer's audience was no longer workers but liberal intellectuals, so he couched his agitprop in the language of old Viennese popular comedy. Highly verbal and fantastical, his full-length Mittel-stücke are, as Horst Jarka puts it, "modern experimental theater inspired by resistance," a cross between Shaw and Karl Valentin. One of Soyfer's shorter pieces, *The Most Loyal Citizen of Baghdad*, a comment on the situation of the Jews in an increasingly fascist Austria, was first played at the Regenbogen ABC in the fall of 1937.

The next year, during the Anschluss, Soyfer tried to escape—on skis—but was arrested and interned in Dachau, where he went on writing songs. He died there of typhoid fever a few days before immigration papers to the United States arrived for him.

The Most Loyal Citizen of Baghdad

(Der treueste Bürger Bagdads)

An Oriental Fairy Tale

1937

by

Jura Soyfer

CHARACTERS

Scheherazade
Harun al Rashid, Caliph
The voice of the Grand Vizier
Omar   ⎫
Zuleika   ⎬ Traders
Ruben   ⎭
Chorus

SCHEHERAZADE (*before the curtain*): . . . And now the thousand
and one nights are all up, and my lord and master, instead of
beheading me as he had originally intended, has, lulled by the
gentle sound of my tales, returned to the bosom of the Prophet,
where exquisite houris await him; but meanwhile I have grown
so downright accustomed to story-telling that short stories
gush from my mouth of themselves like fountains in the garden
of Allah, and since it thus befalls, I shall tell you a tale, ye
faithful and pilgrims to Mecca, on the thousand and second
night.
    The tale is called "The Most Loyal Citizen of Baghdad"; and
verily, it is protected by the strictest copyright, including all
rights to film and radio adaptations, so should any of you make
so bold as to lay your godless hand on it, may the sentence of

the law overtake your gold and your cattle, your menials, maids
and wives, and may you be accursed unto the third and fourth
editions.

And now the story begins:

One day the Caliph Harun al Rashid, defender of the faithful
and terror of the infidel, decided to mingle once more unrec-
ognized amid the common folk. For this had become a favorite
hobby of his and a pet complex. Concealed beneath the leprous
tatters of a state-licensed ass driver, he left his palace in the wee
morning hours.

*(The curtain goes up. The stage represents a street in Baghdad. The street
is empty. Harun al Rashid, whose song has rung out during the storytell-
er's last word, enters. Tune: an orientally tinged "Little Streetsinger.")*

HARUN *(singing)*:
> I'm but a poor man who asses drives,
> With one ass and no luck for his pain.
> So meanly poor, I've but two wives,
> Who'll never see their youth again.

SCHEHERAZADE: The muezzin struck eight-thirty. *(A gong is
struck.)* But this was the hour when the Baghdad International
Model Bazaar was to open. Now there resounded through the
streets the last opening suras spoken by the Grand Vizier on
this, as on every occasion—

VOICE OF THE GRAND VIZIER: . . . And so may this Model
Bazaar light the way for the whole Oriental-Islamic world as a
model example of Near Eastern trade, Near Eastern commerce,
and Near Eastern fatalism! Kismet!

CHORUS: Kismet!

SCHEHERAZADE: . . . and the typical Oriental street scene
came to full and colorful life. Innumerable tradesmen streamed
by and set up their tents amid the lively banter.

*(Omar, Ruben, and Zuleika have entered. They set up their tents and put
their wares on display, hang out shop signs—e.g., "Omar's Assorted Re-
tail Goods"—etc.)*

OMAR *(dolefully)*: It's the times!

ZULEIKA *(dolefully)*: It's the prices!

RUBEN *(dolefully)*: It's business!

SCHEHERAZADE: And hearkening to suchlike things, Harun the

Kindhearted mingled with the people, with a view to experiencing their woes and offering prompt assistance . . .

HARUN: Salem!

OMAR, ZULEIKA, RUBEN: Aleikum!

OMAR: Why dost thou hang out here with thine ugly mouth agape, thou nephew of a jackal and son of a process-server?

HARUN: I'm an ass-driver, sir—

ZULEIKA: I call thee no ass-driver, but a customer-driver-awayer. Begone from hence and clear out of thence! I have a better sign to hang out than thy degenerate mug and better publicity than thy voice!

HARUN: I do not take your hard words amiss, for rightly I am called the Kindhearted. And *I* wouldn't want to talk to an ass-driver either.

ZULEIKA: Dost thou have a license, may thine eyes be blest?

HARUN: No, I must confess.

RUBEN (*gently*): What? And dost thou drive asses without one?

HARUN: Ah! So, prithee, let not your knowledge ruin me nor your perception lead to my denunciation!

ZULEIKA: Hark at him! So thou art another black-marketeer and an ass-bungler! Yet I, an honest tradeswoman, have to look on while the guild inspector, cursed be his name, circles my shop like birds of ill omen around the tower of silence.

RUBEN (*gently*): To whom do you say that?

ZULEIKA: May Shaitan torture thee, thou arch-nebbish and chieftain of all tax-embezzlers!

HARUN: Well-a-day! Now that I have acquired your confidences in this manner, ye good if common people, I shall pose ye three riddles.

ZULEIKA: Oh, go to! Tomorrow my husband declares bankruptcy, and thou wilt ask me riddles? But the oriental mentality exerts its prerogative. Ask then, for thou canst do naught else.

HARUN: Why then, my first question goes: Are ye happy?

OMAR: Oh, heaven! Dost know no harder riddle, black-marketeer? Happy? So little am I that not even the cockamamie question can make me unhappier! Seven times have I sent my son on the pilgrimage to Mecca; no expense have I spared that he might be something better than his father! He was to be a first-class hadji! And now? Woe is me, he goes without sandals and hasn't two rupees in his purse for a little hashish!

HARUN: And thou, Zuleika, whose husband is declaring bankruptcy, art thou happy?

ZULEIKA: A person could weep at thy stupidity, for it is as boundless as the Arabian deserts and bitter as the waters of the Dead Sea! Dost know how many wives my poor husband has?

HARUN: How could I?

ZULEIKA: One! And I'm it! Not a single second wife can we afford nowadays, being small-time traders! Seven times seven years we've been saving up for a little hunchbacked woman and still can't get out of this cheerless monogamy! I, his one and only! Oh, God, what a disgrace!

HARUN: Well-a-day, and thou, silent Ruben! Art thou happy?

RUBEN: Thou asketh me, oh friend? What should I say to thee? Why should I be happy? But verily: why should I be unhappy? Nowadays shouldn't a man be glad he's alive? But look you: to whom am I talking?

HARUN: This answer methinks is the wisest. And now the second question: What, my uncouth Omar, dost thou consider the root of all evil? Are the taxes perhaps too low?

OMAR: Seldom, oh stranger, have I taken part in such an idiotic open competition! Too low? Even the process-server, cursed be his appearance, would shake with laughter at such stupidity, yea and verily, for everyone in Baghdad knows the taxes are higher than the cedars of Lebanon and heavier to bear than the torments of Gehenna!

HARUN: Look you then. Dost thou share his opinion, garrulous Zuleika?

ZULEIKA: In no way do I. Not too high are the taxes nor too heavy methinks them, but even so high that they grow over one's head, and even so heavy that one suffocates beneath them. Ah, one is bent double like a crescent moon beneath them.

HARUN: That's what we heard before. And how dost thou solve the riddle, wise Ruben?

RUBEN: What does it mean, how do I solve it, my friend? What does it mean, the taxes are too high? And also: what does it mean, the taxes are too low? Are they perchance too low for me and too high for the Lord High Finance Vizier? Or is the opposite perchance the case? In truth look you then: if the opposite is the case, what availeth it to proclaim they are too high for me? What availeth it and what profiteth it me thereby? But verily: to whom am I talking?

HARUN: Yet again thou hast spoken the wisest . . .

SCHEHERAZADE: . . . said the kind-hearted Caliph in his deft disguise. And he posed the third riddle. But this was the leading question, and for its sake had the Caliph mingled with the people where they were commonest . . .

HARUN: Now answer me the third, ye good if uncouth persons! What think ye the basic evil of all evils and what means would ye propose to bring happiness and contentment to the faithful?

OMAR: The first sensible riddle! Now: my cast-iron proposal for the salvation of the people of Baghdad is that they cut out the tongue of the kindhearted Caliph Harun al Rashid. For truth to tell, he eats much too much, and were he to eat less, something would fall to the lot of us, and that is the solution to the riddle. Basta!

HARUN: Hot damn—

SCHEHERAZADE: . . . murmured the Caliph in surprise.

HARUN: Dost thou partake of his opinion, garrulous Zuleika?

ZULEIKA: In no way, ass-driver. I take the diametrically opposite point of view. My conviction is that the kindhearted Caliph Harun al Rashid should be emasculated with the utmost dispatch; he has too many wives and were he to have fewer or none, something might fall to the lot of my husband. There's the rub. Period.

HARUN: Well-a-day—

SCHEHERAZADE: . . . sighed the Caliph, moved to his innermost heart.

HARUN: Which version dost thou cleave to, wise Ruben?

RUBEN: What does it mean, which do I cleave to, my friend? Do I not know that there are two parties in Baghdad, which contend mightily with one another, whether the Caliph should be emasculated or lose his tongue? And am I not, to be brief, torn this way and that? And does it then behoove me to make myself unpleasantly conspicuous one way or the other? But were I to cleave to neither camp, what then ensues? Does it mean that I stand for the Caliph's being neither emasculated nor tongue-tortured? Or does it follow that I consent to both measures? And what would hap if I as one torn both ways made a decision?

Indeed were I to make it—what then ensues? Nothing or less than nothing? Or both? And what of it? And for the third time: to whom am I talking?

HARUN: This was the most profound of your answers!

SCHEHERAZADE: . . . exclaimed the Caliph, enraptured.

HARUN: Not only the wisest, no: the most loyal citizen of Baghdad do I dub thee! But ye have not yet learned my name. I am the Caliph Harun al Rashid!

OMAR AND ZULEIKA: Woe is us! (*rush back and forth*).

HARUN: That's so in any case. And now to thee, wise Ruben. Thou art the only one of the three to lay claim to that oriental fatalism so befitting the racial characteristics of the people of Baghdad. Teach me the secret of thy resignation, and thou shalt have rich reward in thy bank balance unto the third and fourth end of the month.

RUBEN: The secret of my fatalism, sire? What else could I be but fatalistic, in thy presence?

HARUN: What's that? Was I not an ass-driver in your eyes?

RUBEN: Why, wast thou indeed an ass-driver? Great is the empire of the Caliph and all-powerful his trade regulations. And they stretch from sunrise to sunset of commerce and show no loopholes, let alone a back door. If such a one drives asses in the Caliph's empire and has no license—who could he be except the Caliph himself, Harun al Rashid the Kind, Defender of the Faithful and Terror of the Infidel?

HARUN: Not bad . . .

SCHEHERAZADE: . . . replied the Caliph with a grin.

HARUN: For the second time thou hast shown thyself to be the most loyal of my subjects. And that I may reward thee as befits thy merit, tell me now: To which sect of the faithful dost thou belong? For if thou art a Sunnite, I shall exempt thee from taxes for a year. But if thou art a Shiite, and therefore one of the recreant, in my great tolerance I shall strike off all thy back taxes, so that thou shalt be immaculate in the sight of my tax collectors and thy menials and cattle shall remain free of their distraining stamps. Wherefore art thou silent, Ruben?

RUBEN: Well, wherefore am I silent?

HARUN: Dost thou belong in fact to the most recreant of recreants? Ah, that would pain me in my kidneys and would make my gallbladder ache! For then thou must depart from hence to thence well and truly unrewarded as thou came. Say then swiftly: art thou an Ismaelite?

RUBEN: With an "r," sire . . .

SCHEHERAZADE: Then Harun the Kind-hearted was taken aback and sank into deep rumination.

HARUN: Embarrassing . . .

SCHEHERAZADE: . . . he sighed after a while, before falling back into woeful brooding.

HARUN: Most embarrassing . . .

SCHEHERAZADE: . . . he insisted at last. To retreat again into despondent meditation.

HARUN: Extremely embarrassing . . .

SCHEHERAZADE: . . . he announced at last.

HARUN: That thou art the most loyal citizen of Baghdad is for me a disgrace without end and a bitterness without bottom. However, in the great graciousness of my nickname I wish to leave thee as thou wert. But canst thou assure me for the third time that thou art worthy of this?

RUBEN: Can I, sire?

HARUN: Thou canst, my most loyal one. Shout in a loud and ringing voice "Down with Harun!" For if thou dost shout it, then thou wilt rightfully be punished with the bastinado and my embarrassingly long familiarity with thee will come to its only worthy conclusion.

RUBEN: And what would hap, sire, if I did not shout "Down with Harun?"

HARUN: Then thou wilt be rightfully dragged to the bastinado in any case. For thou wouldst have disobeyed the command of thy kindhearted master, who is righteous and remains so however much things may change. Now, which dost thou choose, my most loyal one? Be aware how embarrassing this is for me, for I cannot leave this place until the case is decided one way or the other.

SCHEHERAZADE: But before he could make a decision, the most loyal citizen of Baghdad felt the tears well up in him, salty and bitter as the waters of the Dead Sea. And he wept long and unchecked, until Harun al Rashid in his inordinate kindness asked him:

HARUN: What distresses thee, my most loyal one? And when wilt thou at last release me from this ever embarrassing situation?

SCHEHERAZADE: Then spake Ruben the tradesman, and his words faltered with a grief that mingled gloom with bitterness . . .
RUBEN: It's hard . . .
HARUN: What is hard?
RUBEN: It's hard to be a Caliph . . .

Translator's Notes

An Oriental Fairy Tale. Despite the Arabian Nights pastiche, Soyfer's focus is on Austria. Baghdad is Vienna, the Model Bazaar is the Vienna Fair, the Grand Vizier is the President of the Republic, the Oriental-Islamic world is the Christian West, Near Eastern equals Austrian. Fatalism equates to the Austrian phrase, "Can't be done."

"Little Streetsinger" was a hit song of the 1930s.

"Hard to be a Caliph" is an allusion to the Yiddish saying, "Hard to be a Jew." It gained currency from Sholom Aleichem's play of that title, *Shver tzu Zayn a Yid,* performed in Yiddish theaters throughout the world.

A MINIATURE DESCENDANT OF THE MUSICAL FARCES OF NES-troy, the Mittelstück had been devised by a former bookseller, Rudolf Weys (1898–1978). In 1933 Weys founded the Union of Young Austrian Authors, and wrote for such satiric cabarets as the Stachelbeere (Gooseberry) and Literatur am Naschmarkt (Literature in the Sweets Market). The most famous Mittelstück was his own *Pratermärchen* (*Amusement Park Fairy Tale*), which was performed over five hundred times. The tale of a pickpocket and a city girl persecuted by a small businessman, its satiric point was blunted by its compensating sentimentality.

The Liebe Augustin had attacked Hitler in 1935 with an allegory, *Reynard the Fox,* and a song, "The Legend of the Unknown Soldier," performed by Herbert Berghof, which commented on the Nazi attempt to remove the names of Jewish war-dead from memorial monuments. But with the arrival of the Germans in 1938, this cabaret closed and its company disbanded. Stella Kadmon went to Palestine, Berghof to New York.

But Rudolf Weys had been a secret fellow-traveller of the Nazis since 1934, when the party was still illegal in Austria. So with the permission of his new masters, he opened the Wiener Werkel (Viennese Workshop) in 1938, trying hard to preserve some of the old Viennese spirit and even putting on pseudonymous works by proscribed colleagues: most of the material was actually written by "non-Aryans," including Hammerschlag. So, paradoxically, an anti-Nazi cabaret operated under the protection of an idealistic Nazi management. For all the cooperation of the "Aryan Department," Weys found it difficult to get around the censorship, though he tried hard, using Viennese dialect, Greek myths, and standard fairy tales as camouflage. As late as 1942, Hammerschlag contributed verses to a song, before he was deported eastwards and probably gassed.

In Weys's Mittelstück *Ein Lord träumt* (*A Lord Dreams*), the pretext is the dream of an English press baron like Beaverbrook. The oneiric framing device enabled Weys to allude to the Sudeten crisis, European rearmament, the problem of refugees from Germany, and the humiliating peace treaty of Laxenburg. In the third scene, translated here, the various neighborhoods of Vienna are treated as if they were sovereign European states.

The Federal Republic of Hernals
(Scene 3 from Ein Lord träumt)
1938
by
Rudolf Weys

(*Government office with a large coat of arms of "The Federal Republic of Hernals." A police official is officiating at the desk.*)

OFFICIAL (*leafing through papers*): Twelve official documents just for traffic passing through the Archduchy of Wieden! New passport regulations for the Voivodom of Währing, stamp fees for the Penal Colony of Leopoldstadt—I'll go batty if this keeps up. (*A knock at the door.*) Come in! (*A lady enters.*) Can't you read? Preferred parties are to enter the passport bureau without knocking!

LADY: Excuse me, I didn't know . . .

OFFICIAL: But you ought to know! That, among other things, is what distinguishes the Federal Republic of Hernals from the People's Republic of Ottakring. *They* knock; we don't. So whadya want?

LADY: Excusemeplease, it concerns a move from Larkfield Street to Nuthill Street.

OFFICIAL: Ah, you want to emigrate? Why didn't ya say so right away? Have ya got a *P* in your passport?

LADY (*timidly*): No, I'm sorry, not yet. I . . .

OFFICIAL: Holy-moly, don't you know that all Protestants from that side of the zone and this side of the intersection not only have to have a *P* in their passports, but also have to take the Christian name *Pepi*.

LADY: Yes, but my husband . . .

OFFICIAL: That don't matter! Even if your respected spouse belongs to the neopagan religion, he is and remains a Pepi. Unless his grandfather prior to the deadline of April 17, 1909, was a follower of Lueger?!

LADY: Unfortunately not.

OFFICIAL: Then I'm sorry, but I can't assimilate you into Hernals. (*Calls.*) Next! (*A gentleman enters.*)

LADY (*as she exits, furious*): Sooner than waste my time making applications all over the place, I'll leave my furniture in Larkfield Street and cross the border illegally on the front platform of a caboose! (*Exits.*)

OFFICIAL (*calling after her*): You! I didn't hear that! (*Leafing through the gentleman's papers.*) What do you want?? A luxury trip to the Furtwängler concert next Sunday? Are you nuts? You think we have hard currency for that sort of thing? You can take seventeen Hernalian groats with you, and that's all. And only in paper money.

GENTLEMAN: I'm awfully sorry, but that won't be enough even for the streetcar!

OFFICIAL: What am I supposed to do? I didn't conclude the disgraceful peace treaty of Laxenburg. Go complain to the Epsom salts office, not me.

GENTLEMAN: Then, under what circumstances can one travel to Downtown County today?

OFFICIAL: My dear friend, there are three hundred and fifty-two regulations governing that matter and they cancel one another out. Anyway, the Ducal County of Downtown is a territory with a high rate of exchange, the same as Neustadt Empire, and entries thereto are permitted only when bringing foreign currency back into Hernals.

GENTLEMAN: So a person can get to the concert hall, so to speak, only when that person is giving a concert himself?

OFFICIAL: That's right, sure. Just for the sake of being in the audience, it's not worth the trouble of hanging entry-, exit-, and four transit-visas around your neck. Unless you suffer from masochistic tendencies. And besides you don't belong to me, but to Steinhof. Now that lies in the Empire of Hietzing, and the plutocrats there'll make sure you don't get in.

GENTLEMAN: Nowadays you can't even go nuts in an orderly fashion!

OFFICIAL: Not until we've converted the municipal bathhouse to a district insane asylum. However, cold showers are always readily available for those suffering grievously from political conditions. Good afternoon.

GENTLEMAN (*saluting*): Hernals über alles, if only it will. (*Exits.*)

OFFICIAL: Thanks, same to you! (*The telephone rings. He picks it up.*) Hello, Passport Bureau, Federal Republic of Hernals. Who's this? Archdiocese Klosterneuburg? God bless you! What?? You caught a swimmer in the Sultanate of Kritzendorf? Well, all right! What? A bather without a country? Naturally that's very aggravating if he lives in Bath. Resident of Watt Street and therefore belongs to us? Just a sec', lemme take a look . . . (*Leafs through his card-file.*) Kri-, Kre-, Kratochwill . . . , there he is all right . . . (*Reads.*) Ah, this'll be fun! First, he's without a country, and therefore he's a bum. Second, he's not supposed to go anywhere without papers; third, six months ago we deported him, and in addition, anyone who swims any more, strictly for his own needs, is detrimental to the welfare of the Hernalian people and a parasite. It would have been better if you'd let the subhuman drown plain and simple. Anyway we won't take him back! (*Is about to hang up.*) Hello! Yes?? But send back the bathing-suit! We're waging a fierce war against decadence!! Sbeenmypleasure! (*Hangs up, leans back pensively.*) Somehow—, I don't think things can go on like this much longer . . . !

CURTAIN

Translator's Note

P on the passport . . . Pepi. A reference to the fact that Jews in the Third Reich had to have a capital *J* in their passports and bear the generic names Israel and Sara. "Pepi" is a standard Viennese nickname and is to Austrians what "Joe" is to Americans.

Lueger. Richard Lueger, the popular prewar mayor of Vienna, used anti-Semitism as a plank in his political platform.

VALESKA GERT EMIGRATED TO SWITZERLAND BEFORE MOV-
ing on to New York in 1938. After some time as a dishwasher,
nude model, and nightclub dancer, she opened the Beggar Bar in
Greenwich Village, which sustained a shaky existence, since Gert
had regular run-ins with the police, the licensing agencies, and
the Mafia. The performers were considerably more amateurish
than those she had been used to in Berlin, but Gert herself kept
launching new songs and dance pantomimes. One of these was *The
Strange Journey of Professor Blitz,* which she describes in her memoirs. After the Beggar Bar closed for financial and legal reasons,
she opened another cabaret in Provincetown, where her performance of *Professor Blitz* was interrupted by a hail of bottles. The
police forced an eleven o'clock curfew on her, one hour earlier than
other bars, and so ended her American experiments. After the war
she returned to Berlin and successfully managed two more cabarets.

The Strange Journey of Professor Blitz
(Die seltsame Reise des Professor Blitz)
1940
by
Valeska Gert

The Professor wants to travel to the moon. His colleagues shoot him into space in a rocket. He feels sick, leans out the window, and throws up. The oxygen in the rocket escapes, and the Professor falls out of the rocket. Anyone who gets into the moon's gravitational orbit has to circle it. He circles. The scientists observe him through a big telescope and notice how desperately he gestures that he is tired, hungry, and thirsty. They shoot a couch under his behind, and sardines (*close-up of a sardine*) and whisky and gin into his clutching, outstretched hands. His wife, Anna, lies in bed and moans in passion for her husband. She remembers her pledge to follow him whithersoever he goeth and asks the scientists to shoot her to her husband; they fulfill her wish, shoot, and she lands happily in the arms of her beloved husband. For two years they circle, and it starts to get boring. It's boring enough to be married on earth sometimes, but how much more boring to circle the moon for years on end on a couch. Then one day a huge meteor hurls right past them. With great presence of mind the professor clutches his wife to him and leaps with her onto the meteor. The force of the fall is great, and the meteor crashes far below the sea, into Hell. They get into the elevator, which carries them even deeper down. The elevator boy of Hell calls, "Sixth floor! Politicians, actors, overreachers!"—"Eighth floor! Money-grubbers, whores, libertines, racing cyclists!"—"Tenth floor! Poets, writers, gluttons, guzzlers, bicycle racers, jockeys!" Here the couple get out. At a round table sits a fat man who gobbles and gobbles, moans and groans; a supernaturally large hand keeps shoving more food into his mouth and forces him to keep eating. He gobbles and groans, but cannot stop. He explodes. Chickens and pigs crawl out of his belly. Two gigantic hands sew the two halves of his body together at a sewing machine, and he keeps gobbling. A little girl slurps ice cream nonstop. She cries horribly but has to go on licking, whether she wants to or not. Yes, even ice cream can become a vice; everything one does can be done without stopping. At the same table sits an old soak. His body is so full of alcohol that the excess liquor spurts out of his head. The Professor and his wife are terrified and go down another story. A garishly painted whore shimmies past them, with a lapdog on a leash; a man follows her with weak knees. A racing cyclist pants and rests; he must, he must be the first one to reach the finish line. A gigantic gold piece rolls by; a little pygmy with outstretched arms runs after it. The cyclist gets thinner and thinner; two gigantic hands pump him up until he is distended. He has to go on pedaling. The Professor and his wife cannot stand the torments of the damned any longer. They too belong to the possessed; they have gone much too far. A volcanic eruption blows them upwards. Like two soap bubbles they hover above the entrance to Hell. A gust of wind seizes them and pulls them across meadows, fields, and woods, until they reach their own country and land in the midst of their friends, who have been waiting for them.

A UNIQUE VOICE IN THE BERLIN CABARET WAS THAT OF WER-
ner Finck (1902–78), conférencier of the Katakombe. The Cata-
combs cabaret had been founded in 1929 by Finck and other
young actors as a counterblast to the KadeKo, or Kaberett der
Komiker (Comics' Cabaret), a huge restaurant, more music hall
than cabaret, whose performers appeared in formal attire. At the
Katakombe, the performers, whom Finck described as "a progressive commune of unknown young artists," wore baggy street
clothes and scuffed shoes. Hanns Eisler played the piano accom-
paniments.

Finck had come to Berlin in 1928, to recite poetry in cabaret.
He soon became known as a subtly witty M.C., who attacked his
targets obliquely with evasive humor and innuendo. Puns, wordplay, unfinished sentences, and ambiguous remarks were his forte.
As a result, he was appreciated by right and left and was able to
continue performing well into the Nazi era, since the stool pigeons assigned to report on his act were hard put to pinpoint
where the offense lay.

As the regime grew more oppressive, Finck became bolder. His
greeting to the audience, "Heil Hitler—and good evening to the
other ninety-eight per cent of you!" was met with cheering and
applause. In one sketch, a patient refused to open his mouth for
the dentist: "How can I open my mouth? I hardly know you."
Finck would begin to leave the stage: "As you all know, in the past
there have been some truly great names: Napoleon, Frederick the
Great, Goethe, and Bismarck. They were truly great subjects for
writers. There was much to be said about them and they liked to
hear men express themselves. But now—you know," he was almost in the wings, "now . . . Oh, yes, that would be so nice."
Even bolder was his delivery of the Nazi salute; with his right arm
up in the air, he would remark, "That's how deep we are in the
shit."

His humor began to be rebuked by the authorities and occasionally by party members in the audience. "You shameless Jew

buffoon," shouted one irate spectator. "What can I do?" replied Finck. "I don't happen to be Jewish. Can I help it if I look that intelligent?"

The last straw for the authorities was the Tailor sketch, translated here, performed in March 1935 by Finck and Ivo Veit. A couple of months later, before the act break, Finck announced, "My friends, there will be a fifteen-minute intermission. If I'm not back at the end of that time, you'll know—well, at least you can *guess* where I am." This was met with dead silence. A week after that, Finck was "transferred" to Esterwegen concentration camp.

The Tailor Fragment

(Das Fragment vom Schneider)

1935

by

Werner Finck

(*Werner Finck comes to a tailor as a customer.*)

TAILOR: How can I serve you?

CUSTOMER (*aside*): He's talking about serving too? (*Aloud.*) I'd like to get a suit. Something seasonable . . . (*Pregnant pause. Then thoughtfully.*) Because I think we're in for a big blow.

TAILOR: Good—

CUSTOMER: Whether it's good or not—Well, I don't know . . .

TAILOR (*a bit impatient*): What would you like then? Sportswear? Something for camping?

CUSTOMER: Everyone's winding up in camps these days.

TAILOR: Would you like it all one color or with stripes?

CUSTOMER: We've had enough of all one color. But no stripes by any means!

TAILOR: Shawl collar and turn-up cuffs?

CUSTOMER: If you're wearing stripes, it means you've been collared and you get cuffed. (*Resigned.*) I suppose a stripe down the pants can't be helped . . .

TAILOR: Let's start with the jacket first. How would you like a military tunic with chevrons and shoulder flaps?

CUSTOMER: Oh, you mean a straitjacket.

TAILOR: Whatever you want to call it. First-class material or second-class?

CUSTOMER: I don't care. So long as it's not cheap and natsi,— uh, nasty.

TAILOR: How do you want the lapels?

CUSTOMER: Very wide, with lots of room for medals and don't spare the material. Maybe we'll all be spared. As the Crown Prince used to say: Once more into the breeches!

TAILOR: Then may I size you up now?

CUSTOMER: Sure, sure, we're used to it.

(*The customer strikes a pose; the tailor stands beside him with a tape measure. He takes measurements, while the customer puts his hands along the seams of his trouser legs.*)

TAILOR (*looking at the tape*): 14/18—Ah, please, take a stand.

CUSTOMER: Who for?

TAILOR: That's it—fine . . . And now up with the right arm— fist clenched. 18/19. And now with the hand wide open . . . 33 . . . All right, why don't you put your arm down? What's that supposed to mean?

CUSTOMER: Upholding the right . . .

Translator's Notes

All one color. Brown, the National Socialist color.

Cheap and natsi. In German the tailor asks the customer if he wants it single- or double-breasted—*einreihig* or *zweireihig.* Finck answers, "So long as it's not *diesreihig*" pronounced to sound like "This Reich."

Lots of room for medals. A reference to Field-Marshal Goering's passion for medals and the general inflation in decorations.

14/18. Service in the Imperial Army during the Great War.

18/19. The years of the Revolution that established the Weimar Republic.

33. The year of Hitler's accession to the Chancellorship.

THANKS TO THE INTERCESSION OF THE ACTRESS KÄTE Dorsch, mistress of Hermann Goering, who was at that time on the outs with Propaganda Minister Goebbels, Werner Finck and his colleagues were acquitted of offenses against the antilibel law, despite considerable evidence against them. Finck was, however, forbidden to appear on stage for a year. The Katakombe and the Tingeltangel Theater had been closed at the time of his arrest; four years later, the KadeKo, the only Berlin cabaret still extant, was shut down on Goebbels's order. Its building was demolished by bombing during the war.

Nazi newspapers kept protesting more and more loudly against "artists' license to be fools," "mockery by Jewish intellectuals," even against allusions to proscribed performers. The upshot in 1941 was an official decree from the Ministry of Propaganda, forbidding any performance by conférenciers. In essence, it was a death sentence for the European cabaret that was carried out over the next four years. But the cabaret was not easy to slay; its seeming death was merely dormancy. No sooner had the Germans been defeated than a thriving cabaret sprang up in the American-occupied zone of Berlin. And that was just the beginning.

Order Prohibiting Masters of Ceremonies and Commentary from the Stage
(Anordnung betreffend Verbot des Conférence-und Ansagewesens)
1941
by
Joseph Goebbels

Despite my repeated ordinances of 8 December 1937, 6 May 1939, and 11 December 1940, in which I urgently stated a requirement that cabaret and performance matters be assimilated to the demands of public taste and especially those of the war, so-called conférenciers, masters of ceremony, and cabaretists, as I am informed from a multitude of nuisances both in this country and, above all, at the front, continue to practice their mischief. They indulge in cheap and frivolous vilification of the conditions of public life entailed by the necessity of war. In so-called political jokes they offer open or covert criticism of politics and the economic and cultural leadership of the Reich. They scoff at the indigenous characteristics of our people's unique race and thereby contribute to imperiling the inner unity of the nation, which is the most important prerequisite for the victorious conclusion of this war. Considering that my repeated, earnestly enjoined admonitions have obviously borne no fruit and the old defects and shortcomings of a form of public entertainment engendered by a liberal-democratic style of government continue to surface afresh, I find myself compelled more than ever to take decisive measures at the Fuehrer's behest.

By virtue of §25 of Ordinance One for effecting the Reich

Chamber of Culture law of 1 November 1933 (Reich Law Bulletin I p. 797) I hereby order:

1. Any and every so-called conférencier performance or commentary is immediately and fundamentally forbidden for the entire public. It makes no difference whether it means to deal with matters of politics, economy, culture, or any other concerns of public or private life.
2. Comments, including the allegedly well-meaning, on personalities, circumstances, or events of public life, are forbidden in theaters, cabarets, variety shows, and any other places of entertainment.
3. The press is most vigorously advised to avoid as punctiliously as possible dealing with questions irrelevant to life, which might trouble or upset the German people unnecessarily.
4. It is forbidden to play one race off against another, one city against another, or one part of the Reich against another, even if in an allegedly well-intentioned manner. All the forces of public life must be directed to the unity of the people. Problems which needlessly inflame emotions and which are of subordinate significance to the victorious carrying-out of the war will be barred from public discussion. This decree represents an ultimate, earnest, and urgent admonition. At the Fuehrer's behest, transgressions will be punished with the harshest penalties.

Berlin, 30 January 1941.

signed: Dr. Goebbels

*Erika Mann as
M.C. at the
Peppermill.*

Therese Giehse as a national "prophetess" at the Peppermill.

Max Werner Lenz as the Man without a Passport, 1935.

Caricature of Jura Soyfer, by Willi Spira.

Caricature of Rudolf Weys, by Hugo Gottschlich.

Werner Finck as M.C. at the Katakombe.